Recipes from La Isla

RECIPES FROM LA ISLA
New & Traditional Puerto Rican Cuisine

by

Robert Rosado and
Judith Healy Rosado

Lowell House
Los Angeles

Contemporary Books
Chicago

Library of Congress Cataloging-in-Publication Data

Rosado, Robert.
    Recipes from La Isla : new & traditional Puerto Rican cuisine / by Robert
and Judith Healy Rosado.
        p.   cm.
    Includes bibliographical references and index.
    ISBN 1-56565-339-4 (hardcover)
    ISBN 1-56565-476-5 (paperback)
    1. Cookery, Puerto Rican.   2. Cookery—Puerto Rico.   I. Rosado,
Judith.   II. Title.
    TX716.P8R66   1995   95-31564
    641.597295—dc20   CIP

Requests for such permissions should be addressed to:
Lowell House
2029 Century Park East, Suite 3290
Los Angeles, CA 90067

Lowell House books can be purchased at special discounts when ordered in bulk for
premiums and special sales. Contact Department TC at the address above.

Publisher: Jack Artenstein
General Manager, Lowell House Adult: Bud Sperry
Text Design: Nancy Freeborn
Typesetting and Layout: Michele Lanci-Altomare

Manufactured in the United States of America

10 9 8 7 6 5 4 3 2 1

Dedication

This book is, first of all, lovingly dedicated to our mothers,
Lydia Cuascut Rosado and Margaret Ruth Healy,
for in their own ways they planted the seeds.

And to our son, Adam Robert Rosado, age seven,
whose loving nature, humor and creativity inspired us,
and whose patience and support during the time we spent
working on this book revealed a maturity beyond his years.

———

This book is also dedicated to my big brother, Mikey Rosado,
because we lived through many of these experiences together.
And to my son, Aaron T. Rosado—
embrace the currents of our culture and listen to your heart. (RR)

Acknowledgments

Many friends and family members gave their support during the time we spent writing this book. Our friend and editor, Karen Warmdahl, helped us over some hurdles and prepared final versions of the manuscript for our publisher—thank you for the great job, Karen! Many others helped, in ways too numerous to mention: Phyllis Rosado Arlotta, Nancy Cloud, Peter Z Orton, Jack and Christine Lamb Parker, and Adena Siegel. Thanks also to our agent, Nicole Aragi, of Watkins-Loomis Agency; our editor at Lowell House, Maria Magallanes; Nélida Pérez of the Center for Puerto Rican Studies at Hunter College in New York; Roberto Trujillo, Latin America curator at the Stanford University Libraries; and Gloria Paniagua, of the Institute for Puerto Rican Culture for their special assistance. And thanks to all our other friends who "hung in there" with us over the past couple of years, faithfully asking from time to time, "How's the book?"

The authors gratefully acknowledge the following sources:

Introduction to Chapter I, "The Borinqueños," from *Borinquen—An Anthology of Puerto Rican Literature*, edited by María Teresa Babín and Stan Steiner, copyright 1974, Alfred A. Knopf, Inc. Reprinted by permission of Vera John-Steiner.

"Return," by José Gautier Benítez, from *Poesias*, 1880. Reprinted in *Poesias*, Editorial Campos, San Juan, Puerto Rico, 1955. Excerpt translated by Robert Rosado.

"La Borinqueña," by Manuel Fernández Juncos. Puerto Rican National Anthem. Excerpt translated by Robert Rosado.

"To the Beautiful and Felicitous Island of San Juan de Puerto Rico," by Juan Rodríguez Calderón, from *Memorias, Geográficas, Históricas, Económicas y Estadísticas*

CONTENTS

What is Puerto Rican Cuisine, Anyway? • XIII

What is Puerto Rican Cuisine, Anyway?

When we first toyed with the idea of writing a book on traditional Puerto Rican food, as a means of preserving authentic recipes from Robert's side of our family, we didn't realize we were embarking on such an exciting challenge. It wasn't the technical aspects of putting together a cookbook that raised so many questions, but rather the fact that so little seems to be known about Puerto Rican food.

We came to the Bay Area from Puerto Rico in May of 1987. Because each of us had lived at times in large cities, we took for granted the great variety of ethnic foods available. But both of us were quick to realize that a Puerto Rican influence was definitely absent. Even a city as cosmopolitan as San Francisco didn't seem to have a restaurant claiming to be Puerto Rican. There were restaurants representing all kinds of Asian and Latin American cultures, and plenty from Europe, of course, and even Africa. No wonder our friends in The City so often asked us about Puerto Rican cuisine. Was it spicy like Mexican food? Were there a lot of root dishes, like Hawaiian poi? Were Puerto Ricans fond of meat turnovers or wrapped pastries, as are so many other cultures?

Spending time in the ethnic cooking sections of bookstores led us to ask ourselves similar questions about the lack of a Puerto Rican presence. Where were the cookbooks representing the beloved island we had recently left? It seemed odd that despite the special relationship of Puerto Rico to the United States, or the recent interest in Caribbean food, little seemed to be known about Puerto Rican cuisine or culture. So we felt compelled to write this book as a way of proudly representing Puerto Rican culture for those who knew so little about it.

What is Puerto Rican food? Ask a Puerto Rican and he or she will tell you that it is *lechón asado*—pig roasted over an open pit; or *pasteles*—meat pies made with a root vegetable batter and wrapped in banana leaves; or *mofongo al pilón*—fried green plantains seasoned and mashed with garlic sauce and served in a mortar. Or, put even more simply: rice and beans.

It is all of these. And much more! For those who were born and raised on the island of Puerto Rico, and who have migrated to the mainland and adopted the

American way of life, traditional Puerto Rican food arouses nostalgic passions and childhood memories of the *campos*, green and fertile mountains with clear streams and rivers running through them. Many Puerto Ricans from The Island can remember running in the fields against warm and gentle breezes blowing in from the Caribbean Sea, permeating the air with the sweet smell of sugar cane, oranges, limes, and mangoes.

The Puerto Rican diet was and still is rich in naturally healthy ingredients, and provides a spectacular array of unique and colorful fruits and vegetables. Tuberous vegetables such as cassava, taro root, and sweet potatoes, vegetables whose frequent use distinguishes Puerto Rican cuisine from that of the United States, though not from other Caribbean cuisines, are an important ingredient of the daily diets of both city and country dwellers. Citrus trees grow abundantly on The Island and provide the population with fresh fruit that is eaten whole, or squeezed and served as juice. The abundance and variety of plantain and banana plants also make an important contribution to the Puerto Rican diet. These fruits are prepared and cooked in dishes that range from appetizers to desserts. Herbs and other cultivated plants thrive, their leaves often growing twice the size that cooks and gardeners in the United States might be used to seeing.

Poultry, fish, and seafood figure prominently in Island eating. While not preferred exclusively over pork or beef, chicken and turkey are eaten regularly, and are still raised in the backyards of country dwellers—sometimes even in coops by city dwellers in towns like San Juan or Ponce. Fish and other seafood are eaten daily, especially along the coastal areas. Both the Puerto Rican climate and soil have provided its inhabitants with an abundant variety of tasty natural foods.

On the downside, however, the Puerto Rican diet of the past often consisted of many foods fried in animal fat. Frequently a big tub of *manteca*, lard made from the fat of pig meat, sat in the patio near the outside cooking area and was used for frying fish, poultry, meat, pastries, and other finger foods. Because of the warm Caribbean climate, islanders preferred cooking on grills or stoves outside their houses.

We have not stayed clear of all fried foods in this collection, as this is a book filled with many traditional Puerto Rican recipes. But instead of animal fat these recipes call for olive oil. Most of the time suggestions are given for broiling or grilling instead of frying. In many instances, Robert has developed baking alternatives to traditionally fried items such as *alcapurrias* or *tostones*. Also, in an attempt to eat healthier, recipes for such unique foods as *morcilla* (blood sausage), or *chicharrones* (crispy fried pig skin) have been left out.

Taste instead the fish and root vegetables of Puerto Rico, the fruits or the rice and beans. In recent years there has been a higher consciousness on The Island, as there is throughout the world, of the need for less salt and fewer saturated fats in our diets. You will find whole foods and fresh vegetables here, many of which have been eaten since the time the Taino Indians lived on The Island. Using basic ingredients found in the region, we have modified the methods of preparation in the interest of better health. Where a traditional recipe called for too much salt by today's standards, Robert has worked with the seasonings in order to produce a delicious taste equivalent to the traditional. This book does not claim to be a complete collection of every dish the Puerto Rican kitchen has to offer. But it is the best of the traditional, and the best of the new.

Puerto Rico is an island, but it is not an island unto itself. Outside influences have helped form the Puerto Rican diet since the time when Caribbean tribes traveled throughout the area in their canoes. The cuisine from *La Isla* shares commonalities with other Caribbean island neighbors. Fritters, dried codfish, rice, crab and other seafood, meat pies, tuberous vegetables, meat or vegetable pastries wrapped in leaves or surrounded by flaky dough—all can be found in most island cuisines. But Puerto Rican food is never as hot as the curries of Trinidad or the Jamaican jerk, both influenced by East Indian cookery. Instead, it is flavored with its own blends of *sofrito*, a sauce made from fresh tomato, garlic, oregano, and onion, and used to flavor beans, rice, or meats, the favorite of which is pork.

But Puerto Rican cuisine has its own decidedly native elements: *asopao*, *pasteles*, *bacalaitos*, *arroz* and *gandules*, most made even tastier by the special flavors of Puerto Rican *sofrito*. The "national bean" is the *gandule*, the pigeon pea. Where Cubans would probably name rice with black beans as their most typical dish, Puerto Ricans would think immediately of rice with pigeon peas, or red beans with rice. Today's Puerto Rican cuisine has been influenced by Spain, Africa, Europe, and the United States. This is a universal cuisine, but it has its own distinct flavor and essence, finding the most similarities with other Spanish-Caribbean island cuisines.

Within the island, small though it is, different regions exist whose diets emphasize one or another food item. The southern coast, whose "pearl" is Ponce, a major hub of immigration, import, and export, has long been the place where many cultures meld together. Its cuisine, naturally, has always maintained a rather cosmopolitan flavor. When the northern port of San Juan became an international city and eventually the capital, it too began to reflect these relationships in its cuisine. Now the center of tourism on The Island, this large city can offer the visitor everything from pizza or Argentinean beef, to the dishes featured in this book.

In Puerto Rico, on Sunday mornings, it is commonplace to see scores of people heading to the seashore, hoping to secure the ideal spots where the fish and finger foods are excellent, the prices affordable, and the scenery enchanting. These *playas* contain the most abundant supply of marine life The Island has to offer—fish, conch, octopus, oysters, clams, squids, shrimps, and gray land crabs. The two large cities on the west and east coast of Puerto Rico—Mayagüez and Fajardo—are famous for their seafood menus. We loved driving to Fajardo for an early Sunday afternoon dinner.

In mountainous regions on The Island, the Puerto Rican farmers, the *jíbaros*, raise livestock, poultry, and small crops. Their diet includes more pork and beef, but poultry and seafood are not neglected. The freshest of tubers and other vegetables have always been readily available to them, and the beautiful and attractive country dish known as *serenata* appears on the rustic tables of *jíbaros* who live in these lush mountains.

All over The Island, one finds the Puerto Rican tradition of sharing in the preparation and cooking of succulent dishes whenever family and friends come by for a visit, and on special occasions such as a wedding, the birth of a child, or for a christening or a wake. Whenever a group of Puerto Ricans get together, it is always a merry feast of cooking, drinking, dancing, singing, sharing, and embracing. Good and hard times are celebrated together, always with the optimistic philosophy of a "better tomorrow," coupled with the warmest and most sincere wishes: *mi casa es su casa* ("my house is your house") and *buen provecho* ("good eating").

We would not only like to share Puerto Rican hospitality with you in this book, we'd also like to acquaint you with the warmth and physical beauty of Puerto Rico—the sights, sounds, music, and fragrances of the land, city, and kitchen. Gaze outside our window with us and you will see the rose and yellow sunsets, and the lush green hills dotted with orange and purple flowers. Wait until dusk and hear the Puerto Rican tree frog, the *coquí*, singing its nightly serenade to darkness and moist earth— *ko-kee!; ko-kee! ko-kee!* Look up and see the tiny lizards darting out suddenly from a crack in the wall and "freezing" on the ceiling. Travel, too, down winding backroads and see the flaming red blossoms of the *flamboyan*, a tree that bursts its passionate flowers in springtime throughout Puerto Rico, giving rise to story and song, and to sighs of *ah, que bella*.

There are gentle warm tropical evenings in Puerto Rico, when you may be inclined to join in with the beat of *salsa*, and dance. And there are the hot, hot days when you want nothing more than to sit at a shady outside table and enjoy an ice cold drink. There is laughter and singing and dancing on our island. And everyday life. Whatever you come to learn about Puerto Rico and its culture by reading this book, and making these traditional and newly created recipes, we are sure you will come to treasure. Perhaps we cannot fully answer why the world has not yet truly discovered our lovely island, but if you find Puerto Rico, you will wonder why it has taken you so long to get there.

We would also like to share with you the warmth of our kitchen, with its good smells and good feelings and the laughter of adults and children. Enjoy these dishes: make them and eat them with friends and family; have a cup of strong coffee or a fruit juice or cold beer. Relax and enjoy Puerto Rico. The recipes are Robert's. The memories are ours—and yours too, once you taste and visit *La Isla*.

Recipes from La Isla

Puerto Rico's History in a Coconut Cup

Boriké the Beautiful

The island known as Boriké by its inhabitants was a tranquil place until Columbus landed. Upon discovery, the Old World found another world as old as itself, rich in primitive culture and natural beauty. At first the explorers must have been astonished at seeing the new varieties of trees, plants, and tropical fruits and vegetables that grew in the dark, fertile soil. When they wandered into the exotic rainforests that sheltered lizards, frogs, parrots and other colorful birds, and when they saw the giant-leafed plants, moist and shady, lush in their greenness, they must have stopped, perhaps in reverence, and listened to the music and magic of this new land.

The Caribbean islands are often thought of as something akin to paradise. Their warm weather and white sandy beaches, shaded by tall palms, must have enchanted other Caribbean people long before Spanish explorers sailed into their clear aqua waters. For centuries Indians had lived on the islands as far north as Cuba and south to Trinidad, sometimes separating into individual island groups like the Igneris and the Caribs. Archeological remains found in southern Puerto Rico place the Igneri Indians, known as ostionoides—shellfish eaters—there as early as 300 B.C. The Tibes Indian Ceremonial Center, a restored archaeological site near Ponce, Puerto Rico's largest southern city, provides evidence of their existence and has been called one of the largest ancient burial grounds in the Caribbean.

The Taino Indians who met the ships of Columbus shouting "Taino, Taino!" traveled by *canoa* (canoe) between the neighboring islands, often to trade with other island tribes. On this island, only 3400 square miles, the Tainos had little need for complex housing or clothing. They lived in *bohios* (small hutches) made from palm leaves and wood, and often slept in *hamacas* (hammocks). The climate was warm and hospitable, at least until the god *Hurakán* sent fury upon them. They lived in villages based around a central courtyard, sometimes near the sea, sometimes further inland.

Like other contemporary people of the region, the Tainos lived in a subsistence economy and raised vegetables in a form of agriculture known as *conuco*—raising tuberous plants in large mounds of soil. To work the *conucos* Indians first burned dry plants before the rainy season, in typical slash-and-burn fashion. Then they piled the resulting soil, now made more nutritious with ash and burnt remains of former plant life, into mounds, each mound about 3 feet high and 6 to 9 feet around. They made fields of these mounds, and used long sticks called *coa* to plant the root vegetables in the mounds. The principal crops were cassava (*yuca*) and sweet potato (*batata*), but arrowroot, peanuts, peppers, and gourds were raised too. *Conucos* provided natural drainage and prevented erosion, and could be used for farming either on hills or flat land, sometimes for as long as ten to fifteen years.

The women made cassava bread, *casabe*, which they processed from the root vegetable known to us today as cassava. When grated, drained, and strained through handmade woven baskets, cassava was processed into pulp, formed into loaves and baked on small clay griddles over an open fire. The bread could be kept a long time in the hot tropical climate. *Casabe* was a main staple of the Taino diet and *Yúcahu*, the spirit of the cassava and the sea, was worshipped.

Christopher Columbus observed the Tainos making the *casabe* and made note of it in his diary on December 16, 1492. *Casabe* is still made the same way in Puerto Rico and other places in the Caribbean to this day. It is an unleavened bread, like a cracker bread or matzoh. In Puerto Rico the cassava is also grated and used in batters to make *alcapurrias* and *pasteles*, and is served as a vegetable in large chunks alongside pieces of sweet potatoes, potatoes, taro, and plantains in the colorful dish called *serenata* (serenade).

Tainos also grew some seed plants like tobacco, corn, beans, and squash. Living near the ocean, they were able to supplement their diets with shellfish and fish. Using bows and arrows and stone weapons, they may have caught manatees or turtles, and an occasional parrot, pigeon or iguana. They also ate tropical fruits like pineapple, mamey, and guava. As a forerunner of future Caribbean cooking methods, the Tainos threw the meat or fish into what was called a pepper pot, along with other juices and vegetables like the *yuca* and simmered them continuously over a fire. This open air cooking over fire was called *barbacoa* (barbeque).

Arrival of the Spanish

In 1492, Christopher Columbus made his famous first voyage to the Caribbean region, sailing from Spain after that country's recent conquest of Granada, and other Spanish lands held for centuries by the conquering Moors. During his second voyage to the Indies in 1493 he sailed into Boriké's waters on November 19th, naming the island San Juan Bautista after the son of Queen Isabella and King Ferdinand. The Spaniards later modified the Taino name of the island to Borinquen.

Intending to further colonize the New World for the Spanish, Columbus brought with him the seeds, crop plants, and animals that were destined to mix the Old World and the New together forever. Pigs, cattle and horses, citrus plants, melons, wheat, barley, vegetables, and, of course, sugar cane, all made their way to the New World and eventually to the creation of a new Caribbean cuisine. The Moors had taught the Spanish how to raise rice, and when the Spanish transferred this knowledge to their new lands they introduced one of the most basic elements of today's Puerto Rican diet. Pigeon peas, *gandules*, destined to become Puerto Rico's "national bean," came from the Moors as well. We can imagine the Puerto Rican favorite of *arroz con gandules* (rice and pigeon peas) being inspired at this time. Many plants and animals prospered in the gentle climate and fertile soil. Spanish pigs and other cattle increased a hundredfold in a short time. Citrus and melons became part of the daily diet.

The Search For Gold

But what the Spaniards really wanted was gold. Explorers had seen the Indians wearing golden jewelry and assumed that the island was rich in this precious metal. Columbus forced the Tainos into mining, demanding that Indians produce a specified amount of gold before being able to engage in their own farming. This soon disrupted production on the *conucos*, and the Tainos began to go hungry, eventually dying as frequently from overwork and malnutrition as they had from more direct forms of Spanish cruelty.

In 1508, Ponce de León made his first trip to Puerto Rico from Santo Domingo, on the island of Hispaniola directly to the west. Ordered by Queen Isabella and King Ferdinand to continue the search for gold, Ponce de León, the island's first governor, soon converted the island's economy to one based on mining. Because of the widespread rumors of gold on the island, San Juan Bautista came to be known as Puerto Rico, or "rich port." Ponce de León employed Indian labor in the search for gold but the indigenous population continued to die out from murder, suicide, overwork, disease, and assimilation. Many Spaniards married Indian women, blurring the distinction between Tainos and Spanish. Bartholome de las Casas, a Spanish priest who traveled with the Spanish conquerors, urged them to use other labor, white or black, in gold mining and agricultural production so that the Indian population would not be completely annihilated. But within a hundred years the Tainos were almost extinct.

Agriculture and Commerce in Southern Puerto Rico

Bordered by the Atlantic ocean on the north and the Caribbean on the south, Puerto Rico lies east of the two larger islands of Cuba and Hispaniola—the latter is known today as the countries of Haiti and the Dominican Republic. On the southeast side of Borinquen lay the Lesser Antilles—the Virgin Islands, Saba, Antigua, to name a few. Explorers to The Island usually came first to its southern ports like San Germán and Ponce, later the western port of Mayagüez and northern San Juan. As time went on the southern areas became agriculturally rich and active ports. Sugar, ginger, coffee, tobacco, and cattle were raised for both consumption and export.

Presumably, the diet of these islanders began changing as Spanish cooks worked to recreate their own favorite dishes with new ingredients. We can imagine that many elements of the cuisine of Catalonia, in northern Spain, contributed to the Puerto Rican diet after explorers from there traveled to Puerto Rico. A look at any cookbook from the Catalonian region reveals many elements also found in Puerto Rican cuisine: *sofrito*, garlic, dried salted codfish (*bacalao*), and other wines, spices, and herbs.

Along with the native tropical ingredients that they found on The Island, these new cooks were creating the cuisine we know today as Puerto Rican.

Africans Enrich the Island

There turned out to be very little gold on Puerto Rico, or on any Caribbean island for that matter. Instead, the first attempt at large-scale sugar production began in the mid-1500s on Puerto Rico and neighboring islands as a means of developing export crops to enrich the Spanish Crown. Everything connected with sugar production was imported—the technology, the plantation system, the sugar cane, and the African slaves. Africans, whether slaves or free men, brought cola nuts, periwinkle, okra, black-eyed peas, bananas, plantains, and watermelons to the Americas. Tamarind and millet also originated in Africa. Those Africans who already knew about growing rice, also contributed their knowledge of basketweaving as a means of carrying the rice between field and pepper pot. Their methods of pottery making and cooking were another contribution. Although their labor helped build the Americas, they're still not given credit for their many cultural influences.

Beginnings of *Criollismo*

Sugar production in this era did not last long, and when it stopped the Puerto Rican population became more unified. With the demise of the sugar industry on The Island in the early 1600s, slaves, slave-owners, and plantations also disappeared from Puerto Rico. As the population intermarried, Puerto Rico's people became distinctly creole, bronze in skin tone and more racially mixed than in many other countries where slavery had existed. The Spanish word used to describe the Puerto Rican people, *criollo*, is still used today to describe the population, the culture, and the cuisine.

In the eighteenth and nineteenth centuries, agriculture flourished in the southern regions. Although Puerto Rico was a country that produced mainly for consumption and its trade was regulated by the Spanish, sugar, coffee, ginger, tobacco, and cattle were raised, and traders came in ships from all over the world to purchase these goods. Puerto Rican coffee was in demand in Europe and Spain, and thought of as the best by coffee lovers of the Spanish ruling class. Ponce grew as The Island's southern seat of culture, agriculture, and the arts. Frenchmen, South Americans, and other Europeans all contributed their share to the culture and cuisine of the southern area. Whereas San Juan to the north was the seat of government, law and order, Ponce became known for having a more liberal air. It was a melting pot where immigration was encouraged and cultural diversity was appreciated. Many who came were connected with the sugar trade, but art and music, architecture and cuisine were influenced by a multitude of sources. Ships from Spain, Portugal, France and England came to trade wine, cast-iron pots, and other Old World necessities for ginger, coffee, fruits, and hides produced in Puerto Rico.

By the early 1800s sugar production was in a surge of growth, the hub of activity still in Ponce. Despite a brief reappearance of the African slave trade to provide labor for small plantations, slavery was fully and finally abolished in 1873, more than likely hurried to its end by the influence the *criollos* had on the Spanish Crown. Later, separatists demanding the right to control their own trade almost won complete autonomy for Puerto Rico from Spain in the 1800s. But then, after only several days of enjoying the right to self determination, the island was handed over to the United States at the end of the Spanish-American war.

Puerto Rico's Relationship with the United States

The United States initiated the second era of large-scale sugar production, lasting until World War II. In 1917 all Puerto Ricans were given U.S. citizenship as a "benefit" resulting from their country's colonial status. Even today, Puerto Ricans are eligible for the draft in the U.S. armed forces but cannot vote in U.S. presidential elections. Later, with industrialization, the United States put an end to large-scale agricultural production on the island, replacing it with smaller industries such as pharmaceuticals and computer parts assembly plants. Tragically, where once Puerto Rico exported sugar and coffee for foreign markets, today more of these products are imported than exported. Many still argue that industry is imported into the country for the purposes of cheap production, and that Puerto Rico is kept in a colonial status so that the United States can enjoy a military outpost in the Caribbean.

In 1952 Puerto Rico was declared a "commonwealth," self-governing in local matters only, still not completely independent. On The Island the status debate never ends. In the early 1950s, hearing that there were more jobs north, huge numbers of

Puerto Ricans left The Island and moved to the large industrialized areas in the eastern United States. Since that time, migration from and to The Island has never ceased.

Today's Puerto Rican Eating Habits

On The Island now you will find plenty of American fast-food restaurants, an unfortunate contribution one might say, but you will also find *come y vetes* (eat-and-run establishments) and other small open-door eating places serving a dish that is typically *puertorriqueño*—rice and beans, or crab with rice, or *alcapurrias*. There are, as well, finer restaurants that show the influence of fresh and healthy California cuisine, the fine foods of Spain, France and Italy, as well as homebred restaurants with healthier foods, expensive menus and fine wines.

With industrialization, the longer lunch and rest time in the afternoon, still typical in most Latin American countries, has gone the way of many other old world pleasures in Puerto Rico. Today a lunch hour, especially in the cosmopolitan area of San Juan, is like lunch time in any U.S. city. Workers bring their lunches from home or buy them at an outdoor cafe or restaurant. They may eat a hamburger, a salad, or a plate of rice and beans—anything goes!

As for food shopping, many marketplaces have gone the way of the lunch hour. Marketplaces still exist, but in most cities poor and rich alike shop at large supermarkets (*supermercados*). We shopped at both. Near our apartment was one of the best produce markets, the Santurce Market; it is often pictured in colorful photographs of life in Puerto Rico. We shopped very early on Saturday mornings, hoping to beat both crowds and heat. We loved walking between rows of huge avocados, papayas, and mangoes that grow on The Island, along with the herbs, soaps, and incense proclaimed for their spiritual as well as medicinal value. But for most non-food items we went the way of both citizens and tourists and shopped at our local *supermercado*.

Food Unites Us All

Food separates us, and food unites us. Although wars have been fought over a rise in coffee prices, or a chance to produce sugar at a lower cost in a different country, food also brings us together. If you are Puerto Rican, and whether you are for independence, statehood, or a continuation of the Commonwealth, you have more than likely eaten rice and *gandules* many times and have probably helped your family make *pasteles* during the Christmas holidays. If you are not Puerto Rican, and are not associated in some way with The Island or someone from it, you may very well have never tasted its delights. If you live in New York City, you may associate Puerto Rican cuisine with *cuchifritos*, fried innards. If you live in the west or the midwest, you may have dined at a restaurant claiming to serve Caribbean food, and seen an item or two on the menu claiming to be Puerto Rican, perhaps a *pionono* or a *pastele*, perhaps a soup called *asopao* or *caldo gallego*.

The reasons why Puerto Rican cuisine is so unknown in the United States can be speculated on, and these speculations can be disturbing to those who know and love Puerto Rico. Perhaps because Puerto Rico has a colonial relationship with the United States, its people, culture and cuisine are less respected by citizens of the fifty states. Or perhaps since many Americans frequently forget that Puerto Ricans are also citizens of their country, they likewise don't think of The Island's cuisine as a neighboring, friendly cuisine. Perhaps it has taken Puerto Ricans themselves too long to proudly and formally present their cuisine to the rest of the world.

Whatever the reasons for the lack of knowledge of Puerto Rican cuisine, let the interest in it start now! Take a taste, take a trip, to Puerto Rico. You will be glad you did.

Tools, Techniques, & Ingredients of the Puerto Rican Kitchen

Freshness For Generations

My love for cooking and appreciation for great food was influenced greatly by my paternal grandmother, whose own grandfather migrated from northern Spain and settled in San Germán, Puerto Rico, during the middle of the eighteenth century. The family later moved to Ponce and acquired property near what is now the center of the old city, next to one of the oldest architectural landmarks on The Island, Hospital Tricoche. The Spanish colonists, especially the Catalonians, were for the most part ethnocentrics. The pride of who they were, where they came from, and their mission in the new colony firmly established the foundation for most of our institutions. Their legacy is present in every aspect of the Puerto Rican way of life—politics, art, architecture, literature, technology, agriculture, commerce and gastronomy.

To be invited to my grandmother's house for dinner was equivalent to being invited to a royal extravaganza whose preparation would sometimes start four days earlier. Everyone invited participated in the preparation. It was during these times that my grandma's Spanish aristocratic make-up would shine through. Masterfully issuing orders and delegating the tasting and inspecting, she did so with so much grace and elegance that every one would intuitively address her as Doña Fela, *doña* being a term of respect.

I always accompanied her to the plaza during shopping trips since I knew my way around and was known by every fresh produce proprietor in the marketplace. To be the son of Miguel, *el carnicero* (the butcher) carried a lot of prestige and benefits, of which my grandmother took full advantage and used as leverage during the haggling segment of the ritual. We always walked away with the best, freshest vegetables, the greenest herbs, and the highest quality nuts and spices.

To find the best cut of salted codfish (*bacalao*), my grandmother sometimes made the vendor open up a new crate, thinking that the one on display had been exposed too long to fresh air. The trick, she used to say, is to know what you want and to recognize it when you see it. The fresh produce vendor would argue that everything he sold was of the highest quality. "Perhaps he was right," my grandmother would say, "but the only one who knows for sure is the hand that is stirring the pot." Many times when she was cooking she would break off a small piece of a particular food item we had bought and stick it gently in my mouth as a gesture of approval, and probably as a reward for my enthusiastic interest when I accompanied her on those shopping trips to the old Ponce marketplace. Although she lived to be over 100 years old, I wish she was still around to see how much her influence and our trips to market affects me to this day.

The key to Puerto Rican cooking, as with any culture's cooking, has a great deal to do with imagination, as well as knowledge. But a little knowledge of the culture will give you the insight for understanding the use of basic herbs and spices, identifying the ingredients, and helping you determine what substitutions to make when certain ingredients are unavailable. Cultural awareness will help direct you to the places where you can purchase the necessary ingredients and, most importantly, help you to prepare them successfully. Equipment is essential, but minimal changes to your culinary "toolshed" are necessary. One of the universal truths of ethnic cooking is that it is time-consuming and ritualistic by nature, when approached in its purest form. The modern time schedule, however, and changing attitudes about how much attention one should devote to kitchen life make it necessary to compromise. Whether or not you approach this new adventure as a purist (as I do), do not be afraid! A little knowledge is the key to overcoming the apprehension, fear of failure or appearing foolish as we contemplate a journey into an area that we know little or nothing about, such as the preparation and cooking of ethnic food.

The way I like to illustrate the dynamics of Puerto Rican culture is with a story that I heard during my childhood. It was about a gypsy who wandered into a village where the inhabitants didn't like strangers, and because they had never seen a gypsy before, and knew nothing about gypsies, the poor fellow was soon surrounded by villagers in the middle of the market square demanding to know who he was, where he came from, and what he wanted. "I am a universal wanderer," he replied. "I am passing through and have stopped to rest and have a bite to eat."

Quickly assessing the situation he smiled and, pointing to a stand of fresh vegetables, passionately exclaimed, *"Que bello! Magnífico!"* He reached back into the sack that slung from his shoulders and pulled out a pot and then a folding iron bar, which he snapped open. With a quick flick of the wrist he formed a stand for holding the kettle and hung it in place before the stand touched the ground, and over the pile of wood that was already burning. Taking advantage of the sudden collective amazement displayed by the villagers watching his uncannily agile movements, he flashed a shining gold earring and proclaimed that it contained special powers and that with it he would create the best mixture ever, for all to enjoy.

But first, he needed water to release the power. "Here is some water!" someone shouted from the back of the crowd. Quickly making his way to the front, the villager brought the water and filled the pot. The water soon started to roar. "The power is released! It needs to be contained quickly! I need some bones with straps of flesh attached to it. "Here is the best leg of mutton I have," replied the butcher. The mutton was quickly diced into one-inch cubes. "I need garlic and onions—red, green and yellow—carrots, potatoes, turnips, sage, parsley . . . " and soon every villager was lined up in front of the pot, passing in parade form, adding a little bit of this and that to the pot, each claiming to contribute what was needed to enrich the quality of the simmering mixture. Finally, the gypsy invited the people to sit and eat. It was as he had promised! Everyone agreed.

The traveler then removed the gold earring from the bottom of the pot, wiped it clean, put it back in his pocket and quietly left the village. The villagers were too immersed in dialogue and debate about which one of the precious ingredients had "made" the soup to notice his departure. Thus, despite all the individual claims of perfecting the soup, it had actually been all the culinary contributions that made it so delicious—a true melting pot.

Today's Puerto Rican cuisine, traditionally known as *comida criolla* (creole cuisine) is a fusion of over five hundred years of diverse cultural roots and experiences, a balanced blend of the old world with the new.

Tools and Techniques of *Comida Criolla*

In my cooking I use a mortar and pestle, an eight-inch utility knife, a blender, a food processor, a heavy-duty manual shredder, and four 18 by 18 inch hardwood cutting boards. Most of these items are available in the average kitchen and do not require much discussion, but some, especially the mortar and pestle, may be new tools for some cooks.

I also use glazed ceramic bowls, wooden bowls, cold-to-hot deep glass baking dishes, stainless steel sheet pans, shallow roasting pans, glass jars (mason jars), wooden spoons, wire whisks, and most other standard cooking tools and utensils. For stove cooking I use a 12-inch cast iron skillet and two cast iron kettles—one for cooking rice and rice dishes, and one for cooking beans. The most significant of these basic pieces of equipment is the *caldero*, the cast iron kettle.

Cast Iron Kettle *(Caldero)*

Cast iron kettles are essential because of their ability to absorb heat slowly, retain it, and transmit it evenly. The *caldero* creates the ideal environment for cooking perfect rice dishes, beans, and meats in the Puerto Rican style.

Chopping Boards

I recommend using hardwood boards, and I believe it is best to have four chopping boards—one for vegetables, one for chopping herbs, one for meats, and one for kneading dough. The benefit of using several boards for distinct functions is the prevention of acid residues (which often become trapped in the grain of the wood) mixing with other ingredients during the chopping process.

Food Processor

I am a purist in the kitchen, and enjoy using basic tools, like the knife and the mortar and pestle in my daily food preparation. But for dishes that require a lot of grinding, grating, or mixing, there is nothing like the modern food processor. Using our Cuisinart makes preparation of *pasteles* a much quicker process. And a food processor will grate tubers, like *yuca* or *malanga*, much more easily than will a hand grater.

Mortar and Pestle *(Pilón y Maceta)*

The mortar and pestle has been around since the beginning of time. I think of it as a truly universal tool. Fashioned out of every medium, from stone, seashells, tree trunks, to metals, its basic characteristic is that it is a cylindrical or shallow shaped bowl, varying in size, hollow in the center and balanced on the bottom by a flat base. Just about every culture has its own interpretation, sometimes designed for many specific applications. The common denominator of the *pilón* is its purpose, which is to trap a combination of ingredients inside the belly of the mortar while a cylinder-shaped shaft (the pestle) is manually thrust up and down continuously, pounding and fusing together the ingredients. I also use the *pilón* for cracking open cloves of garlic or other hard vegetables.

   The Spanish colonists had their version of the *pilón*, made of glazed clay and used for light pounding, and grinding nuts and garlic, and other ingredients for their *picada*, a pasty base used to flavor other dishes. The Tainos used a *pilón* carved from stone for heavy pounding of grains, roots, and seeds. *Pilóns* made of wood and gourds were used for light pounding and delicate mixing. The Africans also use the lighter version of the mortar and pestle as an on-the-spot prepping, serving, and eating bowl. This method of preparing and serving *mofongo* (see recipe on page 214) is still in use today.

Although the mortar and pestle remain a standard kitchen accessory in most Puerto Rican homes, modern technology has limited their use by the irresistible presence of the blender and food processor, as well as the availability of commercially packaged condiments and base mixes. In Puerto Rico the process of fixing herbs and spices in the *pilón* is called *machacando* (pounding), and is also known as *moliendo* (milling or grinding).

I use the *pilón* in my everyday cooking routine. It saves me time because I don't need to assemble it, nor take it apart to wash. But most importantly, it keeps the integrity of my herbs and spices uncompromised; there is no loss of the natural chemistry and no aftertaste or oxidation from contact with the cold blade of a knife or blender attachment. The *pilón* is ideal, especially when quantities of ingredients are small.

The *pilón*, fashioned out of wood or metal, in varied sizes, can be purchased at just about any Latin American produce store. Those made from ceramic or marble can be found in any major department store, or specialty cookware shops in the United States. I recommend the ones made from wood, especially the wood of cedar, oak or teak, 8 to 10 inches tall; the exact diameter and weight is relative to the size of the *pilón*.

Curing. This process helps eliminate the raw taste, smell, and protective coating of the new wood. To cure the *pilón*, combine one cup of hot water with ½ cup of white vinegar, and fill the belly of the *pilón* with the solution. Allow to sit for about an hour, then discard the solution and wipe the *pilón* dry. Take 4 cloves of garlic, one at a time, and practice *machacando*. To prevent the garlic from spinning out, place the cupped palm of your hand over the rim of the mortar and pound in a vertical motion.

Never, never wash the *pilón* again. Wipe it clean immediately after each use, place a paper bag over it and store in a dry place. Before each use you may want to dampen a cloth with a bit of vinegar and wipe the inside of the bowl clean.

When to use the *pilón*. Use the *pilón* every chance you get. It won't take long before you become proficient in the technique of its use and discover its true potential. When making marinades, sauces, and pastes, and whenever a recipe calls for pulverized, minced, ground, cracked, or crushed ingredients, use the *pilón* in the preparation. Use it when making the *sofritos*, or when making bread crumbs or cracker meal, or to pound nuts, seeds, and grains for producing a coarse or fine flour or meal. Chunks of meat can be tenderized with a mortar and pestle, and small amounts of fresh juices and acids from fruit and vegetables can be extracted.

How to use the *pilón*. Always place the largest dry pieces (e.g., garlic cloves) into the belly first, followed by the most textured (rock salt or peppercorns). You may combine all the textured ingredients at once, or in sequence. Then, taking the pestle in one hand, place it in the center of the mortar while cupping the top with the palm of your other hand and begin the thrusting movement up and down slowly, and from side to side. Stop every few seconds to add what remaining ingredients you may have and to monitor the texture you want to achieve. The last ingredients to add will be the liquids, such as vinegar, olive oil, or fruit juices, etc. Then use a wooden spoon to blend, stirring slowly from the bottom up while scraping the sides. Once the task is completed, cover the *pilón* with a small clean kitchen towel and set it aside until ready to use. This will help prevent the aromas from escaping through evaporation. Do not transfer the mixture. The attributes of a cured *pilón* will enhance the complexity of the herbs and spices. Generally, I let my *pilón* sit for an hour or so next to a warm spot on top of the stove, especially when I'm fixing a garlic *mojo* for bread or a topping for hot vegetables.

Essential Ingredients of *Comida Criolla*

These are the ingredients that are essential to our cuisine. Many of them you may find in your own kitchen. Others can be obtained in ethnic markets, Latino or Asian. Or don't be afraid to substitute if you cannot find a particular item. If I think that an ingredient may be difficult to obtain, I offer substitutes that will work well.

Adobo

Adobo is a compound condiment, made from a combination of crushed fresh garlic, sea salt, black ground pepper, and ground cumin. The *adobo* mixture is excellent as a base for marinades, as a deep seasoning agent, and an instant and temporary preservative for meat, poultry, and fish. This preparatory technique of coloring and flavoring food is known as *adobar* and consists simply of rubbing or coating by brushing the *adobo* onto the food items, whether meats or vegetables.

When roasting large cuts of meat, the deep seasoning technique is employed. The purpose is to trap the seasoning agents deep inside the cavities where they will interact with and infuse the natural juices released by the meat during the roasting process. The trapped seasoned juices also become a self-basting element for the roast. This benefit will prevent a significant loss of flavor and helps to slow down the dehydration of the meat.

To employ the *adobar* method, lay the cut of meat flat on the roasting pan. Using a boning knife in the flat position, insert the knife and drive it at an angle from the sides of the meat to the center, or as far as to where the bone is located. The cavities should be spaced approximately six inches apart. When using this technique the *adobo* ingredients are usually mixed whole, or very coarse (see *Adobo* recipe on page 294). The refined *adobo* is commonly prepared fresh in the kitchen, but also can be purchased in small commercially packaged quantities at most supermarkets. There are accents and seasoned salts with varying ingredients, most of which are compounds of powders from dehydrated ingredients, synthetics and chemical preservatives.

I prefer to mix a fresh batch of *adobo* whenever it is needed, because it allows me full control of the amounts of ingredients in proportion to each other, and because I ensure that no chemical preservatives are involved. The amounts and quality of the ingredients are important, particularly when I'm looking to decrease or highlight the accent of a particular dish. Using commercially prepared and packaged seasoning does not compare to the flavors and aromas obtained from rock salt crystals, whole peppercorns, fresh garlic, ground cumin seeds, etc., when freshly milled or processed in a mortar.

Annatto *(Achiote)*

The use of *achiote* emulsion as a technique for food coloring and flavoring has always been an important aspect in the preparation of traditional food in the Puerto Rican kitchen. The Tainos called it *bixa*. This emulsion, when infused with other herbs and spices, fortifies the flavors, aromas and textures which gives Puerto Rican cooked food its distinct, regional characteristics.

The mildly pungent flavor of the annato seed is released when mixed with lard in a saucepan and cooked over intense heat. In addition to this distinct flavor, a deep orange-colored dye is also released from the seeds, transforming the opaque melting lard into an intensely yellow-colored composition.

The seeds are then removed by straining the mixture through a fine sieve. The emulsion is then placed in a jar or container and reserved for many uses in the kitchen. When used in conjunction with the *adobo* for marinating white meats, it induces a finished golden brown color and texture to the cooked white meat dishes, especially pork and poultry. It also adds character and complexity to vegetables such as *yuca* and potatoes.

The emulsion is also broadly used to intensify the color and texture of mixed rice dishes, such as *Arroz con Pollo*, or *Arroz con Bacalao*. It is used to accent bean stocks in the absence of tomatoes or tomato puree. The implementation of the *achiote* as a coloring and flavoring agent was the best way to deal with the many necessities not found in the kitchens of Spanish colonial Puerto Rico. When the cook of that era discovered that saffron, an essential ingredient of the Spanish kitchen, was not readily available in the New World, the *achiote* seed became an excellent substitute. These *achiote* seed-producing shrubs were soon transported to most of the tropical countries in the world and are sometimes referred to as the "poor people's saffron."

In this book I use no animal fat or heavy vegetable oils. In my recipes the use of *achiote* emulsion is substituted by a lighter emulsion made from pure olive oil and Spanish paprika. With this combination I am able to obtain the same color and texture as with the *achiote*, along with a mild peppery flavor, plus the obvious benefits of lighter and healthier dishes by eliminating the use of lard or fatty vegetable oils.

Coconut *(Coco)*

The coconut has many uses in most of the households in the coastal regions of Puerto Rico. The coconut is separated into two categories: *fresco de agua* (ripe with water) and *seco* (dry). The ripe-with-water coconuts contain soft meat and are used in the creation of desserts and sweet toppings, glazes and sauces. The water content is drained out and used as a fresh beverage, or a mixer for rum drinks. Today, and in the past, it is combined with boiled coconut palm roots and other medicinal plants as a remedy to treat certain ailments, from flushing out the kidneys to breaking up gallstones.

The coco *seco* (dry) is used for intense flavoring and/or for texture in cooked dishes such as Island Goat (see recipe), and for coconut milk and coconut oil extracts. When I was a child, and for hundreds of years before that, the shell of the dry coconut was fashioned into drinking cups and serving bowls. Today these utensils are made as folk art. I have included at least one example of a dry coconut-based recipe in each of the cooking categories to illustrate the endless possibilities of working with coconut meat and coconut milk.

Dry coconuts are available just about everywhere in Puerto Rico and mainland United States. The important factor to consider when buying a coconut is its freshness. To determine the suitability of the coconut take these steps: (1) inspect the coconut for cracks on the outer shell; (2) place the coconut close to the ear and shake it, listening for the heavy sound of slushing water; (3) feel and slightly scratch with your fingernail around the eye of the coconut, and sniff.

The coconut is invariably rancid when: (1) a crack is present (regardless of the size of the crack); (2) the sound of the water is hollow and light, producing an echo effect; and, (3) the area around the eye and the eye itself are slightly soft and spongy, and you can detect a mildew scent after scratching the surface.

To work with the coconut. Use a clean nail and a hammer to puncture a point in each of the coconut eyes; then finish the perforation by inserting a corkscrew through each eye until the coconut has been deeply penetrated. Turn the coconut upside down, slanted slightly over a bowl to catch the outpouring of coconut water. It may be necessary to shake the coconut to ensure that all the water has been released. The water will have coconut fiber specks which can be eliminated by running the water through a fine mesh cloth or linen strainer. Taste the water to be certain the coconut is not rancid. The water should taste and smell sweet, and void of any hint of sourness.

To crack open the shell, gently tap the belly of the coconut with a hammer, rotating the coconut while at the same time increasing the blow of the hammer until the coconut splits open. The meat inside the coconut shell should be completely white. Separate the meat from the shell by placing the split coconut into a skillet or shallow pan (meat side up) with 2 cups of water. Cover and place over medium heat to simmer until most of the water evaporates. Remove from heat and allow to cool to the touch, then insert the point of a shucking knife between the meat and the shell, exerting upward pressure until the meat is separated from the shell. The coconut meat should then be placed in a bowl and rinsed under cold running water.

Coconut milk can be extracted by using a heavy-duty grater or food processor. Shred the coconut meat, then place in a stock pot with 6 cups of water. Place over high heat and bring to a quick boil, then reset the heat to low and continue to simmer until the mixture begins to rise. Remove from the burner and allow it to cool.

To extract the milk, place a linen cloth inside a sieve and filter through the cloth, draining the liquid through. Carefully pick up the linen cloth by the four corners and twirl it into a ball, twisting and squeezing the coconut pulp dry. To obtain the maximum amount of milk, do a second pressing by repeating the process and using two cups of water. I suggest freezing the milk in ice cube trays for future use.

Although I recommend the use of fresh dry coconut in my recipes, I have obtained great results by using commercially packaged coconut milk and cream, both the frozen and canned varieties. I do not recommend the dry shredded coconut for extracting milk, as the volume and the quality of the milk yield is not worth the time spent.

Dry Salted Codfish (*Bacalao*)

Bacalao is dried codfish, preserved by a drying and salting process that has its origins in the Scandinavian countries. The codfish became a staple all over the Mediterranean and found its way to the New World during the early explorations. The Spanish colonists introduced *bacalao* to Puerto Rico in the early sixteenth century and it has remained a popular staple ever since.

The many ways that dried codfish can be prepared, cooked and served gives it the distinction of being the "old reliable" in most Puerto Rican kitchens. I have included instructions for some of the many ways in which *bacalao* is fixed and served in different regions of The Island, from the fritters of the coastal towns to the country-style stew of the central mountain regions.

Salt cod is sold in most Latino, Mediterranean, and Asian produce stores in the United States and, of course, in supermarkets in Puerto Rico. We have also seen, in supermarkets catering to the gourmet trade, a variety from Canada that is sold in small, sealed wooden boxes. The pieces inside are much smaller than the slabs we find in Latino markets. The kind that I use and recommend is the salt cod fillet, because it is boneless and widely available. It is sold in bulk, and you can choose the cut you want. We buy it at Latin American markets, where we find cartons filled with small and large slabs of the fish. Ask for the middle section, because it is the most layered and fleshy part, and its flaky integrity will be preserved during the cooking process. I explain the method of preparing and "de-salting" the codfish in the recipe section.

To store the raw codfish for any length of time, place it in a tight lidded glass container or plastic wrap, and refrigerate. It will keep for several months.

Garlic (*Ajo*)

Garlic is one of the oldest known cultivated plants in the world and a member of the lily family, as are onions, shallots, leeks and chives. It dates back five thousand years. Its many uses for both cooking and medicinal purposes have spread throughout the world. There are probably as many claims attesting to the powers of garlic as there are cultures.

The Spanish colonists introduced garlic to Puerto Rico, and with each passing generation, the list of garlic uses became so extensive that the plant became known as *arrasa con todo*, or "cure-all." The prestige of house cooks soared depending upon their ability to exploit herbs and plants, garlic being one of them. It was believed capable of curing toothaches and earaches, used for dressing wounds, curing fungus, impotency, bronchial congestions, and insect bites, just to name a few. My mother often said, "seven little cloves of garlic and let nature do the rest." I first became acquainted with garlic's "magical healing powers" at the age of seven, while attending a traditional family picnic on one of our favorite banks of the Maragüey River in Ponce.

Five minutes after our arrival my older brother and two cousins left the picnic site to go foraging for tamarinds and mangoes that grew wild at the bottom of a nearby ravine. I insisted on following them and they, in turn, did everything possible to discourage me from tagging along. They ran and hid and made terrifying sounds to scare me into turning back, but I was persistent. Then they spotted a nest of pigmy wasps hanging from the branch of a guava tree and, while sidestepping it themselves, they urged me to walk on, under the tree.

Completely unaware of their malicious intent, I followed the path straight under the guava tree, only to feel an immediate explosion on my forehead and intense heat on my back and chest, produced by the numerous and incessant stings of what felt like thousands of angry wasps. Confused, crying, and hurling a barrage of grownup curses at my brother and cousins, I ran as fast as I could back to the picnic area where my mother was able to figure out what had happened from my incoherent jabberings. She immediately covered my wounded body with a quickly concocted mixture of garlic and wild aloe vera while comforting and reassuring me that the magic power of the garlic would be released instantly and that the pain would vanish quickly. It worked! I ate garlic most of that day and I haven't stopped eating garlic since!

Preparing and Using Garlic. While I am not prepared to offer the reader any medicinal recipes for using garlic, I include this ingredient as the primary seasoning in most of my dishes, the catalyst to hold together the repertoire of herbs and spices.

The quantity, the method of preparation, and the sequence used in the cooking process will determine the outcome of the flavor of the dishes being prepared. Fresh garlic is inherently pungent. Maximum pungency will be present when the garlic clove is crushed, minced or liquefied. The intensity of the garlic flavor and aroma is proportionate to the amounts used and to the reduction of the garlic during cooking time. The larger the pieces and the longer it cooks, the softer the flavor becomes, while the aroma zooms to a peak, then gradually descends into a subtle fragrance.

It is during this process of releasing the spirit of the garlic that I chart the course for the rest of the ingredients to follow. As an aromatic agent I combine it with onions, mint, sage, or lime. As a condiment I combine it with rock salt, cayenne pepper, black peppercorns, and fresh ginger; as an emulsifier I mix it with oil, vinegar, lemon, or lime juice. I combine it with green herbs high in chlorophyll content such as fresh cilantro, parsley, oregano, or marjoram. There is no limitation to the many flavor possibilities one can achieve when using garlic as a foundation.

There are several methods for peeling garlic. My choice is the following: hold the clove with the fingers of one hand while holding the pestle in your other hand, tapping the clove with enough force to crack the shell open. Then separate the peel from the clove by peeling away the covering. For obtaining thin layers that will melt upon touching the hot surface of a skillet, cut the cloves in half lengthwise, remove the peel and cross cut slices with a razor thin blade.

You can peel the garlic ahead of time and keep it fresh for at least three months in a glass jar filled with olive oil, tightly sealed and stored in a dry, cool place. Also, fresh garlic can remain fresh and strong without olive oil if you keep it in a dry, cool place away from sunlight or heat. It is all right to use a piece of garlic that may display a green sprout growing from it; the strength is not as great, but it is workable. On the other hand, soft or wilted garlic should be discarded.

Gingerroot (*Jengibre*)

Ginger is a central figure in the mosaic of herbs and spices upon which I draw to create the subtle undertones of my sauces. It is the main ingredient in the Island Bouquet Garni. When combined with garlic in the right proportions, what will be produced is a subtle, piquant effect without the high level of acidity and palate discomfort we sometimes experience when eating foods laced with chili peppers. The ginger can be controlled at every step of the cooking process, in the same way garlic is controlled, to produce the proper aroma, texture, flavor, accent and complexity.

Ginger was commercially cultivated on the southeastern part of The Island until the beginning of the nineteenth century, when it was replaced by sugar cane and the plantation system. The demand for ginger continued to grow as greater discoveries of its potential for use in meats, sauces, gravies, pastries, candies, and beverages occurred in kitchens throughout the world. The Puerto Rican gingerroot is smaller and much more pungent and flavorful than other commercially available ginger that I have tried. Although still in abundance in Puerto Rico's farmers' markets, chances are that you may not find this variety in U.S. mainland markets. However, the fresh ginger found in most Asian and Middle Eastern produce stores and supermarkets can still do the job.

Gingerroot works best when it is fresh and crispy. Make the test by snapping a piece off the same way you would snap a piece of dry twig. It should break easily without bending, like rubber. When working with ginger, peel it with a knife on top of a cutting board, not with a vegetable peeler. Save the skin for tea or for garni bouquet. Once peeled, wrap the ginger in a cold damp towel until ready to use. Chop or slice just prior to use; this will help preserve all its power.

When purchasing fresh gingerroot it's wise not to exceed the quantity needed for immediate use. Fresh gingerroot can keep for weeks when properly stored. However, you don't really know how long the ginger has been sitting in the store bins, so I suggest buying only what is needed for immediate use. Keep it in a cool, dry place. I don't recommend refrigeration, because the cold moist air will enhance fermentation and cause the root to become soggy and stringy. Different stages of aging will greatly influence the natural attributes of the fresh ginger, and consequently will limit its action in the cooking process. The transformation of the ginger during cooking will be evident when the texture changes from crispy to fibrous, from a moderate pungency to spicy hot, and from an invigorating aroma to a soft fragrance.

Green Onions (*Cebollín*)

Green onions, or scallions, are delicate and effective in subtle flavoring of sauces, salads, meat, fish, and poultry. The high moisture content of the green onions is a benefit when sautéing with fresh herbs as it will provide some liquid to the drier ingredients, and help prevent excess dehydration. Garlic, for example, will toast rather quickly upon touching the hot surface of a skillet, and the moisture released by the onions will slow down the reaction of the garlic to the hot surface. The same thing occurs with other fresh and green herbs, such as oregano and sage.

Aside from the more obvious use of green onions as a seasoning, they can also be used to neutralize the strong odors sometimes given off by fresh lamb, goat or seafood during the cooking process. To do this, take a deep pan or stock pot and prepare a solution with the following ingredients: 2 quarts of water, 1 tablespoon cider vinegar, 1/3 cup of lime juice, 1 tablespoon coarse rock salt.

Submerge the meat in the solution for approximately 15 minutes, then discard the solution and rinse the meat under cold running water. Take 12 green onions and cut them in half vertically and layer the inside of a glass bowl or pan with half the onions. Place your meat or fish on top of the onions, then add the remaining green onions on top. Press down slightly with the palm of your hand. Cover with a kitchen towel and refrigerate for approximately 2 hours.

The green onions will absorb most of the unpleasant odors. Once the green onions have done their job, remove them and discard. Now your meat or fish is ready to be processed as per the recipe.

Ham (*Jamón*)

Smoked cured ham has many uses in the Puerto Rican kitchen, and due to its smoky quality and intense flavor and texture, it is indispensable as a base in the preparation of *sofrito*, and for soups, rice, beans, stuffings, appetizers, and entree dishes. I have included at least one sample recipe in which the use of ham, fresh or cured, can be employed to obtain different and delectable results for different occasions.

Fresh ham (*pernil trasero*) is used for pork meat fillings in *pasteles*, *alcapurrias*, *empanadas* and *piononos*. *Pernil delantero*, a shoulder cut, is used for roasting, as is baked sugar-cured ham. The fresh and cured hams that I suggest in the recipes can be purchased at any meat market. In the recipes I recommend a specific ham for a specific use.

Olive Oil (*Aceite de Oliva*)

My memories of my relationship with my grandmother are as many as they are pleasant. I will never forget how wonderful her fresh food tasted. My favorite dish was a plate of freshly cooked *vianda* (boiled vegetables, like *Serenata*) laced with olive oil and eaten under a shady tree, using our fingers as utensils. "The goodness is in the olive oil," she would say.

In earlier centuries, olive oil was much in demand in the New World and Puerto Rico, not only for cooking purposes but as fuel for lamps, lubricants for machinery and weapons, and medicinal uses. The Spanish trade route to the New World was devastated at times as Spanish cargo and supply ships fell prey to the pirates operating throughout the Caribbean, leaving the colonies without raw materials and basic necessities for long periods. Sometimes it would be one or two years before a cargo ship would manage to reach The Island. The limited supplies caused prices to soar and the goods were available only to those who were able to afford the exorbitant prices. Olive oil, like a fine wine, was highly prized and priced. Its use in the kitchen was limited to special occasions, and to this day we refer to it as *aceite de comer* (eating oil).

Olive oil has always been indispensable in Puerto Rican kitchens, both for cooking and for use on the table alongside vinegar as a condiment for seasoning salads and vegetables. In my recipes I suggest the use of Spanish olive oils because I find them to be light and intensely flavored. For salads and cold dressings my preference is the extra virgin oils. For prepping and cooking I prefer the pure olive oils, because they are refined and have a slightly higher acidity, which holds pretty well when mixed with other ingredients during the cooking process, leaving no oily aftertaste while the subtle, fruity flavor of the olive is prevalent.

Most commercial brands imported to the United States are of good to excellent quality and can be found in any well-stocked supermarket, specialty store, or Latino market. Most oils will last for an indefinite amount of time stored in a cool dark place away from direct heat or sunlight; the temperature can vary between 50 to 60 degrees Farenheit.

Olives and Capers (*Alcaparrado*)

Alcaparrado is a combination of olives and capers preserved in a salt and vinegar solution and commercially packaged in glass jars. Olives and capers have been used traditionally in most *rellenos* (stuffings and fillings) and dishes, such as *pasteles*, salads and marinated meat dishes. In my recipes the use of the olives and capers transcend the function of a filler. When combined with raisins in a *pionono* or *pastelillo* shell, the olives and the pickled quality of the capers mix with the sweetness of the raisins, providing the palate with a burst of complex flavors and a nutty texture. The experience is always unique from dish to dish.

Although the pimiento stuffed olives are commonly used, I prefer the fresh green olives or sun ripened varieties sold in bulk at the local farmers market or in specialty stores. Spanish, Greek, or Italian olives will do the job.

To preserve the olives for any length of time, I pack them in a jar with a good quality extra virgin olive oil and store the jar in a dark cool place until ready to use.

Capers can be purchased at most supermarkets. Although I prefer the capers of Spanish origin, any variety of these small berries packed in vinegar will be fine. Some brands contain higher acidity levels than others, so I recommend first tasting the capers as a way to check the acidity level prior to using. Should the capers prove to be too bitter for your taste, soak them in a bowl of cool water for a few seconds, then strain them and pat dry. This method will minimize some of the acidity.

Onions *(Cebollas)*

Onions are a must ingredient in most cooked Puerto Rican dishes. The foundation for the original *sofritos* consisted of caramelizing onions with olive oil, and later evolved into a much more complex method for seasoning food. (See the chapter on Sauces and Marinades.)

Lightly sauteed onions are used in dishes such as the *Biftec Encebollado* (Puerto Rican steak), *Bacalao Guisado* (stewed codfish), and *Pescado en Escabeche* (marinated fish). Green, red, yellow, and white onions have their own distinct flavors and textures which I take advantage of when preparing most of my dishes. I use them not only as an aromatic but as agents to minimize and neutralize the strong odors of fish, lamb, or goat, in the earliest stages of preparation.

I use red onions for their sweetness, supple texture, and appealing color. They are a lively and elegant way to adorn salads and complement other garnishes. I use chopped yellow or white onions during the cooking process to work in combination with garlic for flavor complexity. As the garlic breaks down, its essence is captured and fused by the action of caramelizing onions, rendering a nicely balanced perfume and subtle pungent flavor to the finished cooked dish.

Store onions in a cool and dry place. Never wash an onion before of after peeling; washing will greatly minimize its depth of flavor. When cutting onions on a cutting board, breathe through your mouth and not your nose. This will help keep you from "crying" as you work with onions.

Pimiento Morrones

Spanish roasted peppers are flavorful and slightly peppery. Their name translates more exactly to Moorish peppers. Traditionally used as a flavoring agent and as a garnish in most Puerto Rican dishes, this item is available in cans or glass jars, and can be purchased at most supermarkets.

Most processed pimientos are of good quality and can come in handy when needed in a hurry. But they do tend to be soft and difficult to "prep." Therefore, in order to maintain the integrity of a fresh-cooked dish with only fresh ingredients, I have substituted the canned Spanish pimiento with fresh green, red, and yellow bell peppers. Using these fresh peppers also allows for crisp, manageable textures when fine chopping, dicing, and slicing.

Techniques for Roasting Peppers

There is very little work involved in roasting peppers. During the spring, summer, and early fall, I set up my barbecue grill in the backyard, keeping it handy to roast fresh peppers at a moment's notice. They lend a unique and smoky flavor to a variety of dishes.

Place whole peppers on the grill approximately 4 inches from the nest of hot coals. Do not place the hood over the grill or cover the peppers. They will cook under hot pressure, dehydrate, and become too soft. Crispy peppers are best to work with and taste so much better. Once the peppers are superficially blistered on the outside, remove them from the grill and scrape off the blistered skin with a knife. Then return them to the grill and further expose the peeled peppers to the heat until charred lines begin to form; this will create the smoky taste. Then, while the peppers are still hot, quickly submerge them in olive oil infused with freshly mashed garlic. Cover and refrigerate the peppers until ready to use.

To prepare one or two peppers indoors on top of the stove, hook the peppers with a utility fork and roast them over the open flame of your burner, rotating the position for uniform effect. Then place the peppers inside a paper bag and close the bag by tightly twisting the open end. Shake vigorously for approximately 30 seconds. Remove the peppers from the bag and set them on top of a kitchen towel; wipe off the excess charred skin. Core the peppers and place them in a bowl with olive oil and refrigerate until ready to use.

During the winter months I do a lot of baking and take advantage of the hot oven by broiling and roasting items which can be refrigerated and preserved for another day or another meal. I take the peppers, core, seed, and butterfly them, then lay them flat on a sheet pan and place them under the broiler section of the oven until the skin is blackened (charred). Then I cover the peppers with a cool, damp kitchen towel and gently rub off the blistered skin. I then transfer the broiled peppers to a glass bowl with an olive oil and garlic mixture, cover and refrigerate.

Do not wash peppers after broiling, roasting or barbecuing or you will destroy much of their flavor and smoky quality. There is no substitute for fresh roasted peppers.

Rice *(Arroz)*

Rice is the primary food source on which most Puerto Rican meals are based, making The Island's rice market and consumption per capita one of the highest in the world among rice consuming cultures. Unfortunately, The Island does not have the acreage available to produce a significant quantity for local use, and thus relies on U.S. imports to satisfy its demand for this precious commodity.

Rice is a way of life, and Puerto Ricans have been able to exploit the grain's volatile quality to a superior level of excellence and gusto. From San Juan's *asopaos* (brothy rice dishes) to Ponce's *arroz con dulce*, whether white or yellow, brown or black, rice dishes will always be present at the dinner table.

Rice was introduced to The Island by Spanish colonists, and through the centuries, the many ways of cooking rice has also been contributed to by African, East Indian, and Asian cultures. The preparation and cooking of rice is a task which requires a conscientious approach in the Puerto Rican kitchen. One of the first kitchen tasks that a female member of the family was taught at a very early age was to cook perfect rice. Hopefully, we have come a bit farther in this day and age, and are teaching our sons the secrets of good rice as well. I like to think of this book as a step toward that end.

Saffron *(Azafrán)*

Azafrán, as it is known in Spanish, is probably the most exotic, sophisticated and expensive of all the spices in the world. The plant is a native of Asia; its cultivation and use was introduced by the Spanish Moors. The word *zafran* derives from the Arabic, meaning yellow, the color it gives to the cooking process of rice and other foods. Saffron comes in both thread and powdered form. I prefer to use the threads in my recipes; although they are much more expensive, the results are more gratifying. The powdered form sometimes can be of a lower quality and somewhat adulterated, making a vast difference in the outcome of the dish being prepared.

To obtain maximum results when using saffron, I place the threads in my mortar and crush them; then I add twice the amount of warm water and let the mixture sit for about ten minutes to extract and further intensify the flavor. It is important to control the amount used, as too much will produce a medicine-like quality in the flavor. I use saffron in combination with Spanish paprika, cayenne pepper, and Spanish sherry in my yellow dishes, such as *Arroz con Pollo*, *Arroz con Bacalao*, and *Arroz con Jamón* to obtain a burst of flavor, and for color intensity. Saffron can be purchased at many specialty food stores in relatively small and affordable quantities. It will keep for a couple of years in an air-tight container, away from direct sunshine, humidity and extreme temperatures.

Salt *(Sal)*

Salt, says the dietitian and medical practitioner of the twentieth century, is bad for one's health. Therefore, in the interest of good health, not only have I reduced the quantities of salt in my recipes, but I also consistently use and recommend the use of rock salt (sea salt).

Rock salt disperses further when it is mixed and dissolved by the natural juices of foods during the cooking process, and because of its intense flavor, the amount required in a recipe is less than with commercially processed salts. It is sold in both coarse and fine crystals at many health food stores and specialty shops.

I prefer to work with coarse crystals (pebbles) because it enables me to have greater control of the amounts to be employed while assembling a meat dish for roasting or baking, or open-pit roasting and barbecuing of pork, turkey, lamb, goat, and large cuts of beef. Whenever I need soft salt, I use the mortar and pestle and pound the coarse crystals to obtain the size of granules I want.

Traditionally, Puerto Ricans have enjoyed their meats cooked "well done and well seasoned," succulently tasty and tender on the inside, crisp and flavorful on the outside. No burning is allowed. The key to achieve the perfect balance is by using rock salt crystals in the *adobo*.

The meat sweats and the moisture dissolves the salt, which in turn is absorbed by the meat (see *adobo* and *adobar* techniques).

Sofrito

There is no adequate English translation for *sofrito*. The essence of Puerto Rican cooking, most Puerto Ricans will say, is in this very special combination of ingredients. Ask where the *sofrito* came from and most will reply, "My mother's kitchen." The *sofrito* will always be found in the kitchen, made ahead of time and packed in glass jars with tightly closed lids and preserved for future use.

The basic *sofrito* has its origin in northern Spain where it was called *sofregit* and consisted of caramelized onions in olive oil. The introduction of its use in Puerto Rico can be attributed to the Catalonian colonists who migrated from northern Spain in the middle of the sixteenth century and settled in the southern part of the island in San Germán and my hometown, Ponce. The word *sofregit* translates into "slow, lengthy cooking." The *sofrito* soon came to take its rightful place in the Puerto Rican kitchen and, like its Catalonian originator, became a dominant force in Puerto Rican culinary culture. After three hundred years of cultural transformation, by the middle of the nineteenth century the *sofregit* had become *sofrito criollo*, a gastronomical expression of the pride of the new breed of *criollos*, and the soul of Puerto Rican cuisine.

Sofrito Criollo

Made in the traditional Puerto Rican way, *sofrito* consists of garlic cloves, black pepper, salt, onions, sweet peppers, cilantro, oregano, and tomatoes, pounded together in the belly of a mortar to a paste-like consistency. This mix is then transferred to a frying pan, to be combined with diced fat back, diced ham shank and *manteca de achiote* (a lard emulsion mixed with annatto oil), and reduced to a rich paste, bursting with flavors and aromas, to be used as the base for all mixed dishes.

In this book I suggest a lighter and healthier alternative to the traditional *sofrito*, which I have dubbed as *neo-sofrito*. In order that we may appreciate the special qualities of the *sofrito*, and for the purpose of obtaining new and fresh flavors, aromas, textures and color schemes, I have modified the method in which the ingredients are combined and prepared.

By chopping, dicing, slicing and mincing instead of pounding into a paste, I control the accent and texture of the fresh ingredients such as garlic, peppers, onions, tomatoes, fresh oregano, and cilantro.

Olive oil has been substituted for lard, fat back by broiled dry bacon, and lean smoke-cured ham or honey-cured ham for ham shanks. I have also described in the recipes, methods for added complexity by varying combinations of herbs and spices such as mint, fresh ginger, saffron, Spanish paprika, cayenne pepper, and cooking spirits such as brandy, rum, sherry, red and white wines. (See the recipe for *Neo-Sofrito*.)

Spirits and Deglazing

While the technique of deglazing is generally applied to cooking off the alcohol in wines or spirits and leaving the essence of its flavor in the pan, I like to take advantage of the aromatic moisture as it rises, and trap the main ingredients by covering the pot or skillet. Not only does this capture the essence of the wine, brandy or beer in the cooked dish, but also the subtle effect it has on the individual ingredients that make up the dish. I have suggested the use of Spanish sherry, brandy, and white or red wine to enhance the integrity of the dishes. The use of a good quality spirit produces the best results. It will also come in handy when things get rough in the kitchen!

Sweet Peppers (*Aji Dulce*)

Sweet peppers are an essential element of Puerto Rican cuisine. Unfortunately, the variety that has been cultivated on The Island for centuries is not available commercially in most of the United States. The delicate berry-size pepper known as *aji dulce* is used for its aroma and exotic flavors that burst forth when they come into contact with a hot surface. The *aji* comes in different colors: green, yellow, orange, and red, and with each color is a varying degree of texture and taste. The green is the most intense, and is mashed in the mortar as part of the *recao* (the green components of the *sofrito*), while the yellow, orange and red are chopped, diced, sliced, or tossed in whole at the last minute into finished dishes for texture, accents and garnishes.

I have rarely found Puerto Rican sweet peppers in U.S. markets. However, I have found an almost comparable item at one of the leading retail food supermarkets on the west coast. The pepper is called *habanero*. It is expensive and somewhat larger and more pungent than the Puerto Rican *aji dulce* but can be made to work as well.

Tomatoes (*Tomates*)

When we say salad, we usually picture lettuce and tomatoes. When we say *salsa*, the picture is of a red sauce, the base of which is the *sofrito*, an infusion of all the herbs and spices held together in emulsified tomatoes. The tomatoes that I prefer to use in my recipes are organically grown, vine-ripened tomatoes, and the Roma Plum tomatoes. I prefer these varieties for their pronounced flavor and firm fleshy texture which holds up very well when exposed to direct heat and prolonged cooking. But anyone who is fond of tomatoes knows that there is nothing like those that are home-grown. Once you have tasted them, you will be disappointed with store bought tomatoes.

Tomatoes should be firm and plump when purchased. To slow down the ripening process, refrigerate them. To accelerate the ripening process, leave tomatoes out at room temperature, exposed to light, until they turn deep red.

To peel tomatoes, make a 4-way superficial incision with a sharp knife at the base. Insert a fork through the center of the core and immerse the tomato in a pot of boiling water for about 5 seconds; the skin tissue should curl back. Allow to cool for a few seconds, then finish separating the skin with a paring knife or your fingertips.

To peel by roasting on an open flame, score the tomato, then insert the points of a fork through the center of the core (the navel). Apply a light coat of olive oil with a brush, then hold the tomato over the flame, rotating continuously until the skin blisters. Allow to cool to the touch and then finish removing the skin with a knife or your fingertips. This method is ideal when a smoky accent is sought in a tomato-based dish.

For removing the seeds, cross-cut the tomato and use the points of a fork to eliminate the seeds. I do not recommend washing the seeds away; by so doing you'll eliminate the natural juices and end up with just dry pulp and shell instead of a delicate, full-bodied and flavorful fruit.

Use of Fresh Herbs and Spices

Fresh herbs such as coriander, oregano, sage, mint, and marjoram are widely used in our cuisine. Fortunately, these are found sometimes fresh, in most supermarkets and produce stores. In Puerto Rico we have different varieties of these herbs. One type of oregano called *oregano brujo*, which means "witch's oregano," grows wild, has large leaves, and a more pungent taste and aroma than commercially cultivated oregano. If you do not have access to fresh oregano, sweet marjoram may be substituted, and if neither is available in fresh form, the dried variety of either oregano or marjoram will do.

We have two varieties of *cilantro*: common *cilantro* (coriander) and *culantro*, a wide-leafed coriander. These fresh herbs can be found all year round in many produce stores. Crushed, dry coriander seeds can also be used.

When substituting fresh herbs with dried herbs, I recommend soaking the dry ingredients for approximately five minutes with an equal amount of warm water. Dry ingredients require longer cooking time to release their full flavor and aroma; through soaking this process is accelerated. But remember, there is no substitute for freshly grown herbs.

Spices that appear prominently in our cuisine are black pepper, cayenne pepper, paprika, chili pepper, cinnamon, cloves, nutmeg, vanilla, and star anise. We use these ingredients in both their whole and ground forms. In combination with other natural ingredients from the region, such as coconuts, almonds, rice or seafood, they form the flavors known as "tropical." All are intrinsic to the Caribbean Basin and imperative to our distinctive Puerto Rican cuisine.

Appetizers
& Finger Foods

Aperitivos

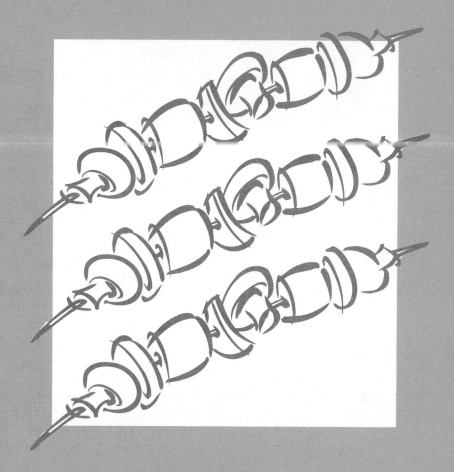

> *At last, dear heart, at last*
> *a breath of hope,*
> *for between the crimson clouds*
> *my land can be seen*
> *upon the horizon.*
>
> .....
>
> *And there against the dark background*
> *of silhouetted mountains,*
> *under a pure and handsome sky*
> *enclosed within the whiteness of her walls*
> *my most beautiful San Juan.*
>
> JOSÉ GAUTIER BENÍTEZ

The plane ride to Puerto Rico is always exciting, not only because of the natural excitement one feels when traveling, but also because of the Puerto Ricans on the plane who are returning to their island. As the plane starts its descent, the walls of the famous fortress, *El Morro*, come into view, and all the Puerto Ricans on board begin to clap and cheer. It is a moment truly worthy of all the sentiment expressed by the nineteenth century poet, José Gautier Benítez, in his poem, written as he returned by boat to Puerto Rico.

But from there the journey has only just begun. In Puerto Rico many finger foods are sold at beach hut restaurants and *kioskos* (roadside stands) near the airports, and along all the well-traveled roads throughout The Island. When a Puerto Rican returns after having been away a long time, his or her first stop will be at one of these stands to indulge in their first delicious taste of home.

Upon my numerous returns to The Island, I usually drove from San Juan to Ponce, a trip that ordinarily takes an hour and fifteen minutes. But because of my country's delicious finger foods, the drive frequently turned into a twenty-four hour adventure of fun and eating as my companions and I traveled coast to coast, stopping along the way at every *kiosko* that boasted of making the "best" of what The Island had to offer. I was never disappointed. We would continue into the interior, up and down serpentine winding roads, through backroads that revealed green *campos* and fertile lands, and every so often stopped to collect gingerroot, sweet chili peppers, *oregano brujo* (oregano), and *culantro* (cilantro) growing wild on the side of the roads.

Along the way we always marveled at the simplicity and hospitality of the people, how these qualities still prevailed despite the modern, faster pace of life in the larger cities, and how the natural beauty of The Island still serves as an enhancement to the beauty of the people.

Frituras, deep-fried finger foods, will always represent the embodiment of everything that was home to me, the gratifying sensorial experiences I had as a child walking through my mother's garden, enticed by the aromas and textures of the herbs, spices and medicinal plants that flourished unattended, as if placed there by magic for our indulgence and delight. "Stop eating my plants," my mother would shout from the other end of the patio. "God did not put them there for you to make a meal out of in one sitting. Give them a chance to grow, tomorrow is another day." I would carefully pluck the young leaves of some, and the mature leaves of others—yellows, reds, light greens—always combining the textures and colors and discovering endless possibilities in the combinations of flavors and complexity. It was not until years later, when my mother taught me the many ways she combines and blends basic herbs and spices with other ingredients to come up with a delightful array of dishes, that I finally came to understand and appreciate the true value of my mother's garden, her Creole legacy, and her gastronomical knowledge.

Finger foods are often referred to as *mata hambre*, or food taken to "kill hunger." While not necessarily a full meal in themselves, they can be eaten as a light snack or made into a full meal by adding a soup, salad or another dish. I have designed the recipes to produce small portions in case you want to serve them as appetizers to a main meal or enjoy them as a light snack.

Traditionally, most finger foods in Puerto Rico, and throughout the Caribbean, have been deep-fried in animal fat and fatty oils, a practice that by today's standards is considered unhealthy. I believe it is this cooking method that alienates a number of health-conscious individuals from ever sampling and enjoying the variety of wonderful foods from the Puerto Rican kitchen. Instead, I have concentrated on devising delicious recipes for appetizers that are baked, and call these new finger foods *neo-frituras*.

I hope that you enjoy these and other appetizers—the *alcapurrias* and *pinchos*, the filled pastries (*pastelillos*), and the fritters, and the *piononos* and *surullos*—and that you delight in serving them to friends and family.

YUCA DUMPLINGS
Alcapurrias

Alcapurrias are similar to stuffed dumplings or piroshkis. But the dough that surrounds the filling is not made from flour, but from a *yuca* batter. *Yuca*, also known as cassava, or manioc, was one of the staples that the native Caribbean people cultivated, and on which they based much of their diet. *Yuca* is also indigenous to most of the south and central American countries. One of the many uses of *yuca* in Puerto Rico is in the making of *alcapurrias*.

Traditionally, *alcapurrias* are fried, but the ones I offer in this book are baked. My approach is to provide a healthier alternative in preparing the *alcapurria* to those who would be turned off by the traditional deep-frying method of cooking, and therefore miss out on one of Puerto Rico's most delicious culinary experiences.

The *alcapurrias* are made with a batter highlighted by the grated *yuca's* unique texture, which creates the "dough-like batter" that is a perfect baking vehicle for the fillings of meat or seafood and blended herbs and spices. As with most ethnic dishes prepared with fresh ingredients, time and patience is required. But you will find that these wonderful *alcapurrias* are worth every bit of extra effort it takes to prepare the fresh *yuca* and various fillings.

Yuca Dumplings

Alcapurrias

MAKES 8 *ALCAPURRIAS*

BASIC DOUGH

- 2 pounds of yuca (cassava), fresh or frozen
- 2 teaspoons rock salt, pulverized
- 1/4 teaspoon cayenne pepper
- 1 tablespoon olive oil
- 2 teaspoons paprika
- 1/3 cup coconut milk
- 1 whole egg
- 2 cups of filling (see filling recipes)
- 1/3 cup coconut egg wash (1 beaten egg blended with 1/3 cup coconut milk)

1. To peel the *yucas*, trim the ends and divide the *yucas* in halves. Using a paring knife, make four vertical incisions on the bark, one on each side. Then, using a knife with a rounded point, peel the bark by inserting the knife at an angle and pushing back against it. Repeat the process until the *yuca* is completely peeled. *Yucas* should be all white, with no pink showing after peeling and no gray spots or fibers. If the *yuca* is not all white, discard it. After you have finished peeling, let the vegetables sit in a bowl of cold water until ready to grate.

2. To grate the *yuca* use a heavy-duty manual grater on the fine texture side or a food processor with the grating attachment, followed by additional processing with the steel blade. *Yuca* will need to be finely grated. When using the frozen variety of the cassava, which usually comes already peeled, allow to thaw before grating.

3. Next, strain the grated *yuca* by spreading a linen cloth inside a colander and placing the grated *yuca* in the center of the cloth. Close the cloth, holding up the four ends, and twist with a circular motion until all the moisture has been removed. Transfer to a mixing bowl.

4. To prepare the dough, combine the grated, strained cassava in a mixing bowl; add the salt, cayenne pepper, olive oil, paprika, coconut milk and egg. Using your hand and fingers, work all the ingredients together, until a dough-like batter is achieved.

5. To make the *alcapurrias*, first layer a sheet pan with baking parchment. Using a 2-ounce scoop, place balls of dough onto the sheet pan, leaving a 2-inch space between each ball. Use the bottom of a teaspoon to press down approximately 1/2-inch deep, to create an oval-shaped well in the center of each ball. Fill each well with a generous tablespoon of filling. (See filling recipes that follow.)

6. To pack and seal the *alcapurrias*, press down gently with a teaspoon and spread the dough over the well. Dip the flat part of the spoon into the coconut egg wash and coat all sides of the dumpling. The surface and sides should be smooth and tight. The assembled dumpling should have the oval appearance of a football or an egg.

7. To bake, preheat the oven to 375° for 10 minutes. Cover *alcapurrias* with foil and bake for 15 minutes, then remove foil and finish baking for an additional 15 minutes, until *alcapurrias* are golden brown. Allow to cool for a couple of minutes prior to separating from parchment.

Chicken Filling for Yuca Dumplings

Alcapurrias de Pollo

MAKES FILLING FOR 8 *ALCAPURRIAS*

Small chunks of chicken blended with sherry, spices, fresh tomatoes, and red bell peppers make these *alcapurrias* extremely tasty, yet inexpensive to prepare.

1/3 cup Spanish olive oil

4 garlic cloves, minced

1 teaspoon minced fresh gingerroot

1 pound chicken breast, chopped

2 teaspoons chopped fresh oregano (1 teaspoon dry)

1/4 teaspoon saffron threads

1 teaspoon paprika

1/4 teaspoon cayenne pepper

1 teaspoon pulverized rock salt

1/3 cup Spanish sherry

3 green onions, chopped

1 tablespoon chopped fresh cilantro

1 medium tomato, chopped

1/2 medium red bell pepper, chopped

1/2 medium green bell pepper, chopped

1/2 medium yellow bell pepper, chopped

8 green Spanish olives, pitted and sliced

1/3 cup Spanish capers

1. In a preheated skillet, combine and sauté for 3 minutes the olive oil, garlic, gingerroot, chopped chicken, oregano, saffron, paprika, cayenne pepper, and salt. Stir in the onions and sherry, lower the heat, and continue to cook for five minutes. Then add the cilantro, tomato, red, green and yellow peppers, olives and capers. Remove from heat and allow to cool before filling the *alcapurrias*.

2. Use 1 generous tablespoon of filling for each dumpling.

Beef Filling for Yuca Dumplings

Alcapurrias de Res

MAKES FILLING FOR 8 *ALCAPURRIAS*

In Puerto Rico you find these *alcapurrias* in *kioskos* and coffee shops on city streets. I didn't care much for *yuca* dumplings until I tasted Robert's baked variety. The deep fried ones seemed to absorb too much oil. These *alcapurrias* are great as a brunch item with a glass of *maví* on the side.

1/3	cup Spanish olive oil
4	garlic cloves, minced
1	teaspoon minced fresh gingerroot
1	pound ground sirloin
2	teaspoons chopped fresh oregano (1 teaspoon dry)
3	minced small chili peppers
1/3	cup raisins
1/2	teaspoon pulverized rock salt
1/3	cup burgundy wine
3	green onions, chopped
1	tablespoon chopped fresh cilantro
1	medium tomato, chopped
1/2	medium red bell pepper, chopped
1/2	chopped medium green bell pepper
8	pitted and sliced green Spanish olives
1/3	cup Spanish capers

1. In a preheated skillet, on low to medium heat, add olive oil, garlic, ginger, ground sirloin, oregano, chili pepper, raisins, and salt. Stir until beef turns brown, then stir in burgundy and onions and cook down for 2 minutes. Remove from heat and allow to cool, then fold in the cilantro, tomato, red and green peppers, olives, and capers.

2. To fill the *alcapurrias*, use 1 heaping tablespoon of filling.

Crabmeat and Coconut Milk Filling for Yuca Dumplings

Alcapurrias de Juey

MAKES FILLING FOR 8 *ALCAPURRIAS*

Crabmeat *alcapurrias* are often sold in oceanside *kioskos*, especially on the northern coast near San Juan, at Piñones, where the meat of the regional mangrove land crab is used. Because this crab is not available in the United States, I suggest using Dungeness crabmeat as an excellent substitute. Combined with coconut milk, the crabmeat and spices produce a superb blend of a northern climate ingredient with a tropical twist.

1/3 cup Spanish olive oil

4 garlic cloves, minced

1 teaspoon minced fresh gingerroot

1/2 pound fresh crabmeat

2 teaspoons chopped fresh oregano (1 teaspoon dry)

1 tablespoon fresh lime juice

1/4 teaspoon cayenne pepper

1/2 teaspoon pulverized rock salt

2/3 cup coconut milk

3 green onions, chopped

1 tablespoon chopped fresh cilantro

1/2 medium red bell pepper, chopped

1/2 medium green bell pepper, chopped

1/2 medium yellow bell pepper, chopped

1. In a preheated skillet on low to medium heat, add oil, garlic, gingerroot, crabmeat, oregano, lime juice, cayenne pepper, and salt. Sauté lightly for 1 minute. Add coconut milk, then stir, cover and cook down for 2 minutes on low heat. Then remove from heat and fold in onions, cilantro, red, green, and yellow peppers.

2. To fill *alcapurrias*, use 1 generous tablespoon of crab mixture per dumpling.

Lobster or Shrimp Filling for Yuca Dumplings

Alcapurrias de Langosta o Camarones

MAKES FILLING FOR 8 *ALCAPURRIAS*

These delicious seafood *alcapurrias* are *picante* (mildly hot). For shrimp filling, substitute one pound medium shrimps, shelled, deveined and chopped.

$1/3$	cup Spanish olive oil
4	garlic cloves, minced
1	teaspoon minced fresh gingerroot
1	pound chopped lobster meat
1	tablespoon fresh lime juice
2	teaspoons chopped fresh oregano (or 1 teaspoon dry)
$1/4$	teaspoon saffron threads
$1/4$	teaspoon cayenne pepper
$1/2$	teaspoon pulverized rock salt
3	green onions, chopped
$1/3$	cup Spanish sherry
1	tablespoon chopped fresh cilantro
1	medium tomato, chopped
$1/2$	medium red bell pepper, chopped
$1/2$	medium green bell pepper, chopped
$1/2$	medium yellow bell pepper, chopped
8	green Spanish olives, pitted & sliced
$1/3$	cup Spanish capers

1. In a preheated skillet over low to medium heat, combine olive oil, garlic, gingerroot, lobster meat, lime juice, oregano, saffron, cayenne pepper, and salt. Sauté for 3 minutes. Stir in green onions and sherry. Cook down for an additional 2 minutes and fold in cilantro, tomato, red, green, and yellow peppers. Remove from heat and allow to cool prior to filling *alcapurrias*.

2. Use 1 generous tablespoon of filling for each *yuca* dumpling.

STUFFED PLANTAIN SHELLS
Piononos

Traditional *piononos* are shells made from ripe plantains sliced lengthwise and rolled into a circle, held together by a toothpick. A filling is made by cooking meat, chicken, or fish with herbs, spices and vegetables. Once the shell is filled a batter is spread over each end, and the entire *plátano* is deep-fried. These recipes, however, are for baked *piononos.*

Puerto Ricans and other Caribbean island dwellers find endless uses for plantains. *Piononos* are a good example. The sweetness of the *plátano* (plantain) complements the spiciness of the meat or fish mixture, and the batter holds the entire appetizer together like a unique "sandwich." Robert's mother knows them as *plátanos rellenos.* Whatever the true source and whatever name is used, the essence is a stuffed ripe plantain shell.

In Puerto Rico, *piononos* are often sold at food stands along the beaches, especially on the beach near the Piñones Forest. You can buy a *pionono* and a tropical beverage and sit on the sand under a tall, lanky palm tree and watch the surf roll gently in and out. How the rest of the world has gotten along without *piononos* I'll never know. Three years ago when my mother was eighty, she first tried one of Robert's filled *plátano* shells, and she's been requesting them ever since.

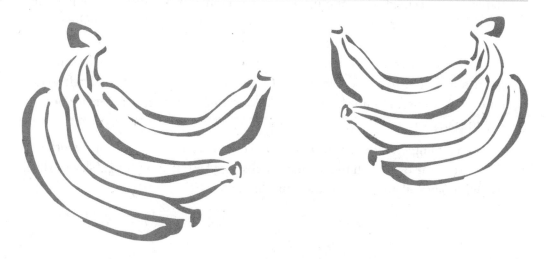

Stuffed Yellow Plantain Shells

Piononos

MAKES 8 *PIONONOS*

BASIC RECIPE FOR SHELLS

- 2 *large yellow plantains, peeled and sliced lengthwise in five slices*
- 1 *cup flour*
- 1/2 *teaspoon salt*
- 2 *teaspoons paprika*
- 1/4 *teaspoon ground nutmeg*
- 2 *eggs, beaten*
- 2 *tablespoons olive oil*
- 1/4 *cup coconut milk*
- 1/2 *cup water*

Garnish: *avocado slices, lemon wedges, cherry tomatoes*

1. In a bowl, combine the flour, salt, paprika, and nutmeg, and mix well. In a separate mixing bowl, whisk together the eggs, olive oil, and coconut milk. Stir cream mixture into dry ingredients, until a thick batter is achieved. Add 1/2 cup of water to thin down the batter to a smooth consistency. Refrigerate until ready to use.

2. To make the ripe plantain shells, take one slice of plantain and make a ring. This step is best executed by wrapping the slice around 3 or 4 fingers of the left hand (assuming you are right-handed), and overlapping the ends (tips). Holding down the ends in position with the thumb to fasten the ring, carefully insert a toothpick diagonally through the overlapping layers. Place on a flat tray and continue the process until the batch is completed. Cover with kitchen towel and refrigerate until ready to use. Do not handle the delicate rings more than necessary or they will break apart.

3. Once the filling is made, preheat oven to 375° for 15 minutes. Set up a work station next to the oven with the plantain shells, egg batter, and filling. Glaze a sheet pan with olive oil and preheat for 8 minutes.

4. Using a tablespoon, scoop out 8 patties onto the pan, leaving a 2-inch space in between. Place one plantain shell on top of each patty, pressing down gently to secure the foundation. Using a teaspoon, very carefully pack the shells with the filling.

5. Quickly spread ½ tablespoon of batter on top of each *pionono* (use a circular motion) then place in oven for 5 minutes. Turn over gently and bake for another 10 minutes. Remove from oven and let cool for one minute.

6. Serve on top of a nest of watercress that you have lightly tossed in an olive oil and lime juice dressing.

Beef and Spanish Sausage Filling for Stuffed Plantain Rings
Piononos de Carne y Chorizo
MAKES FILLING FOR 8 *PIONONOS*

This is a delectable filling—slightly spicy, slightly sweet. The kind of *pionono* you're most likely to find throughout Puerto Rico.

1/3	cup Spanish olive oil
3	minced garlic cloves
2	teaspoons minced fresh gingerroot
1	pound ground sirloin
4	Spanish sausages, chopped
3	green onions, chopped
2	teaspoons chopped fresh oregano (1 teaspoon dry)
2	small red chili peppers, seeded and minced
1	teaspoon pulverized rock salt
1/3	cup burgundy wine
1	tablespoon chopped fresh cilantro
1	medium tomato, cored and chopped

> $^1/_2$ *medium red bell pepper, diced into $^1/_2$-inch pieces*
>
> $^1/_2$ *medium green bell pepper, diced into $^1/_2$-inch pieces*
>
> 8 *green pitted Spanish olives (cut in halves)*
>
> $^1/_3$ *cup raisins*
>
> $^1/_3$ *cup cooked garbanzo beans*

1. Preheat skillet on low to medium heat; add olive oil, garlic, ginger, ground sirloin, and sausage, and stir until beef is brown. Add onions, oregano, chili pepper and salt. Stir in the wine and cook down for 3 minutes, then remove from heat, allow to cool, and fold in the remaining ingredients.

2. To fill *piononos*, divide the mixture into 8 equal parts and follow method for baking outlined in the basic recipe.

Chicken Filling for Plantain Shells
Piononos de Pollo
MAKES FILLING FOR 8 *PIONONOS*

This is an exotic way to enjoy chicken. Tender pieces of chicken breast made succulent by cooking with spices, sherry, red pepper, olives, and raisins. Surrounded by the sweet *plátano*, these *piononos* will make you want to enjoy chicken and plantain together frequently.

> $1^1/_2$ *pounds chicken breast, boneless, skinless*
>
> $^1/_3$ *cup Spanish olive oil*
>
> 1 *tablespoon lime juice*
>
> 3 *garlic cloves, minced*
>
> 3 *green onions, chopped*
>
> $^1/_2$ *teaspoon minced fresh gingerroot*
>
> 1 *tablespoon chopped fresh cilantro*
>
> 2 *teaspoons chopped fresh oregano (1 teaspoon dry)*
>
> $^1/_4$ *teaspoon saffron threads*

1   teaspoon paprika

1/2   teaspoon pulverized rock salt

1/4   teaspoon cayenne pepper

1/3   cup Spanish sherry

1   medium red bell pepper, cored, seeded and diced

8   pitted, ripe Spanish olives, cut in halves

1/3   cup raisins

1. Wash chicken breast and pat dry. Transfer to cutting board and cut into 1/2-inch cubes. In a preheated skillet, over low to medium heat, combine olive oil, lime juice, garlic, onions, ginger, and chicken. Sauté until chicken meat turns white.

2. Stir in the cilantro, oregano, saffron, paprika, salt, cayenne pepper, and sherry. Cover and cook down until most of the liquid has been reduced by half. Then remove from heat and fold in bell pepper, olives, and raisins. Allow to cool prior to filling shells.

3. To fill *piononos*, divide the mixture into 8 equal parts and follow method for filling and baking outlined in basic recipe.

Pork Filling for Stuffed Plantain Shells
Piononos de Cerdo

MAKES FILLING FOR 8 *PIONONOS*

This dish is often found at food stands on The Island's country roads, where the fragrance of fresh roasted pork wafts through the air. *Kioskos* on country roads frequently feature appetizers made from the produce of the nearby farms and fields.

1/3   cup Spanish olive oil

3   garlic cloves, minced

1 1/2   pounds of. pork butt (trim excess fat), cubed into 1/2-inch pieces

1   teaspoon pulverized rock salt

1/2   teaspoon minced fresh gingerroot

2 small red chili peppers, seeded and minced

2 teaspoons chopped fresh oregano (1 teaspoon dry)

1/3 cup raisins

3 green onions, chopped

1/3 cup Spanish brandy

2 medium tomatoes, chopped

1/2 cup diced red bell pepper

1/2 cup diced green bell pepper

8 ripe Spanish olives, pitted and cut into halves

1/3 cup capers

1 tablespoon chopped fresh cilantro

1. Preheat skillet on low to medium heat. Add olive oil, garlic, diced pork, salt, gingerroot, chili peppers, and oregano. Sauté until meat turns white. Add raisins, onions, and stir in brandy. Set heat to low, cover and finish cooking. When pork is fully cooked and tender, remove from heat. Allow to cool, then fold in the remaining ingredients.

2. To fill *piononos*, divide the mixture into 8 equal parts and follow method for baking outlined in basic recipe.

Lobster, Crab or Shrimp Filling for Piononos

Piononos del Mar

MAKES FILLING FOR 8 *PIONONOS*

These were the first *piononos* I ever ate, one Sunday morning when Robert took me to Loiza Beach. The *kiosko* owners were just setting up, and the aroma of food preparation was beginning to drift over the quiet tropical morning air, filling it with the bouquet of herbs and spices, freshly cut *plátanos*, and seafood. In these *Piononos del Mar*, the gentle yet distinctive flavor of the seafood is enhanced by the fresh spices and the Spanish sherry and olives.

1 pound lobster meat, cubed

1 tablespoon lime juice

1/3 cup Spanish olive oil

4 garlic cloves, minced

3 green onions, finely chopped

1 teaspoon minced fresh gingerroot

1 tablespoon chopped fresh cilantro

2 teaspoons chopped fresh oregano(1 teaspoon dry)

1/2 tablespoon saffron threads

1 teaspoon paprika

1/2 teaspoon salt

1/4 teaspoon cayenne pepper

1/3 cup Spanish sherry

1 medium red bell pepper, cored and diced

8 ripe Spanish olives, pitted and cut into halves

16 Spanish capers

1. Combine lobster cubes, lime juice, olive oil, garlic, onion, ginger, cilantro, and oregano in a mixing bowl and toss. Cover and refrigerate for 2 hours, then transfer to a preheated skillet and sauté over low to medium heat for 2 minutes; rotate for uniform cooking.

2. Then stir in saffron, paprika, salt, cayenne pepper and sherry. Cover and continue to cook for 4 minutes. Remove from heat and fold in diced pepper, olives and capers.

3. To fill *piononos*, divide the mixture into 8 equal parts and follow the method for baking outlined in the basic recipe.

VARIATION: For shrimp *piononos*, shell and devein 3/4 pound of medium shrimps and cube. For crab *piononos* use 3/4 pound crabmeat and cube the largest pieces.

MEAT TURNOVERS
Pastelillos

Pastelillos are small meat turnovers, made by first creating the pastry dough, shaping it into a turnover, then filling it with a meat, shellfish or sausage stuffing and deep-frying. Because of the frying, these filled turnovers are categorized as *frituras* (*frita* meaning fried). *Frituras* is a collective noun that includes all fried finger foods. Frequently they are served on a banana leaf, sometimes a sea grape leaf, or a napkin.

The *frituras* occupy a very important position in the cultural gastronomy of The Island. *Frituras* are to the Puerto Rican what *lumpias* are to the Filipinos, what the egg roll is to the Chinese, what the taco is to the Mexican, and what the calzone is to the Italian.

In the spirit of universalism, so that I may transcend cultural boundaries with this wonderful dish, I am introducing the *pastelillo* not as deep fried, but as a yeasted dough baked turnover filled with fresh ingredients prevalent in Puerto Rico, and available in the United States. "*Pastelillos*," says my mother, "should be fried. They have always been fried." I agree with her. *Pastelillos* are great fried, but for the sake of eating healthier and lighter foods, it's necessary to make traditional food preparation relevant to the times.

When I think of *pastelillos*, I think of my grammar school days in Ponce. The school was across a gully from a bread bakery—a *panaderia*—and at recess, a couple of my buddies and I used to run down across the gully and through a hole we had made in the fence that belonged to the school. Every day the bakery, which sold its breads and pastries wholesale, would have loads of *pastelillos* sitting on metal racks to cool. In exchange for our promise to return after school to help grease sheet pans for the next day's baking, we would receive our allotment of two *pastelillos* each. You could say that my bakery apprenticeship started at that time. How we loved to eat those hot, flaky turnovers!

Flaky Turnovers
Pastelillos

MAKES PASTRY FOR 12 *PASTELILLOS*

BASIC PASTRY RECIPE

- 1 cup hot water (130°)
- 1 tablespoon sugar
- 1/4 ounce active yeast
- 2/3 cup olive oil
- 3 cups flour
- 1 teaspoon salt
- 2 teaspoons paprika
- 1/4 teaspoon cayenne pepper

1. Mix water, sugar and yeast and let sit for 5 minutes until yeast activates. Then add olive oil. Set aside.

2. In a mixing bowl combine flour, salt, paprika, and cayenne pepper and mix with a wooden spoon. Make a well in the center and add yeast solution and mix until a dough is formed. Scrape sides and bottom. Then, using your hand and fingers, knead dough inside the bowl until it forms a ball.

3. Transfer dough to a board and knead for 5 to 7 minutes or until dough ball is smooth and silky. Place dough in a well greased bowl (use 2 tablespoons of vegetable oil to coat the bowl), spinning the dough ball so that it is completely covered with the oil. Place a lid over the bowl and let dough rise for 1 hour in a draft-free area.

4. Punch dough down and transfer to the board, kneading for 3 minutes. Then, using a dough cutter or a knife, divide the dough in half. Roll each half into cylinders 2 inches in diameter and divide the cylinders into six equal parts. Place the twelve portions on a slightly floured sheet pan, spaced 1/2-inch apart, cover with a damp kitchen towel and allow to rise for 45 minutes.

5. To make the pastry, turn each portion, one at time, on a lightly floured surface. Using a rolling pin, roll out flat to an approximately 7 inch by 7 inch square; flip dough over.

6. To fill, spread 1½ to 2 tablespoons of filling in the center. Fold by taking the upper wing of the pastry with both hands, and with an even stretch, connect to the bottom wing. Press the edges down with the fingertips to secure form. Use a 6-inch soup bowl with a smooth rim to place on top of turnover and press down firmly to seal. With a paring knife, cut the dough using the outer edge of the bowl as a guideline. Separate and put aside the excess dough. Lift the bowl; then, with a fork, press down on the edges to permanently fasten the pastry. Gently using your hand or a spatula, transfer pastry onto the sheet pan to be used for baking. Allow a ½-inch space in between each pastry. Repeat procedure for all *pastelillos*.

7. Prior to baking, generously coat *pastelillos* with garlic egg wash. Bake pastries in a preheated oven at 375° for 12 minutes.

TO MAKE GARLIC EGG WASH: In a blender combine 4 garlic cloves peeled, 2 tablespoons olive oil, ¼ teaspoon salt and liquify. Add one whole egg and ⅔ cup half-and-half; blend at high speed for 20 seconds. Transfer to a bowl and keep refrigerated until ready to use.

Beef and Roasted Pepper Filling for Pastelillos

Pastelillos de Res con Pimientos Asado

MAKES FILLING FOR 12 *PASTELILLOS*

The smoky taste of the roasted bell peppers adds to the overall complexity of this ground beef-filled pastry. Enjoy the *pastelillos* with an Avocado Salad, or even a fruit salad on the side.

> ⅓ cup olive oil
> 4 garlic cloves, minced
> ½ teaspoon minced fresh gingerroot
> 2 teaspoons chopped fresh oregano (or 1 teaspoon dry)
> 2 small red chili peppers, seeded and minced

1 1/2 pounds ground sirloin

1/2 teaspoon pulverized rock salt

3 green onions, chopped

1 cup chopped fresh tomatoes

1 tablespoon chopped fresh cilantro

1/3 cup raisins

1/3 cup burgundy wine

8 medium green olives, sliced in fours

1/3 cup Spanish capers

1 large red bell pepper, roasted, cored, seeded and diced

1 large green bell pepper, roasted, cored, seeded and diced

1. Preheat skillet on low to medium heat. Add oil, garlic, gingerroot, oregano, chili pepper, ground sirloin, salt, and sauté for 2 minutes; then stir in onions, tomatoes, cilantro, and raisins. Stir in burgundy and cook down until liquid is reduced by half.

2. Fold in olives, capers and roasted peppers. Remove from heat. Allow to cool before filling pastries. Use 1 1/2 to 2 tablespoons of filling per *pastelillo*. To assemble, follow instructions 5, 6, and 7 of Basic Pastry recipe.

Filling for Chicken and Ham Flaky Turnovers
Pastelillos de Pollo y Jamón

MAKES FILLING FOR 8 *PASTELILLOS*

Here's another new twist to the basic and typical *pastelillo*. This version is made from a combination of blended herbs and spices, chicken and smoke-cured ham, prunes, sun-dried tomatoes, and mushrooms.

1/3 cup Spanish olive oil

4 garlic cloves, minced

1 teaspoon minced fresh gingerroot

1 1/2 pounds chicken breast, diced, skinless, and boneless

1/4 teaspoon saffron threads

8 sun-dried tomatoes, diced

6 ounces smoke-cured ham, cut julienne style

4 green onions, chopped

2 teaspoons chopped fresh oregano (or 1 teaspoon dry)

1/2 teaspoon pulverized rock salt

1/3 cup Spanish brandy

2 small chili peppers, seeded and minced

8 large Spanish olives, pitted and sliced

1/3 cup Spanish capers

1/3 cup pitted and diced dry prunes

1/4 teaspoon cayenne pepper

8 sliced mushrooms

1 tablespoon chopped fresh cilantro

1/2 cup diced red bell pepper

1/2 cup diced green bell pepper

1. In a preheated skillet over low to medium heat combine oil, garlic, ginger, chicken, saffron and dry tomatoes. Sauté until all chicken pieces turn white. Add, ham, onions, oregano and salt. Continue to sauté for 2 more minutes. Stir in brandy, chili peppers, olives, capers, prunes, cayenne pepper, mushrooms, and cilantro. Cook down for 2 more minutes, or until most of the moisture has been reduced. Fold in red and green peppers and remove from heat. Allow to cool prior to filling pastries. To fill pastries, divide the mixture into eight equal parts.

2. To assemble pastries, follow instructions 5, 6, and 7 in Basic Pastry recipe.

Crabmeat and Coconut Milk Filling for Turnovers

Pastelillos de Jueyes en Leche de Coco

MAKES FILLING FOR 12 *PASTELILLOS*

Complex and slightly spicy, this filling makes absolutely delicious *pastelillos*. The distinctive flavor of the crab and coconut blends with the fresh ingredients and the mildly hot flavors of the garlic, ginger, and cayenne pepper to render a magnificent Caribbean treat.

1/3   cup Spanish olive oil

4   garlic cloves, minced

1   teaspoon minced fresh gingerroot

1   tablespoon lime juice

1   pound fresh crab meat

2   tablespoons Spanish sherry

2/3   cup coconut milk

3   green onions, chopped

1   tablespoon chopped fresh cilantro

2   teaspoons chopped fresh oregano (or 1 teaspoon dry)

1/4   teaspoon saffron threads

1/2   teaspoon pulverized rock salt

1/4   teaspoon cayenne pepper

1/2   medium red bell pepper, diced

1/2   medium green bell pepper, diced

8   pitted ripe Spanish olives, cut in halves

1/3   cup Spanish capers

1. In a preheated skillet, on low to medium heat, add oil, garlic, gingerroot, lime juice, crabmeat, and sherry and sauté lightly for 2 minutes. Add the coconut milk and cook down until moisture is reduced by half, then incorporate the remaining

ingredients. Cover and continue cooking for 3 minutes on low heat, then remove from heat and allow to cool before filling pastries. To assemble follow instructions 5, 6 and 7 of the Basic Pastry recipe.

2. To substitute shrimp for crabmeat, use 1 pound of medium shrimps. Shell, devein and cube. For lobster filling, use 1 pound of lobster meat cubed into 1/2-inch pieces.

Goat Milk Cheese and Honey-Cured Ham Filling for Pastelillos
Pastelillos de Jamón y Queso de Leche de Cabra

MAKES FILLING FOR 12 *PASTELILLOS*

An original recipe for a *pastelillo* combining both the Puerto Rican and California influences.

10	ounces goat milk cheese, crumbled
4	ounces Spanish sharp cheddar cheese, coarsely grated
2	cups fresh spinach, chopped
2	tablespoons olive oil
1/4	pound honey-cured ham, julienned
1/2	teaspoon minced fresh gingerroot
3	green onions, chopped
1	tablespoon sliced hazelnuts
8	ripe Spanish olives, sliced in fours
1/3	cup Spanish brandy
1/3	cup raisins
1	medium red bell pepper, broiled and julienned
1	medium green bell pepper, broiled and julienned

1. In a bowl, combine and fold together the goat milk cheese, cheddar cheese, and spinach. Refrigerate until ready to use.

2. In a preheated skillet on low to medium heat, combine oil, ham, ginger, and onions. Sauté for 1 minute. Add hazelnuts, olives, raisins, and brandy. Stir and sauté for another minute. Remove from heat and allow to cool.

3. Combine julienne strips of red and green peppers.

4. To assemble the *pastelillos*, start with cheese mixture first, and spread a layer onto center of pastry. Then spread the sautéed ham mixture, and top with julienne roasted peppers. Follow procedures 5, 6, and 7 of Basic Pastry recipe.

VARIATION: Use 4 Spanish sausages, sliced to ¼-inch, or dry pepperoni slices instead of ham.

Goat Milk Cheese and Spanish Sausage Filling for Turnovers
Pastelillos de Queso de Cabra y Chorizo
MAKES FILLING FOR 12 *PASTELILLOS*

A luscious, filled pastry—the goat milk cheese, cheddar cheese, sausage and port wine—make this a rich treat, delicious with any salad, and a cold drink of fruit juice or beer.

    10   *ounces goat milk cheese, crumbled*

      4   *ounces Spanish sharp cheddar cheese, grated coarsely*

      1   *tablespoon fresh parsley, chopped*

      1   *tablespoon olive oil*

      4   *Spanish sausages, sliced ¼-inch pieces*

3   green onions, chopped
3   garlic cloves, minced
2   chili peppers, chopped
1   tablespoon sliced almonds
2   tablespoons port wine
8   ripe Spanish olives, sliced in fours
1   tablespoon Spanish capers
1/2   medium red bell pepper, chopped
1/2   medium green bell pepper, chopped
1/2   medium yellow bell pepper, chopped

1. Combine goat milk cheese, cheddar cheese, and parsley, and fold together.

2. In a preheated skillet on low to medium heat, combine oil, Spanish sausage, onions garlic, and chili peppers. Sauté for 2 minutes. Add almonds, port wine, olives and capers. Remove from heat, allow to cool, and fold into the cheese spread.

3. Fold in chopped peppers and refrigerate until ready to use.

4. To fill pastries, scoop out 2 tablespoons of mixture onto the center of the pastry dough and press down gently prior to closing pastry. Follow steps 5, 6, and 7 of Basic Pastry recipe.

Lobster and Sausage Filling for Pastelillos

Pastelillos de Langosta y Chorizo

MAKES FILLING FOR 12 *PASTELILLOS*

You can find *pastelillos* made with either lobster or sausage in Puerto Rico, but never will you find both together. Try this delicious *neo-pastelillo* combination.

1/3   cup Spanish olive oil
4   garlic cloves, minced

1 teaspoon minced fresh gingerroot

1 pound diced lobster meat

4 sausages, sliced

4 green onions, chopped

2 teaspoons chopped fresh oregano (1 teaspoon dry)

1/4 teaspoon saffron threads

1 teaspoon pulverized rock salt

1/3 cup sherry

8 large green Spanish olives, sliced

1/3 cup Spanish capers

1/3 cup raisins

1/4 teaspoon cayenne pepper

8 mushrooms, sliced

1 tablespoon chopped fresh cilantro

1/2 cup diced red bell pepper

1/2 cup diced green bell pepper

2 cups chopped fresh spinach

1. In a preheated skillet over low to medium heat combine oil, garlic, ginger, lobster, sausage, onions, oregano, saffron, and salt. Sauté for 2 minutes. Stir in sherry, olives, capers, raisins, cayenne pepper, mushrooms, and cilantro. Sauté for 2 more minutes. Remove from heat. Fold in red and green peppers, and spinach. Allow to cool prior to filling pastries.

2. To assemble pastries, divide the filling into 12 equal parts. Follow steps 5, 6, and 7 of the Basic Pastry recipe.

FRITTERS
Frituras

Fritters are small fried patties made from batter containing pieces of fish, meat, vegetables or fruits. The fritters that I have included in this book are baked and grilled rather than deep-fried. My method simulates the ancient Taino way of cooking on a hot flat rock, and should satisfy the need for using as little fat as possible to minimize cholesterol intake. This approach, as outlined more carefully in the recipes, is to first preheat the oven, and then heat the sheet pan sufficiently to cook the fritters when they are spooned out.

Every region seems to have its fritters, and the Caribbean has provided the world with an abundance of these delicious treats. Called *frituras* in Puerto Rico, and on other Spanish speaking islands, they are known as "stamp and go" in Jamaica, *accra* in Trinidad, and *acrat* on French islands. Their origin is credited to West Africa. Whatever the source, the common denominator is a batter filled with chunks of delicious tidbits—fish or meat, beans, vegetables, or fruit—and then deep fried in hot oil. We're breaking with tradition by baking instead of deep frying these fritters, but we think you'll appreciate the healthy change.

Fritters are great as snacks, appetizers, breakfast food or even desserts. They can all be made in 3-inch sizes and as smaller, bite-sized pieces as well.

Banana Fritters

Jíbaritos

MAKES 16 *FRITURAS*

These fritters were named in tribute to the Puerto Rican farmer, the *jíbaro*, whose close relationship with his tropical environment, the land he nourished and farmed daily, enabled him to make numerous contributions to the cuisine of The Island. I have eaten these naturally sweet fritters my whole life. In Puerto Rico, we made *jíbaritos* to take advantage of dwarf bananas, *guineos niños*. The entire *guineo* was dipped in a batter and deep fried, and they were so good that I can remember eating five or six at a time. This recipe is different from the traditional one I grew up with because the common banana is used, along with other complex flavorings that I have added.

1	cup flour
2	teaspoons baking powder
1/4	teaspoon ground nutmeg
1	teaspoon cayenne pepper
1/2	teaspoon salt
2	whole eggs
1/3	cup olive oil
1	cup light cream
2	tablespoons brandy
3	garlic cloves, minced
1	tablespoon chopped fresh cilantro
3	green onions, chopped
1/2	red bell pepper, chopped
5	ripe bananas, diced

Garnish: *mint sprigs, orange slices*

1. Using a wire whisk or wooden spoon, combine in a mixing bowl the flour, baking powder, nutmeg, cayenne pepper, and salt. Add eggs, olive oil, light cream, brandy and blend. Then add garlic, cilantro, green onions, bell pepper and blend again. Fold in bananas.

2. Preheat oven 400° for 5 minutes. Glaze a sheet pan with olive oil and preheat for 5 minutes inside the oven. Remove from oven and quickly place on top of stove. Using a tablespoon, scoop batter onto the sheet pan in rows, leaving ½ inch between each fritter. Bake on one side for 8 minutes, then flip and bake on the other side for another 7 minutes.

3. Remove from oven and serve hot. Garnish with orange slices and fresh mint sprigs. Banana fritters are great as a breakfast food, or for dinner alongside rice and beans.

Codfish Fritters
Bacalaitos
MAKES 12+ *BACALAITOS*

Bacalaitos are fun food snacks that, when combined with other items, can be turned into an instant, full-scale meal. Tiny chunks of dried codfish *(bacalao)* in a tasty batter, these fritters have turned many a Sunday snack into an afternoon of eating, drinking, music, and relaxation with friends and family. Codfish fritters, and other typical island "finger foods" are a double treat for most Puerto Rican people, both because of the flavor and the nostalgic feeling they arouse for the "good old days." When we were children, my mother and grandmother would prepare *bacalaitos* in the patio, first setting up the heavy cast iron kettle on top of *carbón de palito* (homemade charcoal). The kettle would then be filled halfway to the top with homemade shortening which would be brought to a roaring boil.

While this was going on, the children were watching or standing by, ready to perform as runners. Our job was to gather the herbs and spices that went into making the *bacalaitos*—wild cilantro and oregano that grew on nearby river banks and in pastures, and fleshed out with wild onions or peppers from a cousin's yard. The incentive was always an extra serving of the dish being prepared, or some other special recognition for the child who came back from the scavenger hunt with the most ingredients. For the children, cooking *bacalaitos* was always a learning experience as well as play. It was participation and interaction with the adults. And best of all, it was good eating.

1 pound dried codfish (salt cured and boneless)

1 quart warm water (110°)

1½ cups all-purpose flour

1½ cups cold tap water

3 tablespoons olive oil

8 garlic cloves, minced

3 teaspoons chopped fresh oregano (2 teaspoons dry)

4 green onions, chopped

⅓ cup chopped green peppers

⅓ cup chopped red bell peppers

1 tablespoon chopped fresh cilantro

¼ teaspoon cayenne pepper

¼ teaspoon ground black pepper

3 teaspoons Spanish paprika

1. Place salted codfish in 1 quart of warm water and set aside. Allow to soak for 10 minutes.

2. Combine flour and cold tap water in a mixing bowl and blend with a wire whisk to form a batter. Then add olive oil, garlic, oregano, green onions, green peppers, red peppers, cilantro, cayenne pepper, black pepper, and paprika.

3. Take the bowl with the water and codfish and discard water. Rinse codfish under warm running water for 30 seconds. Blot excess water from the pieces, then flake the fish into small pieces or chop coarsely. Gently incorporate codfish into batter.

4. Preheat oven to 375° for 15 minutes. Glaze a sheet pan with olive oil and place in the center rack. Preheat the sheet pan in the oven for 10 minutes.

5. Slide the rack halfway out and, using a 1-ounce ladle, scoop the batter onto the sheet pan, leaving a 2-inch space between each fritter. Bake 4 minutes on one side. Use a spatula to flip the fritters and cook for another 4 minutes or until golden brown on the other side.

6. Remove fritters from sheet pan and transfer to a serving platter. Serve with lemon or lime wedges and chilled cocktail sauce on the side. The fritters are best served while still hot and crispy. An ice-cold fruit juice or cold beer is imperative!

Squash Fritters
Fritas de Calabaza

MAKES 16 *FRITURAS*

Use a butternut squash, a banana squash—or the *calabaza* imported from Puerto Rico if you're lucky and can find it—to make these delicious fritters. The *frituras* have a naturally sweet flavor and are an excellent breakfast food. This dish is tasty served alongside fresh salads or seafood.

1	cup flour
2	teaspoons baking powder
1/4	teaspoon ground nutmeg
1	teaspoon ground cinnamon
1/2	teaspoon ground ginger
1/2	teaspoon salt
2	eggs
1/3	cup olive oil
1	cup light cream
2	tablespoons brandy
3	garlic cloves, minced
1	tablespoon chopped fresh cilantro
3	green onions, chopped
1/2	red bell pepper, chopped
3	cups mashed cooked calabasa (squash)

Garnish: fresh pineapple spears, mint sprigs

1. In a mixing bowl, combine and mix the following ingredients with a wooden spoon: flour, baking powder, nutmeg, cinnamon, ginger, and salt. In a separate bowl mix the eggs, olive oil, light cream, brandy, garlic, cilantro, green onions, bell pepper, and squash. Incorporate the dry ingredients with the wet to achieve a batter of medium consistency.

2. Preheat oven to 375° for 15 minutes. Glaze a sheet pan with olive oil and place on the center rack of the oven. Preheat sheet pan in oven for 10 minutes.

3. Slide the rack halfway out and, using a one-ounce ladle, scoop batter onto the sheet pan in rows leaving ½-inch between the fritters. Bake on one side for 8 minutes, then flip and bake on the other side for another 7 minutes. Remove pan from oven and serve the fritters hot.

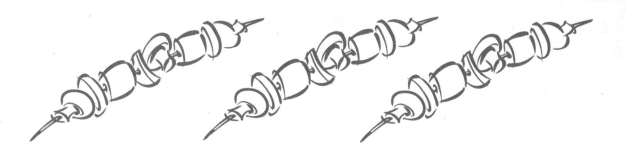

Puerto Rican Shish Kebab

Pinchos

MAKES 4 *PINCHOS*

Try the Puerto Rican version of shish kebab! Pinchos are found in Puerto Rico at roadside stands and at town festivals held during the summertime. Typically, they are made with marinated pork or beef strips and cooked on an outdoor charbroiler (*anafre*). The following recipe is my upscale, indoor version of the *pincho*—delightfully marinated in brandy, herbs, and spices. Although this recipe calls for beef, lamb or chicken may be substituted. For a special treat, combine lobster tail medallions and beef.

> 2 *tablespoons olive oil*
>
> 1 *tablespoon lime juice*
>
> 2/3 *cup Spanish brandy*
>
> 2 *teaspoons brown sugar*

    4   cloves of garlic, minced
 1/2   teaspoon pulverized rock salt
    1   teaspoon cracked peppercorns
    1   teaspoon minced fresh gingerroot
    1   teaspoon chopped fresh oregano
    1   teaspoon chopped fresh mint leaves
    2   teaspoons chopped chives
1 1/2   pounds fillet of beef, cubed into 1-inch pieces, butterflied halfway

1. Combine in a mixing bowl, the oil, lime juice, brandy, sugar, garlic, salt, pepper-
    corns, ginger, oregano, mint, and chives. Mix until all the ingredients are nicely
    blended. Toss in the beef cubes, ensuring that the centers are saturated with the
    dressing. (Use your fingers to pack mixture into the center of each beef cube.)
    Cover and marinate for 2 hours in the refrigerator.

2. Assemble the beef cubes tightly, using 4 to 5 cubes per stick. Use stainless steel
    skewers or bamboo. If using bamboo sticks, soak the sticks in cold water for about
    10 minutes. Then insert the cubes. Prior to roasting, wrap the bamboo end in alu-
    minum foil after skewering the beef cubes. This will prevent the exposed end of
    the sticks from burning while under the broiler.

3. To cook, set your oven to broil and preheat for 10 minutes. Set up a cake drying
    rack on a sheet pan under the broiler, and lay the pinchos on the rack with the
    handles pointing away from the direct flames. For rare to medium-rare, cook 2
    minutes on each side. Use tongs to rotate. Increase the cooking time by 2 min-
    utes on each side for your preferred doneness.

4. Serve with broiled tomatoes, roasted red and green peppers, and plenty of garlic
    bread.

MEAT PIE
Empanada

The name *empanada* translates into "breaded" or "in a breaded form," the word for bread being *pan*. *Empanadas* are said to have been brought to the Americas by the Spanish, and every Spanish-speaking country probably has their own version of this dish. In Puerto Rico, there are many kinds of *empanadas*—with pastry made from flour, corn, or *yuca*, and with every kind of filling imaginable—crab, pork, shrimp, beef, chicken. Here we are presenting our version of the typical *empanada* in the spirit of the new cuisine.

This *empanada* is rather like a large pot pie, and the filling is made from a combination of various meats, seafood, herbs and spices. To cook, the *empanada* is baked in an oven like any other pie. In some countries *empanadas* are made in individual portions, like turnovers, and deep fried.

We thought you would appreciate this healthier alternative.

Meat Pie

Empanada

BASIC PASTRY RECIPE

1   *cup hot water (130°)*
1   *teaspoon sugar*
1/4 *ounce active yeast*
2/3 *cup vegetable oil*
3   *cups flour*

1. Mix water, sugar and yeast and let sit for 5 minutes while yeast activates. Add the oil, then set aside.

2. In a mixing bowl combine half of the flour with all of the yeast solution and mix until forming a batter. Scrape sides and bottom. Add the remaining flour, then, using your hand and fingers, knead dough inside of bowl until it forms a ball.

3. Transfer dough to a board and knead for 5 to 7 minutes or until dough ball is smooth and silky. Coat a large bowl with vegetable oil (approximately 2 tablespoons). Place dough in the bowl, spinning the dough ball so that it is completely covered with the oil. Place a damp kitchen towel over the bowl and let the dough rise for one hour in a draft-free area.

4. Punch dough down and transfer to the board, kneading for 3 minutes. Then, using a dough cutter or knife, divide the dough in half and cover each half with a damp cheesecloth or light linen cloth, and let sit for another 20 minutes.

5. To make the bottom pastry shell, place one dough ball on a lightly floured surface. Using a rolling pin, roll out flat to a 13 inch by 13 inch piece, then arrange in a deep 9 1/2 inch pie pan.

6. To fill, use a slotted spoon to strain the excess moisture and pack well but gently. Once filled, roll out the second dough ball in the same manner and spread on top of the pie to form the top crust. Seal the pie by pressing down with a fork on the outer edges to fuse the bottom and top crust. Perforate the center of the top crust by inserting the points of the fork into the dough. This step will allow internal pressure to escape and prevent the top crust from separating.

7. Generously brush a coat of garlic egg wash to the entire surface of the pie. Bake in a preheated oven at 375° for 1 hour.

8. To serve, allow to cool for a few minutes and cut into wedges. Serve with a salad and your favorite wine.

TO MAKE GARLIC EGG WASH

In a blender combine 4 garlic cloves, peeled, 1/4 teaspoon salt, 1 whole egg, 2/3 cup light cream or half-and-half, and blend at high speed for 60 seconds. Transfer to a bowl and keep refrigerated until ready to use. Stir before using.

Filling for Empanada

MAKES FILLING FOR 9-INCH PIE

1/3 cup Spanish olive oil

4 garlic cloves, minced

1 teaspoon fresh gingerroot, minced

4 green onions, chopped

4 mild hot sausages, cut into 1/2-inch medallions

2 pounds boneless, skinless chicken breast, diced into 1/2-inch pieces

1 pound lobster tail meat, cut into medallions 1/2-inch thick

1/2 pound smoke-cured ham, trimmed and sliced julienne style

1 1/8 tablespoons saffron threads

1 teaspoon paprika

1 cup chopped tomatoes

1 tablespoon chopped fresh cilantro

2 teaspoons chopped fresh oregano (1 teaspoon dry)

1 teaspoon pulverized rock salt

1/4 teaspoon cayenne pepper

1/3 cup sherry

8 large table olives, pitted and cut in fours

1/3 cup Spanish capers

1/3 cup raisins

1 cup thickly sliced mushrooms

1/2 medium red bell pepper, seeded and diced into 1/2-inch pieces

1/2 medium green bell pepper, seeded and diced into 1/2-inch pieces

2 cups chopped fresh spinach leaves

1. Preheat skillet over low to medium heat, then add olive oil, garlic, ginger, onions, sausages and chicken. Saute for 3 minutes, then incorporate lobster, ham, saffron, paprika, tomatoes, cilantro, oregano, salt, cayenne pepper, and sherry. Cook down until liquid has been reduced by half. Fold, remove from heat, and divide the mixture in two.

2. To assemble the *empanada*, make one layer with the first part of the mixture on the bottom crust. Pat down to make the mixture tight. Spread half of the olives, sprinkle half of the capers, and half of the raisins over the mixture. Then layer half of the mushrooms, green and red bell peppers, and spinach. Make a second layer starting with the second part of the mixture and repeat the process.

3. For smaller or larger pies, increase or decrease the amount of ingredients in proportion to the size of the pie. The *empanada* offers a great alternative for salvaging leftovers.

CORNBREAD STICKS
Surullos

One of the earliest cultivated crops in the Caribbean has been a staple in the daily fare of The Islands' inhabitants for centuries. Corn has been eaten not only in bread, meal, flour, and whole cobs and kernels but also as pastes, butters, candies, and liquors. Despite the difficulties that the native people must have had in cultivating and processing maize, it made its way into fritters and cornbreads, sweet or spicy, alongside beans and into chowders.

One of my favorite ways to make corn come to life is by making *surullos*, delicious little sticks of cornbread that can be made into before-dinner appetizers by adding herbs and spices or bits of meat, poultry or seafood to the dough, or sweeter, for a breakfast meal, by dusting with a cinnamon-sugar mixture after cooking.

At home, *surullos* have always held a respectable place at the table. I have fond memories of being roused from sleep early in the morning by my mother's whispered words, "It's *surullo* day today," and then scampering around the patio at five A.M. to gather wood for our *fogón*, the fireplace stove. My mother, meanwhile, was inside making a dough for *surullos* for all seven of us. *Surullos* were made from a rather simple batter of cornmeal, water, and a little brown sugar or molasses, then deep fried in a *caldero* full of hot lard. My mother served us the *surullos*—"heavenly fingers" she called them—sprinkled with a bit of brown sugar and cinnamon, and gave us each a bit of *café con leche* in cups made from coconut shells.

Many years have passed and *surullos* are still a very integral part of our basic diet. I have made my *surrullos* more complex than those in my memory, by adding a variety of different ingredients, and creating new flavors. I hope to present this classic food to a new generation in a fresh and contemporary light. And again, in the interests of good health, I bake the *surullos* rather than deep frying them.

My frequent taster is our young son, Adam, who loves *surullos* partly because they fit so well in his hand, and partly because they taste so good in the morning, warm and with powdered sugar sifted over them. When I see him enjoying *surullos*, I think of all those mornings, long ago, when my mother gave me the same treats.

Cornbread Sticks

Surullos

MAKES 32 CORNBREAD STICKS

1 1/2   cups yellow cornmeal

1 1/2   cups all-purpose flour

1/4   cup sugar

3/4   teaspoon baking powder

1/2   teaspoon salt

3   medium eggs

1/3   cup vegetable oil

1   cup light cream

1/2   teaspoon vanilla

1 2/3   cups lukewarm water

2/3   cup egg wash (1 beaten egg blended with 2/3 cup of milk)

1. Combine dry ingredients in a 2-quart saucepan and mix well.

2. In a separate mixing bowl, combine and blend eggs, vegetable oil, cream and vanilla. Then add to the dry ingredients in the saucepan. Using a wooden spoon, stir and blend well, until batter becomes stiff. Break down with 1 2/3 cups of water, scraping the sides and bottom of the pan.

3. Place pan over medium low heat and stir continuously until a dough ball forms. Remove from heat and continue to roll dough in pan for another minute. Transfer dough to a lightly floured surface (kneading board or tabletop) and knead by slamming, stretching, and rolling for 5 minutes, or until dough is slightly cool, smooth, and silky.

4. Using a dough cutter or a knife, divide the dough into 8 equal parts. Roll each part into a 12-inch cylinder, then cut each cylinder into four 3-inch sticks.

5. Preheat oven at 375° for 10 minutes. Layer a sheet pan with wax paper or baking parchment and align the cornbread sticks, leaving a 1/4-inch space between each stick. Using a pastry brush, generously coat the sticks with egg wash prior to placing inside of oven.

6. Bake at 375° for 17 minutes. Remove from oven and serve hot. These *surullos* can accompany soups or salads. If you want to serve them alone or alongside other breakfast foods, sprinkle them with powdered sugar, or a cinnamon-sugar mixture.

Calypso Cornbread Sticks
Surullos Antillanos
MAKES 32 *SURULLOS*

We call these *Calypso Surullos* because they contain the spices that are grown on the islands where the calypso beat can be heard in the air.

1 1/2 cups yellow cornmeal
1 1/2 cups all-purpose flour
3/4 teaspoon baking powder
1/4 teaspoon salt
1/4 cup light brown sugar
1 teaspoon ground cinnamon
1/2 teaspoon ground ginger
1/4 teaspoon ground nutmeg
1/8 teaspoon ground cloves
3 medium eggs
1/3 cup vegetable oil
1 cup half-and-half
1/2 teaspoon almond extract
1/2 teaspoon vanilla
1 2/3 cups lukewarm water
2/3 cup egg wash (1 beaten egg combined with 2/3 cup of milk)

1. Combine dry ingredients in a 2-quart saucepan and mix well.

2. In a separate mixing bowl, combine and blend eggs, vegetable oil, half-and-half,

almond extract, and vanilla. Once blended, add to dry ingredients in the saucepan. Using a wooden spoon, stir and blend well until batter becomes stiff. Break down with 1²/₃ cups of water, scraping the sides and bottom of the pan.

3. Prepare dough and bake according to instructions 3 through 6 for *basic surullos*.

Coconut Cornbread Sticks
Surullos de Coco

MAKES 32 *SURULLOS*

I created this recipe to show off the wonderful flavor of our Puerto Rican coconuts. These *surullos* are great in the morning with a cup of *café con leche*! In the absence of a Puerto Rican fresh coconut, any good quality package or can of coconut milk, or coconut cream will do the job. Canned coconut cream can be found in many supermarkets, in the gourmet food or drink section.

1¹/₂	cups yellow cornmeal
1¹/₂	cups all-purpose flour
1	tablespoon sugar
³/₄	teaspoon baking powder
¹/₄	teaspoon ground nutmeg
¹/₄	teaspoon salt
3	medium eggs
¹/₃	cup vegetable oil
¹/₄	cup half-and-half
³/₄	cup coconut milk
1²/₃	cups lukewarm water
²/₃	cup egg wash (1 beaten egg combined with ²/₃ cup of milk)

1. Combine dry ingredients in a 2-quart saucepan and mix well.

2. In a separate mixing bowl, combine and blend eggs, vegetable oil, half-and-half, coconut milk, and vanilla. Add liquid mixture to the dry ingredients in the

saucepan. Using a wooden spoon, stir and blend well, until batter becomes stiff. Break down with 1²/₃ cups of water, scraping the sides and bottom of the pan.

3. Complete the cornbread sticks according to Basic Recipe, steps 3 through 6. After baking, sprinkle with powdered sugar.

Cornbread Sticks with Ham
Surullos con Jamón

MAKES 32 *SURULLOS*

The complex flavor and texture of this ham *surullo* makes it one of my favorites. I frequently offer it as a snack or use it to complement and balance a basketful of breads for late or Sunday brunches.

1¹/₂ cups yellow cornmeal

1¹/₂ cups all-purpose flour

³/₄ teaspoon baking powder

1 teaspoon sugar

¹/₂ teaspoon salt

3 medium eggs

¹/₃ cup vegetable oil

1 cup half-and-half

1²/₃ cups lukewarm water

1   tablespoon olive oil

4   minced garlic cloves

2   teaspoons chopped fresh oregano (1 teaspoon dry)

1/2   teaspoon ground black pepper

1   tablespoon chopped fresh cilantro

2   green onions, finely chopped

1/3   cup finely chopped red bell pepper

1   cup minced honey-cured ham

2/3   cup egg wash (Beat 1 egg and blend in 2/3 cup of milk)

1. In a 2-quart saucepan, combine cornmeal, flour, baking powder, and mix.

2. In a separate mixing bowl, combine and blend eggs, vegetable oil, and half-and-half. Using a wooden spoon, stir mixture into dry ingredients until forming a stiff batter. Break down batter with water, scraping all sides and bottom of the pan. Place over low to medium heat while continuously stirring in a circular motion, until dough ball is formed inside the pan.

3. Remove from heat and transfer to lightly floured surface or kneading board, and knead by slamming, stretching, and rolling for 5 minutes, or until dough is silky, smooth, and cool. Make a well in the center of dough and cover with damp cloth.

4. In a preheated skillet, combine olive oil, garlic, oregano, black pepper, cilantro, chopped green onions, chopped red bell pepper, and minced ham. Sauté for 2 minutes. Remove from skillet and allow to cool for 2 minutes, then pour the mixture into the well in the center of dough. Use the tips of your fingers and the palm of your hands to fold and roll the dough and the sautéed ingredients together until the dough is workable again (approximately 3 minutes).

5. Using a dough cutter or a knife, divide the dough into 8 equal parts. Roll parts into 12-inch cylinders, then divide the cylinder into four 3-inch sticks.

6. To bake, preheat oven at 375° for 15 minutes. Layer a sheet pan with wax paper or baking parchment, then arrange sticks in columns leaving a 1/4-inch space between each stick. Using a pastry brush, generously coat the cornbread sticks with egg wash prior to baking. Bake at 375° for 17 minutes.

7. Remove from oven and serve hot with a garlic *mojo* or a spicy cocktail sauce. Or serve simply with Dijon-style mustard, lemon and lime wedges.

Shrimp Cornbread Sticks

Surullos con Camarones

MAKES 32 *SURULLOS*

These shrimp cornbread sticks do very well when served alongside *Sopa de Calabaza* (squash soup) or a *Caldo de Pescado* (fish broth).

1¹/₂ cups yellow cornmeal

1¹/₂ cups all-purpose flour

³/₄ teaspoon baking powder

3 medium eggs

¹/₃ cup vegetable oil

1 cup half-and-half

1²/₃ cups lukewarm water

1 tablespoon olive oil

4 cloves of garlic, minced

2 teaspoons chopped fresh oregano (1 teaspoon dry)

¹/₂ teaspoon cayenne pepper

1 tablespoon chopped fresh cilantro

2 green onions, finely chopped

¹/₃ cup finely chopped red bell pepper

1 tablespoon baby capers, drained and patted dry

1 cup finely chopped shrimp meat

²/₃ cup egg wash (1 beaten egg combined with ²/₃ cup of milk)

1. In a 2-quart saucepan, combine cornmeal, flour, baking powder, and mix.

2. In a separate mixing bowl, combine and blend eggs, vegetable oil, and half-and-half. Using a wooden spoon, stir mixture into dry ingredients until forming a stiff batter. Break down batter with water, scraping all sides and bottom of the pan. Place over low to medium heat while continuously stirring in a circular motion, until dough ball is formed inside the pan.

3. Remove from heat and transfer to lightly floured surface or kneading board, and knead by slamming, stretching, and rolling for 5 minutes, or until dough is silky, smooth, and cool. Make a well in the center of dough and cover with damp cloth.

4. In a preheated skillet, combine olive oil with all the listed herbs and spices, including the capers and shrimp. Sauté for 2 minutes. Remove from skillet and allow to cool for 2 minutes, then pour the mixture into the well in the center of dough. Use the tips of your fingers and the palm of your hands to fold and roll until all the ingredients are nicely blended and the dough is workable again (approximately 3 minutes).

5. Using a dough cutter or a knife, divide the dough into 8 equal parts. Roll parts into 12-inch cylinders, then divide the cylinder into four 3-inch sticks.

6. To bake, follow instructions for basic *surullo* recipe. Then remove from oven and serve hot with a seafood cocktail sauce or garlic *mojo*, and lemon and lime wedges.

Cornbread Sticks with Anchovies
Surullos con Anchoas
MAKES 32 *SURULLOS*

Anchovies in cornbread? If you enjoy anchovies, you'll love fresh cornbread mixed with small chunks of these fish, and the capers and spices folded into the batter. These *surullos* are excellent served with a *Sopa de Calabaza* (Squash Soup) or *Sopa de Habichuelas Blanca* (White Bean Soup). They can also be served along with an avocado dip.

1 1/2 cups yellow cornmeal

1 1/2 cups all-purpose flour

3/4 teaspoon baking powder

3 medium eggs

1/3 cup vegetable oil

1 cup half-and-half

1 2/3 cups lukewarm water

1 tablespoon olive oil

1 teaspoon *lime juice*

5 garlic cloves, *minced*

2 teaspoons *chopped fresh oregano (1 teaspoon dry)*

1/4 teaspoon *cayenne pepper*

1 tablespoon *chopped fresh cilantro*

2 green onions, *finely chopped*

1 tablespoon *chopped red bell pepper*

1 tablespoon *Spanish capers, drained and patted dry*

1 cup *anchovies, chopped*

2/3 cup *egg wash (1 beaten egg combined with 2/3 cup of milk)*

1. In a 2-quart saucepan, combine cornmeal, flour, baking powder, and mix.

2. In a separate mixing bowl, combine and blend eggs, vegetable oil, and half-and-half. Using a wooden spoon, stir mixture into dry ingredients until it forms a stiff batter. Break down batter with water, scraping all sides and bottom of pan. Place over low to medium heat while continuously stirring in a circular motion, until dough ball is formed inside the pan.

3. Remove from heat and transfer to lightly floured surface or kneading board, and knead by slamming, stretching, and rolling for 5 minutes, or until dough is silky, smooth, and cool. Make a well in the center of dough and cover with damp cloth.

4. In a preheated skillet, combine all herbs and spices, including the capers and anchovies, and sauté for 2 minutes. Remove from skillet and allow to cool for 2 minutes, then pour the mixture into the well in the center of dough. Use the tips of your fingers and palm of your hands to fold and roll until all the ingredients are blended together, and the dough is workable again (approximately 3 minutes).

5. Continue with preparation and baking according to steps 5 and 6 of basic *surullo* recipe.

Salads

Ensaladas

> *The land of Borinquen*
> *Where I was born*
> *Is a tropical garden*
> *Of magic splendor.*
>
> MANUEL FERNANDEZ JUNCOS

I grew up enjoying salads at home. Looking back, I realize how lucky I was because I had immediate access to a wonderful source of nutrition right in my own backyard—a pleasure and convenience not available to most city people. My mother's fruit and vegetable garden provided the family with a combination of seasonal, fresh food all year round: lettuce, watercress, *guingambó* (okra), sweet green peppers and chili peppers, tomatoes and onions, chayotes, *calabaza* (squash), eggplants and avocados, green banana plants, and *yautía* (taro root). Most of the fresh produce that we obtained from our garden was supplemented with beans, rice, and other grains purchased at the public marketplace. We also had mangoes, papayas, pineapples, lemons, limes, soursops, and tamarinds.

My mother had a use for everything that grew in our garden, plus she would always create different ways to make a traditional salad seem new and appealing to her children—flavor, color, and texture were always enticing.

Typically, most Puerto Rican salads prepared at home were hearty and not served as appetizers, but rather as part of the main course on a plate alongside rice and beans, or with *tostones* (fried plantain chips) or *vianda* (a combination of boiled tubers). The salads were made from seafood such as octopus, conch meat, crab meat, shrimp, and fish that was cooked, broiled, fried, or boiled, then marinated and served on a bed of lettuce and watercress.

Salads made with codfish or smoked herring were the most popular because they were inexpensive staples, and available all year.

Avocado salads were just as popular, primarily because avocados were abundant during the spring and summer. Whether sliced in a plain avocado salad or combined with other food items, such as chayote, or in a gazpacho with codfish, served hot or cold, or as a dressing, the texture, flavor, and nutritional properties of this fruit made it an ideal way to create hearty, balanced salads that were often part of the Puerto Rican dinner.

After 1950, the presence and influence of the North American culture on The Island has provided a new generation of Islanders with the technology and information to further expand their culinary horizons. The introduction of efficient food preparation appliances, improved storage methods, and greater awareness of health and nutritional values has added a new dimension to the way that Puerto Ricans look at and prepare food.

In the interest of good and healthy eating, and to satisfy both the desire to respect the traditional and the need to experiment, I have recreated many of the old salad favorites. My family and I have always enjoyed them, and I hope you do too!

Basic Avocado Salad
Ensalada de Aguacate

SERVES 4

The avocado is one of the most versatile fruits in existence, and we have Hernando Cortez to thank for spreading the news of its wonders. When he arrived with his expeditionary forces in the land of the Aztecs in Mexico, one of the great gastronomical treasures bestowed upon him by Montezuma's people was the *ahuacatl*, in Puerto Rican Spanish, the *aguacate*.

Although the avocado has its origin in Central America and Mexico, there are countless varieties in the Caribbean Islands and the United States, each with its own appeal and regional characteristics. If you have tried avocados from different tropical locales, you have probably noticed that they vary in size and shape. While most are pear-shaped, some are completely round, and others have long, crooked necks like yellow squash. In California, the Hass variety is most common. This small avocado, with a skin that is black to purple in color and has a gritty, pebbly texture to the touch, is very flavorful. But the amount of meat is relatively little, so a larger quantity of avocados is needed for a recipe. In this book use a 2-to-1 ratio.

In addition to the different species from other regions in the Caribbean, and the Americas, Puerto Rico has its own variety of avocado called "del pais" (from The Island). It is round, about the size of a large orange, and hunter green in color. The thin skin is smooth and shiny. Inside, the seed is small and surrounded by a flavorful, golden green firm pulp.

When I was growing up, it was commonplace to see two or three varieties growing in most backyards. There was always a sense of pride among neighbors when ever the topic of avocados came up in over-the-fence conversations. Of course everyone's tree produced the perfect fruit, and to prove the point, neighbors would share and barter with one another from their small crop, and exchange recipes for new ways to prepare and serve the avocados.

In the following section, I suggest various delicious recipes that are easy to prepare, where the flavor of the avocado is most enjoyed and complemented by the texture of such food items as chayote squash, and the distinct flavors of other ingredients such as *bacalao* and smoked herring. All of these salads can be prepared and served as appetizers or as part of the main course with rice dishes and *viandas* (Puerto Rican style tuberous vegetables).

Avocados imported into the United States from Central America and the Caribbean are larger, greener, and heavier than the varieties typically grown in the western United States. You can find them at Latino fresh produce stores. The technique for choosing from this variety is to hold the fruit close to your ear and carefully shake it. If you hear a crisp hollow sound, the avocado is not ripe. That sound you hear is the seed of the avocado rattling against the crisp unripened flesh. Most vendors will protect the fragile fruit and not allow the customer to squeeze it, but they will have separate batches classified by degrees of maturity. Signs are often posted to identify each batch, for example "ripe" or "ready to eat tomorrow." Avocados take two to three days to ripen to the ideal eating consistency. The best way to enjoy an avocado is at room temperature.

When choosing an avocado for immediate use, it should be ripe but firm and without blemish. To examine the fruit, gently pick up the avocado. Although it may feel soft to the touch on the outside, most avocados in the bins are abused from the constant squeezing by shoppers which renders them soft but not ripe. Tip the avocado bottom side up, use the flat part of your thumb on the center of the bottom and gently press down. If the fruit is ripe, the skin will be resilient to the touch. The neck of the fruit will ripen faster than the bottom, so make sure that it too is also firm.

4 tablespoons olive oil

4 garlic cloves, minced

2 tablespoons red wine vinegar

1 tablespoon lime juice

1/2 teaspoon pulverized rock salt

1/2 teaspoon freshly ground black peppercorns

2 tablespoons chopped fresh cilantro

8 ripe black pitted olives, cut in halves

1/3 cup capers

1 small red onion, sliced julienne

1/2 medium red bell pepper, sliced julienne in 16 pieces

1/2 medium yellow bell pepper, sliced julienne in 16 pieces

1/2 cup shredded red cabbage

3 ripe firm avocados, peeled and diced into 1-inch cubes

8 green lettuce leaves

1 medium tomato, cored and sliced

2 hard-boiled eggs, peeled and cut into 4 wedges

4 lime wedges

1. In a salad bowl, combine olive oil, garlic, red wine vinegar, lime juice, salt, black pepper, cilantro, olives, capers, onion, red and yellow bell peppers, and red cabbage. Mix, then add avocado cubes and toss lightly using your hands.

2. To serve, cover individual salad plates with 2 lettuce leaves each and arrange a mound of salad in the center. Garnish with tomato slices, egg wedges, and lime wedges.

SERVING SUGGESTIONS: Serve with Green Plantain *Tostones* or garlic bread. Wash down with your favorite beverage.

Lobster Salad

Ensalada de Langosta

SERVES 4

The North American presence and influence on The Island has had a great impact on the food industry. With a new market for northern food producers to explore, the United States overwhelmed Puerto Rico with a variety of new consumer products.

I remember the first frozen lobsters that my father brought home—we didn't know what to do with them because the cooking instructions were written in English! My mother suggested cooking each one separately. For the first one, we boiled it and treated it the same way we would a land crab. It worked, except that it was over-cooked and we ended up with a hard, chewy, dry lobster that my father likened to a *barraco* (the flesh of an old hog, so tough it can't be eaten). He then cut it up and mixed the pieces in the glass jar that he kept full of marinated octopus. My mother decided to thaw out the remaining lobsters, separate the meat from the tails, marinate the meat, and broil it the way we would codfish. It worked!

Throughout the years I have prepared and served lobsters in numerous ways. I have also tasted and appreciated lobsters cooked and served by friends and in restaurants. But the only way to prepare this versatile crustacean, in my opinion, is your favorite way. The following recipe is my favorite, unique because the intense sea flavor and texture of the lobster is enhanced by the marinade and broiling. The meat will become tenderized while absorbing the moisture of the marinade and will not require too much time under the broiler. The end result is a delightful salad with a hot, charred, and smoky texture, bursting with the distinct flavor of the cool sea.

Using fresh live lobster is the way to go when preparing your favorite lobster recipe. Although the preparation will require some work on your part, it is well worth the effort. See the "Seafood" chapter for other lobster recipes and preparation tips.

THE MARINADE:

- 6   *garlic cloves, minced*
- 1   *teaspoon crushed rock salt*
- 1   *teaspoon minced fresh gingerroot*
- 1/2 *teaspoon cayenne pepper*
- 1/4 *teaspoon sage*

2　tablespoons olive oil

1/3　cup Spanish sherry

　4　lobster tails, shelled (approximately 6 ounces each)

THE DRESSING:

1/3　cup olive oil

　1　tablespoon white wine vinegar

　1　tablespoon lime juice

　2　teaspoons chopped fresh oregano (1 teaspoon dried)

　8　ripe pitted olives

　1　tablespoon capers

　3　green onions, trimmed to 5 inches and chopped

　1　medium green bell pepper, broiled and diced

　1　medium red bell pepper, broiled and diced

　8　center leaves of romaine lettuce, washed and patted dry,
　　and broken into bite-sized pieces

　1　bunch of watercress, washed and patted dry, with large stems removed

　2　medium tomatoes, cored, seeded, and chopped

　1　tablespoon chopped fresh cilantro

　　Garnish: lemon or lime wedges

1. Make the marinade by combining and blending in a bowl the garlic, salt, ginger, cayenne pepper, sage, olive oil, and sherry. Slice lobster tails into 1-inch medallions and mix well into marinade. Cover and refrigerate for 1 hour.

2. To cook, place the medallions on a sheet pan after draining excess moisture from them. Broil lobster medallions for 2 minutes on each side, making sure to flip pieces over quickly so as not to lose cooking time.

3. In a salad bowl, combine and blend olive oil, wine vinegar, lime juice, and oregano. Fold in broiled lobster meat, olives, capers, green onions, green and red bell peppers.

4. To serve, prepare a mat of lettuce and watercress on a salad plate. Arrange a generous amount of lobster in the center, and then sprinkle chopped tomatoes and cilantro on top.

SERVING SUGGESTIONS: Serve with Green Plantain *Tostones*, Breadfruit *Tostones*, or garlic bread on the side. Enjoy with your favorite wine.

VARIATION: Substitute 6 large, shelled and deveined shrimps for each lobster tail.

Chayote and Avocado Salad with Watercress
Ensalada de Chayote y Aguacate con Berro
SERVES 4

The chayote is a tropical vine-grown, pear-shaped squash that can be easily recognized in the fresh produce bins by its distinctive cactus-like texture and light mint green color. Do not be fooled by the outer appearance of this vegetable. Although its prickly skin gives an unfriendly first impression, it hides an inner, fine, crisp texture that, when cooked, becomes a delicate, delicious, and versatile food item. Whether hot or cold in soups or stews, baked, fried, or in salads, the chayote can be part of any meal.

Chayotes are now available in most large American supermarket chains, and in most Latin American and Asian produce stores almost all year round. Sold individually or in bulk, they are available in different sizes and weights. They weigh from 6 to 10 ounces, and are the size of a large Bartlett pear with an extended neck. Keep in a dry, cool place and away from intense heat. Do not freeze.

I remember, back home in our yard the chayote vines would crawl along a fence, blanketing it, and then like giant green snakes, the vines wound around the trunk and branches of the mango and avocado trees on the far side of the patio. Here, by the fence, I spent most of my leisure time swaying in a hammock made from a burlap sack. I played imaginary games while watching in fascination as the plants and trees came to life. I remember looking for the first-born fruit or vegetable, monitoring their progress every day. I'd take care of it as one would a pet, though at the same time anticipating the day when I would turn it into a delicious treat.

The best chayotes would invariably grow on the vine wrapped around the upper branches of the mango and avocado trees. The weight of the chayotes caused them to rest on the roof of our house. At night, the scraping sound and incessant pounding of the chayotes against the tin roof when the wind blew, drove my parents to distraction. It then became my job to climb a tree to the top of the house and pick the errant chayotes.

My favorite way to eat the chayote was poached in boiling water. Once it was cooked, I would let the chayote cool and peel it like an orange. Ahhh, then I would sit on the hammock and let my mind wander as I swayed back and forth, savoring the fruit of my labor.

With the following recipe, I have combined the chayote, avocado, and watercress to create a truly delectable salad dish to adorn the dinner table or complement dishes on any occasion.

    3   chayotes (approximately 6 to 7 ounces each)
    2   quarts water
  1/3   cup olive oil
    6   garlic cloves, minced
    1   tablespoon white wine vinegar
    1   tablespoon lime juice
  1/2   teaspoon ground black pepper
  1/2   teaspoon pulverized rock salt
    1   tablespoon chopped fresh cilantro
    1   small red onion, julienned
    1   medium green bell pepper, broiled and diced
    1   medium red bell pepper, broiled and diced
   12   ripe black pitted olives, cut in halves
    2   tablespoons capers
    3   avocados, ripe but firm, peeled, and diced into 1-inch cubes
    1   bunch of green lettuce
    1   bunch of watercress, washed, with large stems removed

    Garnish: 2 medium tomatoes, cored and sliced

1. To prepare: cut each chayote in half. Place into a pot with water. Bring to a boil, then simmer at low-to-medium heat for 15 minutes. Remove from direct heat and allow to sit for 5 minutes.

2. Using a colander, carefully strain the chayotes and cool them off by submerging (dunking) the entire colander and chayotes into a cold bath. Repeat the process until the chayotes are cool to the touch.

3. Peel the skin with a sharp paring knife, and dice the chayotes to approximately 1-inch cubes.

4. In a salad bowl, combine and mix olive oil, garlic, vinegar, lime juice, black pepper, salt, cilantro, red onion, green and red bell peppers, olives, and capers.

5. Then carefully fold avocado and chayote into the mixture.

6. To serve: arrange a bed of crisp lettuce leaves on a salad plate followed by a layer of watercress. Place a mound of chayote and avocado salad on top.

SERVING SUGGESTIONS: I enjoy this salad as a light lunch with a basket of hot garlic bread and a red table wine. As a main meal, I serve it with Black Rice, and Red Beans Stewed in Wine Sauce, white wine, and guava shells with slivers of Jarlsberg cheese, and Spanish Coffee with Brandy for dessert.

Chayote and Smoked Herring Salad
Ensalada de Chayote con Arenque
SERVES 6

Arenques are dried, smoke-cured herrings. The intense flavor of the herring is superb when combined with the sweet natural flavors of cheese, tubers, and other vegetables. It also makes an ideal substitute for salted codfish and anchovies.

One of the factors to remember is that *arenque* is very bony, and care must be exercised in removing the bones when working with this dry fish. For those who do not wish to put up with the "fine tuning," fillets of smoke-cured herring are also available at most supermarkets and fish stores in the United States. One of my favorite ways to serve it is combined with crisp marinated chayote slices, and next to a bed of cooked white rice.

3 *medium chayotes*
2 *quarts water*

2   large smoke-cured herrings

1   small red onion, sliced julienne

1   medium green bell pepper, broiled and diced

1   medium red bell pepper, broiled and diced

12 ripe pitted olives

2   tablespoons capers

1/4 cup olive oil

1   tablespoon red wine vinegar

1   tablespoon lime juice

1/2 teaspoon ground black pepper

6   garlic cloves, minced

2   tablespoons chopped cilantro

1/2 small iceberg lettuce

8   green lettuce leaves

1   bunch of watercress

Garnish: lemon wedges, tomato slices

1. Peel chayotes and dice into 1/2-inch pieces.

2. Put in a stockpot, along with the water, and simmer until cooked firm and crisp like an *al dente* potato. Drain and run under cold water. Spread on a platter; cover and refrigerate until needed.

3. Place herrings under the broiler for 2 minutes, each side. Remove and place in a bowl with cold water. Flake the herring carefully while removing the bones.

4. In a glass bowl, combine and mix onion, green bell pepper, red bell pepper, olives, capers, olive oil, vinegar, lime juice, pepper, and cloves. Fold the flaked herring into the dressing, then gently fold the chayote into the herring mixture.

5. Sprinkle chopped cilantro on the salad and refrigerate until ready to serve.

6. Serve on a bed of crisp lettuce and watercress.

SERVING SUGGESTIONS: Serve with a hot, crusty bread or a batch of *surullos*. Wash down with a burgundy wine.

Mango Chicken Salad

Ensalada con Mango y Pollo

SERVES 4

Mango trees once abounded in Puerto Rico, offering cool shade and their delightful fruits. One could walk for miles under a canopy of mango trees that lined both sides of the country roads. In the city, the blistering pavement of high noon would be pacified in places where people had a mango tree growing. During harvest season, when the mango trees were *cargado*—filled with mature fruits ready to be picked—the autumn wind blowing against the tall trees would force the branches, heavy with clusters of mangoes, to sway from side to side like a giant fan. The air was filled with the enticing honey fragrance of ripe mangoes. There were times when the only advance warning of a coming hurricane or a strong tropical rainstorm, in the middle of the night, was the incessant pounding of mangoes on the zinc plank roofs of the houses. Whenever this happened, our entire household was rousted out of bed to make preparations for a quick getaway to my mother's cousin's house. She lived a block away, and her two-story home, constructed of steel bars and reinforced concrete, was used as a shelter by friends and family during tropical storms and other emergencies.

As we waited for the storm to pass, the children huddled together and listened to an endless repertoire of stories exchanged by the adults. The elderly clung to their rosary beads, lit candles, and formed prayer circles around the patron saint Santa Clara. A few women were busy in the kitchen preparing and batch-cooking food. Chicken *asopaos*, *viandas* and quick salads, hot coffee and hot chocolate, cheese and crackers, and mangoes, were usually the menu at hand.

The topics of God, man, children, and the usual exchange of new recipes for preparing mangoes and other fruits and vegetables were discussed in these kitchen *tertulias*. This social activity would last through the night until the sun came out or until it was considered safe to return home. Floods, damaged homes, and power outages were inevitable, and the memories of the last storm would always be relived and retold at the next gathering.

Mangoes come from many different tropical countries in different colors, shapes, and sizes, each with its own distinct taste and texture. Some will exhibit a dull, forest green and purple skin when unripe, but as they ripen, they turn a light yellow to orange color with a smooth texture on the inside. The greener the mango is when ripe, the tighter and firmer the texture. The further the ripe mango is from green, the more the texture of the pulp is stringy and fibrous with a higher content of moisture. This type of mango is not suitable for salads but is great for eating whole and for making juice, desserts, and soups or sauces. This characteristic also applies to the yellow skin mango variety.

The determining factor for ripeness is the fragrance of the tropical mango. To test the aroma, hold the bottom part close to your nose and press gently with your thumb. If the fruit is ripe or near ripe, it will give off its distinctive honey-sweet fragrance. For salads I recommend that the mango be ripe but closer to green for texture and body. Use a very sharp knife when slicing to prevent bruising of the fruit.

Keep a basketful of mangoes in the house whenever you can. This beautiful fruit will adorn your table and fill your house with the fragrance of the tropics.

The following salad is great at any time and for any occasion.

4   *chicken breasts, boneless and skinless, cut into 1-inch cubes*
1/2   *cup Tropical Dressing (see "Sauces" Chapter)*
1/2   *cup shredded red cabbage*
1/2   *medium green bell pepper, diced*
1/2   *medium red bell pepper, diced*
1/2   *medium yellow bell pepper, diced*
1   *small red onion, diced*
4   *spears of celery heart, thinly sliced*
1/3   *cup raisins*
2   *medium mangoes (ripe but firm), peeled and cut into 1/2-inch cubes*
8   *leaves of red lettuce*
1   *bunch watercress, washed and patted dry, with large stems removed*
1   *medium carrot, plumed (thick pieces peeled with a potato peeler)*
1/3   *cup sliced, roasted chestnuts, or 1/3 cup toasted almonds*

TO MAKE MARINADE,
COMBINE THE FOLLOWING IN A MIXING BOWL AND BLEND:
1/3   *cup mango nectar*
1   *tablespoon lime juice*

> 2   *tablespoons olive oil*
> 2   *tablespoons dry sherry*
> 4   *garlic cloves, crushed*
> 1   *teaspoon cracked black peppercorns*
> 1   *tablespoon chopped fresh mint*
> 1   *teaspoon chopped fresh ginger*
> 1   *tablespoon chopped fresh cilantro*
>
> **Garnish:** *orange rings*

1. Toss chicken in marinade. Cover and refrigerate for 1 hour.

2. To cook chicken: spread chicken cubes on a sheet pan, draining the excess marinade back into the bowl. Save for basting. Place the sheet pan under the broiler and cook until chicken cubes begin to sizzle, then flip the cubes with a spatula, and using a basting brush, baste with the leftover marinade and finish cooking. Cubes should appear slightly charred. Remove chicken from broiler and transfer to a cold pan. Set aside and allow to cool.

3. To make salad: combine the following in a salad bowl and toss lightly: Tropical Dressing, red cabbage, broiled chicken cubes, green, red, and yellow bell peppers, red onion, celery, raisins, and mango cubes.

4. To serve: arrange on salad plates red leaf lettuce, watercress, and carrot plumes. Scoop a mound of chicken salad onto each plate, sprinkle sliced roasted chestnuts or toasted almonds on top.

SERVING SUGGESTIONS: Serve *surullos* on the side, or a crusty French bread, and a chilled white wine or fresh coffee.

VARIATIONS: For Papaya Chicken Salad, substitute papayas for mangoes and fresh orange juice for mango nectar.

Broiled Codfish Salad
Ensalada de Bacalao

SERVES 4

Given the choice of either steak and eggs with all the trimmings, or a fresh avocado with a piece of charbroiled codfish for a lazy Sunday morning brunch, for me, there would be no contest—I'd choose the latter!

This recipe was inspired by fond memories of my father and me preparing for the family's Sunday brunch ritual. After attending required church services in the mornings, I'd walk a couple of blocks to my father's butcher shop in the *plaza del mercado* (marketplace) and help him close it up for the day. Then my father and I would shop for the fresh produce on my mother's weekly grocery list. Just spending time with my father on a simple errand was special to me—and he always had a funny new story to tell me.

I especially looked forward to the Sundays when we would bring back the *bacalao*. As soon as we were home, I would gather the charcoal and ready the *anafre* (charcoal pit). My mother would set up the patio table, bring out the eating and cooking utensils, and a basketful of ripe avocados. My father would be responsible for starting the fire and broiling the *bacalao*. He and I took turns at basting the codfish with Puerto Rican beer, and every so often he would allow me to sneak a tiny sip. To my mother's show of concern he would say, "the fish will not taste the same if we don't baste our tongues as well."

When purchasing codfish, always ask for the top to middle portion of the piece because this is the fleshiest and least salty part, and it will retain most of the flaky texture.

After soaking and rinsing the codfish, test for saltiness. If the fish is too salty for your taste buds, rinse again for a couple more minutes after flaking. You want to desalt but not make it insipid by too much rinsing. The appealing attribute of the codfish is the hint of the sea that can be perceived when it's eaten, and which calls for another sip of cold beer or wine as you experience the burst of flavors.

Any leftover codfish that has not been through the desalting process may be kept in the refrigerator for an indefinite amount of time. However, any prepared codfish should be refrigerated and eaten within two or three days. Save it in a plastic container with a tight lid.

$^{3}/_{4}$ pound dry salted codfish fillet (no bones)

2 quarts boiling water

TO MAKE MARINADE:

4 garlic cloves, minced

$^{1}/_{2}$ teaspoon minced fresh gingerroot

1 teaspoon chopped fresh mint

1 tablespoon olive oil

$^{1}/_{3}$ cup beer, room temperature

TO MAKE SALAD DRESSING:

$^{1}/_{3}$ cup olive oil

1 tablespoon white wine vinegar

1 tablespoon lime juice

8 ripe pitted black olives

1 tablespoon capers

1 small red onion, sliced

$^{1}/_{2}$ medium green bell pepper, diced

$^{1}/_{2}$ medium red bell pepper, diced

$^{1}/_{2}$ medium yellow pepper, diced

2 teaspoons chopped fresh oregano leaves (1 teaspoon dried, crushed)

$^{1}/_{2}$ teaspoon cracked black peppercorns

1 tablespoon chopped fresh cilantro

16 fresh spinach leaves, washed, patted dry, and coarsely chopped

2 hard-boiled eggs, sliced

2 medium tomatoes, cored and sliced

Garnish: 4 lemon and 4 lime wedges

1. Soak codfish in boiling-hot water for 20 minutes. Discard water and rinse codfish under running water for 2 minutes, then pat dry and flake into bite-sized pieces. Remove any remaining bones.

2. Make a marinade by combining and blending in a bowl the garlic, ginger, mint, olive oil, and beer. Lay the flaked codfish pieces on a sheet pan and coat well on all sides with the mixture, then cover with foil or plastic wrap and marinate for 1 hour. Drain excess moisture and place under the broiler; broil for 2 minutes and remove.

3. In a salad bowl, combine and mix the olive oil, wine vinegar, lime juice, olives, capers, onion, green, red, and yellow bell peppers, oregano, black pepper, and cilantro. Add the codfish and toss vigorously. Fold in the chopped spinach. Transfer to a salad tray. Garnish with egg and tomato slices, and the lemon and lime wedges.

SERVING SUGGESTIONS: I always serve this salad with White Rice, Simmered Beans, and *amarillos* (Broiled Yellow Plantains). I like a cold beer or a white or red table wine to wash it down. For dessert try Coconut Custard and a cup of freshly brewed Puerto Rican coffee.

VARIATION: To take advantage of the avocado season, choose three ripe avocados and peel. Dice into 1 inch pieces and fold in after adding the spinach.

Octopus Salad
Ensalada de Pulpo

SERVES 4

Since most Puerto Ricans are Catholic and the fundamental teachings of the Church were, traditionally, not to be questioned but acted upon, one of the practices most conscientiously adhered to was the observance of Lent, known as *Cuaresma* or forty days. The peak of this rite was reached during Holy Week when virtually everything stopped and no work was performed. A blanket of pious solemnity would cover The Island, and most hearts and minds were preoccupied with prayers for miracles and the coming and passing of Christ.

Countless tales of redeeming miracles for the true believer were told, and eerie tales of punishment for the transgressors abounded. One of my favorite warnings was, "Do not use the knife or it will turn to blood." I waited many disappointing years to see this metamorphosis! There were times when I was tempted to defy the warning, but I could never muster enough courage to go through with it.

Out of fear and respect, most people abstained from using knives and sharp objects in their homes and at work. Slaughtering of livestock would cease and no meat would be prepared or served. It was during this time that the majority of Puerto Ricans turned to two other logical sources of food: fish from the sea and tubers from the land. The abundance of seafood on the coastal regions of The Island and the availability of springtime fruit and vegetables from the interior during *Cuaresma* provided kitchens with the natural ingredients that were needed to create flavorful and nutritional dishes that easily satisfied the most demanding and holy palate.

Since most salads were destined to be served as main dinner courses, they needed to be hearty, diversified, and healthy, as well as have readily available and affordable ingredients. Refrigeration was limited, so preservation without contamination was an important factor when choosing fresh, raw food. Octopus (*pulpo*) and conch (*carrucho*) became the popular seafood choices. Both are inherently large, chewy, flavorful, and in abundance. With the proper preparation (boiling at high temperatures to kill toxins, and employing the enzymes contained in lemon, lime, and vinegar to cure the meat), and using the preservative properties of combined herbs and spices, the octopus and conch behave very well and can keep for an extended period of time. The longer the curing time (pickling), the softer and more flavorful the fish becomes while submerged in the marinade.

Although one of the popular methods applied was the curing of the live octopus in a spiced rum marinade (see "Seafoods" chapter), I have introduced a more realistic and acceptable salad recipe for the contemporary palate, applying a fast-cooking method along with an on-the-spot marinade. Octopus and conch can be purchased at most fresh fish markets in the United States, especially in Latino or Asian communities. For marinated octopus or conch see the "Seafoods" chapter.

TO PREPARE OCTOPUS:
- *2 pounds raw fresh octopus (large)*
- *4 quarts water*
- *2 teaspoons rock salt*
- *1 teaspoon whole peppercorns*

1 small lemon, cut in half

4 whole garlic cloves, peeled

2 whole bay leaves

2 green onions trimmed to 5 inches whole

THE SALAD:

1/2 medium green bell pepper, diced

1/2 medium red bell pepper, diced

1 small red onion, diced

4 garlic cloves peeled, minced

1/4 teaspoon ground black peppercorns

1 teaspoon pulverized rock salt

2 teaspoons chopped fresh oregano (1 teaspoon dried)

1/3 cup pitted black olives

1/3 cup capers

1/2 cup olive oil

2 teaspoons fresh lime juice

1/3 cup red wine vinegar

4 lettuce leaves, washed and patted dry

1 bunch of watercress, washed, with large stems removed

2 tablespoons chopped fresh cilantro

Garnish: *4 thick slices of tomato, cut in halves, 4 lemon wedges, 4 lime wedges*

1. Rinse octopus thoroughly in warm running water for 1 minute. Then place in a stockpot with 2 to 3 quarts of water. Add whole rock salt, whole peppercorns, lemon, garlic, 2 bay leaves, and green onions.

2. Place on high heat and bring to a boil, reduce heat to medium and continue cooking for approximately 1 hour or until octopus is tender. The octopus must be completely covered with water while cooking; when water level diminishes, add more, otherwise the meat will not become tender.

3. The cooking time will be affected by the size of the octopus. As you check for the

water level, also check for tenderness of the meat by sticking a fork through the fattest part of the tentacles. The fork should go through without effort when the meat is done and ready to be taken out.

4. Once done, transfer octopus to a colander and place under cold running water. Slide your hand up and down the tentacles so as to remove the top layer of the slippery tissues. The octopus head has an inner lining; turn the head inside out and remove the tissue.

5. To make the salad, dice the octopus into pieces approximately ¼-inch thick. Using a glass salad bowl (wood or metal will adversely alter the taste), combine octopus meat, diced green and red peppers, red onion, minced garlic, ground black peppercorns, pulverized salt, oregano, olives, capers, olive oil, lime juice, red wine vinegar, and 3 bay leaves. Toss vigorously, then cover and store at room temperature (but away from direct heat) for at least 1 hour.

6. To serve: layer individual salad plates with green lettuce leaves and a bed of watercress. Using a slotted spoon, scoop a mound of octopus salad onto the plate, then sprinkle chopped cilantro on the top.

SERVING SUGGESTIONS:
For a complete lunch or dinner on a
hot summer day, serve with White Rice,
red beans and boiled plantain, or Yellow Rice,
black beans, and Marinated *Yuca,* or
Breadfruit *Tostones* on the side.

VARIATIONS: For Conch Salad, substitute
octopus with 2 pounds of conch meat.
Using a sharp knife, cut into thin fillets,
then use a meat mallet to pound both sides
of the fillets to tenderize the conch.
Follow the Octopus Salad recipe
instructions for boiling, then coarsely
chop the conch meat and follow the
octopus salad directions for mixing.

Shrimp Salad

Ensalada de Camarones

SERVES 4

Perhaps the most popular and abundant of the shellfish, shrimp turns an ordinary salad into a gourmet main dish. Although shrimp can almost always be substituted for lobster, this dish warrants its own recipe because of its distinct marinade, highlighted by fresh gingerroot, mint, beer, and lime juice. Traditionally, shrimps are steamed or boiled. I have chosen instead to broil the shrimp slightly for a more interesting taste, and also to recapture the experience of freshly-caught sweetwater shrimp roasted over an open pit.

When I was a boy in Ponce, my mother would take all five of us children to the river banks for an afternoon of shrimp catching. Standing in the shallow waters, my mother would scoop down and snatch up the shrimps one by one as they swam by. She dropped each one in the front of her dress that she held up as a makeshift basket, and waited to spot the next one come up near her ankles. What a quick hand she seemed to have. I don't ever think she missed one! We would take all of the shrimps back home and barbeque them in our patio. To this day I have never tasted shrimp that delicious.

THE MARINADE:

- 6   *garlic cloves, minced*
- 2   *tablespoons olive oil*
- 2   *teaspoons minced fresh gingerroot*
- 1/3 *cup beer*
- 1   *tablespoon chopped fresh mint*
- 2   *tablespoons lime juice*
- 1   *teaspoon crushed rock salt*

24 medium shrimps, shelled and deveined

1/3 cup olive oil

1 tablespoon white wine vinegar

1 tablespoon lime juice

2 teaspoons chopped fresh oregano

1/4 teaspoon cayenne pepper

12 ripe pitted olives

2 tablespoons capers

3 green onions, trimmed to 5 inches and chopped

1/2 medium green bell pepper, sliced julienne

1/2 medium red bell pepper, sliced julienne

1/2 medium yellow pepper, sliced julienne

2 medium tomatoes, cored, seeded, and diced

8 center leaves of romaine lettuce, washed and patted dry,
   broken into bite-sized pieces

1 bunch of watercress washed and patted dry, large stems removed

2 tablespoons chopped fresh cilantro

1. Make a marinade by combining in a bowl and blending, garlic, olive oil, ginger, beer, mint, lime juice, and salt. Add shrimp, toss well, cover, and refrigerate for one hour. Drain excess moisture and place under the broiler, broil for 2 minutes on each side.

2. In a salad bowl, combine and blend olive oil, wine vinegar, lime juice, oregano, cayenne pepper. Add and toss: shrimps, olives, capers, onion, green, red, and yellow bell peppers, and diced tomatoes.

3. To serve: arrange a mat of lettuce and watercress on a salad plate and, using a slotted serving spoon, put a copious amount of shrimp salad in the center. Sprinkle chopped cilantro on top.

SERVING SUGGESTIONS: Serve with Green Plantain *Tostones* or Breadfruit *Tostones*, or with garlic bread on the side. And an ice cold beer.

New Puerto Rican Fruit Salad

SERVES 4

A Sunday brunch is never complete without a bowl of chilled fresh fruit salad to refresh the palate. On The Island, a bowl of fresh fruit will invariably occupy a respectable spot on the pantry table in most homes. If one is fortunate enough, there will be several varieties of seasonal fruit growing in one's patio, to be picked and enjoyed at anytime. Whether individually, combined, or as a complement to hot or cold dishes—desserts, soups, and salads—a cook will never go wrong by serving crisp fruits for balance.

Pineapple, mango, papaya, orange, banana, grapefruit, and coconut are the typical fruits we have come to appreciate from the tropics, and which I will use for my chilled champagne-laced tropical fruit salad.

> 1 *small pineapple (1 to 1½ pounds)*
>
> 2 *medium ripe mangoes (firm)*
>
> 1 *ripe papaya*
>
> 2 *navel oranges*
>
> 2 *pink grapefruit*
>
> 2 *ripe bananas*
>
> 4 *teaspoons fresh shredded coconut*

2   *cups chilled dry champagne*

   Garnish: *8 fresh mint leaves*

1. Peel the pineapple, dice into 1-inch cubes, and place cubes, layer fashion, in a deep, square glass pan. Carefully peel the mangoes, dice into 1-inch cubes, and arrange to form a second layer on top of the pineapple. Peel and core the papaya, dice into 1-inch cubes, and layer the papaya cubes on top of the mangoes.

2. Peel oranges and grapefruits, separate into segments free of most of the white membrane covering the flesh. Cut the fruit sections into halves, then cross-cut into thirds and place on top of the mango cubes.

3. Drizzle the champagne over the cut fruit. Shake the pan for uniform distribution of the liquid. Cover and refrigerate for 1 hour.

4. When ready to serve, remove from refrigerator, cross cut bananas into 6 pieces each, add to the fruit salad, and divide the fruit salad into 4 portions.

5. To serve: assemble in 4 frosted sherbet glasses, starting with 3 pieces of bananas. Then continue to build overlapping layers with the other fruit cubes. Spoon in some of the liquid from the salad bowl, then sprinkle with shredded coconut and garnish with mint leaves. Serve immediately.

Soups, Stocks, and Brothy Rice

Caldos, Sopas y Asopaos

Given that Puerto Rico has rich soil and the perfect growing climate for corn, rice, beans, green vegetables, and tubers, it's no surprise that the country's soups and stews are a wonderful way to appreciate The Island's generosity.

Soup is a classical example of a one-pot meal. The word itself sounds like the liquid "souping" into one's mouth from a spoon. The experience of soup gave rise to the word and concept of supper—in early days, a complete dinner entirely from one pot.

The preparing and serving of soups has always been part of the universal gastronomic experience. In all cultures there exist deep-rooted beliefs that soup contains magical, curative powers. And because of its unique attributes, a soup can be served with no other dish. It is one dish where the sum of its ingredients can become a main course meal. My grandmother used to say that soup is "the food that God intended us to eat, that will allow us to live forever." She also believed soup was the antidote for almost every ailment. Whether for a hangover, common cold, or pregnancy, she always offered a specific kind of soup for someone's ailment. The base was made from water and either the bones or innards of an animal, or an old hen.

In this chapter I introduce at least one recipe from the many varieties of soups from the Puerto Rican kitchen. You will find a *caldo*, a broth or clear soup, or a *sopa*, a thicker soup with more ingredients. On the other hand, *asopaos* are thicker soups like gumbos, usually made with rice. These soup categories represent different cooking techniques that emphasize consistency of texture and complexity of taste regardless of what broth or base is used in combination with fresh garden herbs, spices, and vegetables, and accompanying grains, meats, fish, or poultry.

A Puerto Rican soup is a meal by itself, and is great served with bread, *tostones*, or fritters, and avocado slices or a fresh salad on the side.

Chicken Asopao
Asopao de Pollo
SERVES 4

Asopao is also known as "wet rice," a brothy rice or stew similar to that of the jambalaya or gumbo, popular in the southern United States, especially Louisiana. The similarity between these soups is not accidental, as the source of many of the ingredients is Africa. *Asopao* is full of broth, rice, and pieces of seafood or meat. The word *asopao* comes from the Spanish word for soup, *sopa*. This is a delicious dish that can be prepared quickly and will yield enough to serve several people. *Asopao* is a favorite during holidays when unexpected guests drop by and a quick meal is needed. It is a very simple dish, yet quite spectacular.

- 3 tablespoons Spanish olive oil
- 4 garlic cloves, minced
- 1 chicken, 2-3 pounds, skinless and quartered
- 1/2 cup chopped yellow onion
- 1/2 medium green bell pepper, seeded and chopped
- 2 teaspoons chopped fresh oregano (1 teaspoon dried, crushed)
- 2 tablespoons chopped fresh cilantro
- 1/4 teaspoon cayenne pepper
- 1/2 teaspoon cumin
- 1/4 teaspoon saffron threads
- 2 teaspoons paprika
- 1 teaspoon pulverized rock salt
- 1/3 cup dry white wine

2 medium tomatoes, cored and chopped

  8 cups chicken stock (see recipe for Chicken Stock)

1 1/2 cup medium-grain rice, rinsed

  1 large red bell pepper, broiled, seeded, and sliced julienne

  1/2 cup fresh sweet peas, cooked (keep hot)

  1/2 cup chopped fresh carrots, cooked (keep hot)

  2 tablespoons chopped fresh parsley

1. In a preheated kettle on low-to-medium heat, combine olive oil, garlic, and chicken pieces and brown lightly on all sides; then add onion, bell pepper, oregano, cilantro, cayenne pepper, cumin, saffron, paprika, salt, wine, tomatoes, and half of the chicken stock. Bring stock to a boil and stir gently so as not to break the chicken parts. Cover and simmer for 20 minutes, then add rice and remaining stock. Finish cooking for approximately 20 more minutes; chicken parts should be thoroughly cooked and the rice tender. Remove from heat.

2. To serve: use large shallow soup bowls. Place the chicken parts in the center of the bowls, stir the soup and rice mixture to ensure a balanced blend of rice and soup, then ladle out mixture on top of chicken parts. Arrange the strips of broiled peppers on top and sprinkle with peas, carrots, and parsley.

SERVING SUGGESTIONS:
Serve with Avocado Salad, or even plain avocado slices. Or, try with *alcapurrias* or *tostones* on the side.

Shrimp Asopao

Asopao de Camarones

SERVES 4

Puerto Rico is famous throughout the Caribbean for its *asopaos*. The first *asopao* I ever tried was a shrimp version much like this one. Robert and I arose very early one Saturday to gather fresh ingredients for our *asopao*. We went down to the docks and met the fishing boats that were returning with their catch and, after purchasing our share of fresh shrimp, we zipped over to the Santurce Market and fought our way through throngs of shoppers while we searched for fresh oregano, parsley, and cilantro.

The fragrance of the fresh stock and spices simmering made our extra shopping efforts worthwhile, and the tender, tasty fresh shrimp go wonderfully with the brothy rice and garlic. Fresh peppers, red and green, are a "must" for this dish, as are fresh limes and garlic.

24	medium shrimp, peeled and deveined
3	tablespoons Spanish olive oil
4	garlic cloves, minced
2	teaspoons lime juice
1	teaspoon minced fresh gingerroot
1/2	cup chopped yellow onion
2	teaspoons paprika
1/4	teaspoon saffron
2	medium tomatoes, cored and chopped
2	teaspoons chopped fresh oregano (1 teaspoon dried, crushed)
1/2	medium green pepper, seeded and chopped
1/2	teaspoon cayenne pepper
1/2	teaspoon cumin
1	teaspoon pulverized rock salt
1/3	cup Spanish sherry
8	cups Fish Head Stock (page 130)
1 1/2	cups short-grain rice, rinsed

Garnish: 2 tablespoons chopped fresh cilantro

2 red bell peppers, roasted, seeded, and sliced

1. In a preheated kettle, combine shrimp with olive oil and all the herbs, spices, and vegetables, except cilantro and roasted pepper, and sauté until shrimps turn pink. Deglaze with sherry, then add rice and fish stock and stir to blend. Set heat on low and finish cooking for approximately 19 more minutes, or until rice is tender.

2. To serve: dish out with a ladle into large shallow soup bowls, allowing 6 shrimps per serving. Garnish with chopped parsley and sliced roasted peppers.

SERVING SUGGESTIONS: Serve *tostones* and avocado wedges with a lime and garlic sauce on the side.

VARIATION: For lobster *asopao*, substitute 4 lobster tails, ½-pound each, with each tail cut into 6 sections.

Pigeon Pea Asopao with Plantain Puffs
Asopao de Gandules con Bolas de Plátanos
SERVES 4

Gandules abound on The Island during the winter months. The height of the season is in December. A typical scene one might witness on the patios of Puerto Rican homes in the winter are family and friends gathered together, shucking a freshly-picked mound of *gandules*. The pigeon peas are usually saved for cooking in the most popular dish of the season, *Arroz con Gandules*, but another way to take advantage of this seasonal crop's abundance is to make Pigeon Pea *Asopao*. Of course dried or canned pigeon peas may also be used successfully. This dish can be made more complex and hearty by adding ham, sausages, or short beef ribs. Or, as this recipe calls for, made with my favorite combination of pork baby back ribs and plantain puffs.

   2 *tablespoons olive oil*

   4 *garlic cloves, minced*

8   short pork ribs

1   teaspoon pulverized rock salt

2   teaspoons chopped fresh oregano (1 teaspoon dried)

2   tablespoons fresh cilantro, chopped

1/4   teaspoon cayenne pepper

1/2   teaspoon cumin

2   teaspoons Spanish paprika

1/4   teaspoon saffron threads

1/2   cup chopped yellow onion

1/2   medium green bell pepper, seeded and chopped

2   medium tomatoes, peeled, cored, and chopped

8   cups beef stock

1   cup medium-grain rice, rinsed

1/2   pound fresh gandules (pigeon peas)

8   Plantain Puffs (see "Tubers & Vine-Grown Vegetables" chapter)

Garnish: 1 large red bell pepper, broiled, seeded, and julienned

2 tablespoons chopped fresh parsley

1. In a preheated kettle on low-to-medium heat, combine olive oil, garlic, pork spare ribs, salt, oregano, cilantro, cayenne pepper, cumin, paprika, and saffron threads.

2. Stir in onion, peppers, tomatoes, and 4 cups of beef stock. Cook down until ribs begin to curl off the bone at the points. Stir in rice and pigeon peas, and add the remainder of the stock. Heat to bubbling and carefully add the plantain puffs. Reduce heat to low, cover kettle and continue cooking for approximately 20 minutes. Test for doneness using a fork—the ribs should be tender, almost falling off the bone, the rice soft, the plantain puffs firm, and the pigeon peas firm outside, creamy inside.

3. Serve soup in large shallow bowls. Garnish with strips of broiled peppers and sprinkle parsley on top.

SERVING SUGGESTIONS: This *asopao* is delicious served alongside Avocado Salad and *Jíbaritos* (banana fritters).

Fish Head Broth

Caldo de Pescado

SERVES 6 TO 8

Caldo de pescado con mofongo y pescado frito (fish broth with *mofongo* and fried fish) is a typical Sunday morning "special" served throughout The Island, especially in coastal towns. The broth is made and kept hot in coffee dispensers, and served in "to go" cups for the same price as a cup of coffee. A fried fish and a ball of *mofongo* (see recipe for *mofongo* on page 214) is wrapped in banana leaves or tin foil. At that point, it is up to the individual to find the palm tree that he wishes to sit under, and enjoy the fisherman's breakfast "al fresco" (in the fresh air).

At our house, we call this soup Adam's Soup, after our son, Adam, because it was the first soup he ever ate. This is a clear fish stock that can be used as a base for other soups, and also as an appetizer served in small cups.

2 pounds fish head (snapper, perch, or bass), split into 4 pieces
2 quarts water
1 medium yellow onion, cut in quarters
1/2 medium green bell pepper, diced
3 celery spears, sliced
1 large carrot, peeled and diced
8 whole garlic cloves
1 teaspoon rock salt, crushed
1 teaspoon whole peppercorns, cracked
5 sprigs fresh cilantro
1 tablespoon lime juice

Garnish: one each: carrot, celery, green onion, finely chopped cilantro

1. Place all the ingredients in a pot and bring to a boil. Reduce heat and simmer until the meat falls off the bones (approximately 1 to 1½ hours).

2. Strain stock using a fine sieve or tight mesh wire strainer.

3. Serve immediately or freeze for future use. To serve: sprinkle with finely chopped carrots, celery, green onions, and chopped cilantro.

SERVING SUGGESTIONS: Serve in small cups as an appetizer to a full-bodied fish meal. This broth is good alongside oven-fried fish or creole salmon, for example. For a lighter meal, serve this soup with a vegetable *serenata*, or one of the Puerto Rican salads.

Fish Stew with Vegetables
Sopa de Pescado con Vegetales
SERVES 4

Following in the Puerto Rican lineage of hearty soups, this delectable fish stew will make wonderful company during cold winter months. The variety of fresh vegetables turns this soup into a meal of its own. Although I suggest perch or snapper, any fish can be used in the preparation of this dish.

2 tablespoons olive oil

4 garlic cloves, minced

1/3 cup chopped green bell pepper

1/3 cup chopped yellow onion

1/3 cup chopped celery spears

2 large tomatoes, peeled, cored, and chopped

1 tablespoon chopped fresh cilantro

1 1/2 pounds of perch or snapper fillet, cubed into 1-inch pieces

2 teaspoons lime juice

8 cups Fish Head Stock (page 130)

2 medium red potatoes, diced into 1/2-inch pieces

1 large carrot, sliced into 1/4-inch pieces

2 ears of corn, divided into 4 sections each

1/2 pound butternut squash, diced into 1-inch pieces

2 green bananas, peeled and sliced into 1/2-inch pieces

1/2 pound sweet potatoes, peeled and diced into 1/2-inch pieces

1/2 pound celery root, peeled and diced into 1/2-inch pieces

2 medium chayotes, peeled, cored, and diced into 1-inch pieces

Garnish: lemon or lime wedges, sprigs of cilantro

1. In a preheated skillet on low-to-medium heat, combine olive oil, garlic, bell pepper, onion, celery, tomatoes, and cilantro. Gently arrange fish cubes and sauté, turning fish on all sides. Add lime juice and 1 cup of fish stock and cook down for 5 minutes. Set aside.

2. Combine the remainder of the fish stock, potatoes, carrots, corn, squash, green bananas, sweet potatoes, celery root, and chayotes in a soup kettle. Cover and simmer on medium heat until the bananas are tender, then fold in the fish mixture. Cover and cook for another 5 minutes.

3. To serve, use a slotted spoon to catch the solid ingredients and arrange them in a soup bowl. Then use a ladle to dish out the soup liquid over the vegetables. Garnish with lemon or lime wedges and sprigs of cilantro.

SERVING SUGGESTIONS: I would serve this Fish Stew with *Surullos,* or even *jíbaritos,* or a fresh loaf of crusty bread. An Avocado Salad or slices of fresh avocado could be served on the side.

Puerto Rican Beef Stew
Sancocho
SERVES 6

It is said of a person who has been under the sweltering sun that he is *sancochao*—blistering hot or "stewing." This Puerto Rican stew best illustrates the one-step cooking method, a typical food preparation that has prevailed for five hundred years in Puerto Rican homes, primarily because it allows the latitude for batch cooking a nutritious meal in a single pot.

The *barbacoa* technique employed by the Tainos has evolved into a more sophisticated and complex cooking technology, but the spirit and the legacy of the *barbacoa* remain constant as we struggle against the drudgery of the modern work day and subsequent meal preparation. When you come home, why not spend 15 minutes of preparation and 45 minutes of "R and R?" The pot over the heat does the cooking and you end up with a delicious beefy stew.

2	tablespoons olive oil
5	garlic cloves, minced
1 1/2	pounds top round beef, cubed into 1 1/2-inch pieces
1/3	cup chopped yellow onions
1/3	cup chopped green pepper
1/3	cup chopped celery
1	teaspoon minced fresh gingerroot
1	chili pepper, seeded and minced
5	sprigs of cilantro, chopped
1/4	teaspoon ground cumin
1	teaspoon pulverized rock salt
1/4	teaspoon ground white pepper
1/3	cup burgundy wine
4	medium tomatoes, cored and chopped
4	quarts beef stock (see recipe on page 127)
2	green bananas, peeled and sliced into 1-inch pieces
1	yellow plantain, peeled and sliced into 1/2-inch pieces
1	medium sweet potato (1/2 pound), diced into 1-inch pieces
1/2	pound butternut squash, peeled and cubed into 1-inch pieces
3	medium new potatoes, scrubbed clean and quartered
1	large chayote, peeled, cored, and diced into 1-inch pieces
2	ears of white corn, cleaned and sliced into 6 parts each

1. In a preheated kettle over low-to-medium heat, combine olive oil, garlic, beef cubes, and onions, stir until beef is brown on all sides and onions begin to

caramelize. Fold in chopped pepper, celery, gingerroot, chili pepper, cilantro, cumin, salt, white pepper, burgundy wine, tomatoes, and 1 quart of beef stock. Cook down until stock is reduced by half.

2. Stir beef, then fold in all the remaining vegetables and beef stock. Continue to cook until meat is tender and the vegetables soft.

SERVING SUGGESTIONS: Since this soup contains beef and vegetables, it is hearty already. Serve alongside a fresh bread and use the bread to soak up some of this delicious flavor.

Garlic Soup with Plantain Croutons
Sopa de Ajo

SERVES 4

Garlic has always been an essential element of the Puerto Rican diet. The traditional garlic soup was made with layers of large pieces of bread that had been dunked in garlic paste, and toasted over an open flame, before they were incorporated into the garlic broth for body and flavor. For my new and lighter version of garlic soup, I have created plantain croutons to use instead of toasted bread.

16	*cloves of garlic, peeled*
1	*tablespoon olive oil*
2	*green onions, trimmed to 5 inches and chopped*
2	*tablespoons chopped yellow onion*
1	*teaspoon chopped celery*
1	*medium tomato, peeled, seeded, and chopped*
1	*teaspoon chopped fresh oregano*
1	*teaspoon chopped fresh mint*
1	*teaspoon black peppercorns, cracked*
2	*teaspoons chopped fresh cilantro*
1	*teaspoon pulverized rock salt*

1/3 cup Spanish sherry

8 cups chicken stock

2 cups Plantain Croutons (see recipe on page 217)

Garnish: sprig of cilantro

1. Broil garlic cloves until slightly charred, then mince.

2. In a preheated kettle over low-to-medium heat, combine garlic, olive oil, green onions, onion, celery, tomato, oregano, mint, black pepper, cilantro, and salt. Sauté for 3 minutes, deglaze with sherry, then stir in chicken stock. Cover and simmer for 7 minutes. To serve: divide the croutons into four portions and place inside four soup bowls. Ladle garlic soup on top and garnish with a sprig of cilantro.

SERVING SUGGESTIONS: Serve with Avocado and Chayote Salad on the side, or with any main course dish.

Baby Clam and Squab Soup
Sopa de Almejas y Pichón de Paloma
SERVES 4

My uncle used to say that my grandmother was able to make soup out of sea pebbles. That was his term for baby clams. So here's my grandmother's sea pebble and squab soup that she prepared and served whenever there was a birth in our or a neighbor's family. Her sea pebble and squab soup not only provided nourishment and comfort to the laboring mother but was also the catalyst that provided the mystical experience of interacting with nature to safeguard the passage of a new life. Everyone toasted with a cup of Doña Fela's wonderful squab soup.

The squabs that my grandmother used came from a particular species of domesticated pigeons that she bred to be used exclusively in the preparation of soups. They were four to five weeks old and weighed approximately ¾ of a pound.

Pigeon squabs, as a cooking item, are somewhat exotic and can be found in some Asian meat markets in the United States. For the purpose of working with this recipe, I recommend the use of a squab broiler, approximately 8 to 10 weeks old and common in many meat markets. Cornish hens will also do the work and can be found in the frozen food department of most supermarkets.

1 tablespoon olive oil

5 garlic cloves, minced

1 tablespoon lime juice

1/4 teaspoon cayenne pepper

1 squab broiler (1 pound), quartered

2 green onions, finely chopped

1 tablespoon chopped red bell pepper

1 tablespoon chopped green bell pepper

1 tablespoon chopped celery root

2 teaspoons chopped cilantro

2 baby carrots, washed and chopped

1/3 cup chopped yellow squash

1 small sweet potato, diced into small pieces

16 baby clams, scrubbed clean

1 quart of hot fish head stock (page 130)

8 sprigs watercress

1. In a preheated kettle over low to medium heat, combine olive oil, garlic, lime juice, and squab sections, sautéing for approximately 2 minutes on each side.

2. Add onions, red and green bell peppers, celery root, cilantro, baby carrots, and sweet potato. Arrange the baby clams on top and add the hot fish head stock. Cover and allow to simmer on low heat until the squab meat is thoroughly cooked, almost falling off the bones.

3. Serve in dinner bowls, each with 4 clams and 1 squab section. Top with soup and garnish with 2 sprigs of watercress.

SERVING SUGGESTIONS: Serve with Avocado Salad, or Chayote and Avocado Salad. Chunks of *yuca*, covered with a garlic *mojo* are also wonderful alongside this soup.

Squash Soup

Sopa de Calabaza

SERVES 4

The Puerto Rican *calabaza* (the word means squash, or pumpkin) is lighter in flavor and texture than most found in the United States. You may see it in markets—it's called West Indian Pumpkin. I have found that butternut squash and banana squash are comparable to our *calabaza*, and will render excellent results when used for this particular soup dish. The subtle nutty flavor of the squash combined with coconut milk, and the enticing aromatic sweet bouquet of island spices makes this dish a superb first taste in an intimate setting!

  2 *tablespoons olive oil*

  3 *garlic cloves, peeled and minced*

  1/2 *teaspoon fresh minced gingerroot*

  1/4 *teaspoon cayenne pepper*

  1/3 *cup chopped yellow onion*

  1 *tablespoon chopped fresh cilantro*

  1/4 *cup Spanish sherry*

  1 *cup coconut milk*

  6 *cups chicken stock*

  1 *pound butternut squash, peeled and cubed*

  1/8 *teaspoon nutmeg*

  2 *cinnamon sticks*

  1/3 *cup chopped red bell pepper*

  1/3 *cup chopped green bell pepper*

1. In a preheated skillet on low-to-medium heat, combine olive oil, garlic, ginger-root, cayenne pepper, onion, and cilantro. Sauté lightly. Deglaze skillet with sherry and stir in coconut milk; cook down for 1 minute, stir, and remove from heat. Set aside.

2. In a soup kettle over medium heat, combine chicken stock, squash, nutmeg, and cinnamon sticks; cover and simmer until squash is tender, then remove cinnamon sticks. Add the coconut milk mixture, stir to blend, cover, and simmer for another 10 minutes. Remove from heat and add chopped peppers.

SERVING SUGGESTIONS: Serve hot, with Crabmeat *Alcapurrias*, or fresh Lobster Salad on the side.

White Bean Soup with Spanish Sausage
Sopa de Habichuelas Blancas

SERVES 4

Garden fresh white beans make the best soup, but they are rarely found in conventional supermarkets or fresh produce stores in the States. Therefore, I suggest the use of dry beans for this soup. When working with dried beans it's necessary to wash them thoroughly and allow the beans to soak as long as possible prior to cooking. The soft texture of a soaked bean will produce a silky, smooth stock as the beans cook down, but hard dry beans will tend to break down in the cooking process and produce a gritty or rough textured stock.

What makes this soup a popular item in the Puerto Rican kitchen is the subtle nutty flavor of the white beans, and the creamy texture of the broth which bursts with the flavors of garlic, fresh oregano, peppers, and cilantro.

Fine quality Spanish sausages are sometimes difficult to find in the United States. Although the variety that is available in most Latino produce stores will do the job, I recommend an Italian sweet sausage without the fennel, a linguica, or a good quality pepperoni.

3/4   *pound dried white beans*

10   *cups water*

2   *whole garlic cloves, peeled*

1   *small yellow onion, chopped*

1/4   *teaspoon cayenne pepper*

1 teaspoon white wine vinegar

1 teaspoon pulverized rock salt

1 teaspoon olive oil

4 garlic cloves, peeled and minced

2 Spanish sausage (dry), sliced into 1/4-inch pieces

2 medium tomatoes, peeled and chopped

2 teaspoons chopped fresh oregano (1 teaspoon dried, crushed)

1/3 cup Spanish sherry

1 cup banana squash, peeled and cubed into 1/4-inch pieces

3 green onions, trimmed to 5 inches and chopped

5 cups ham bone stock (page 128)

Garnish: 1 tablespoon fresh cilantro, chopped

1/3 cup red bell pepper, seeded and chopped

1. Using a colander and under running water, wash beans thoroughly. Transfer to a soup pot, cover beans with water, and soak for 1 hour. Put back into colander and rinse again under fresh running water.

2. In a stockpot with 10 cups of water, combine beans, whole garlic cloves, onion, cayenne pepper, vinegar, and salt. Place over medium heat and simmer for 30 minutes. (This will cook away approximately half the liquid.)

3. While the beans are simmering, combine the following in a preheated skillet and sauté: olive oil, garlic, and sausage. Stir in tomatoes, oregano, sherry, banana squash, and green onions.

4. Deglaze skillet with one cup of ham bone stock, then transfer sautéed mixture into the pot with the simmering beans. Add the remainder of the ham bone stock, stir to blend, and reduce heat to low. Cook for another 30 minutes. The beans should be tender and the broth thick.

5. Serve in large shallow soup bowls.

SERVING SUGGESTIONS: Serve with *tostones* laced with *mojo* sauce and a watercress and tomato salad.

Black Bean Soup

Sopa de Habichuelas Negras

SERVES 4

Black bean soup, with or without the ham hocks or chunks of ham, is a well-known representative of Caribbean cuisine. This soup is rich and intense with color and flavor. My favorite time of year to serve this soup is during the cold winter months and wet rainy season. Puerto Rico, and its other Caribbean island neighbors, may not experience the same cold winters that many others in the north live through each year, but on The Island, hearty soups such as this one will always be made available, for riding out tropical storms and hurricanes.

3/4 *pound dried black beans*

10 *cups water*

1 *medium ham shank, cracked*

2 *whole garlic cloves, peeled*

1 *bay leaf*

1 *small yellow onion, peeled and quartered*

1/2 *teaspoon black pepper*

1 *teaspoon red wine vinegar*

1/2 *teaspoon pulverized rock salt*

2 *teaspoons olive oil*

4 *garlic cloves, peeled and minced*

1/2 *pound smoke-cured ham, trimmed and cubed to 1/2-inch pieces*

2 *medium tomatoes, peeled and chopped*

1 *teaspoon chopped fresh oregano (1/2 teaspoon dried, crushed)*

1/3 *cup Spanish sherry*

4 *green onions, trimmed to 5 inches and chopped*

Garnish: *1 tablespoon chopped fresh cilantro*
1/3 cup diced red bell pepper

1. Using a colander, place beans under running water and wash thoroughly. Transfer to a soup pot with 10 cups of water. Combine beans, ham shank, whole garlic cloves, bay leaf, onion, black pepper, vinegar, and salt. Place over medium heat and simmer for 45 minutes. Then remove ham shank and bay leaf.

2. While beans are simmering, combine the following in a preheated skillet and sauté: olive oil, minced garlic, ham cubes, tomatoes, oregano, sherry, and green onions. Deglaze skillet with a cup of bean stock and transfer sautéed mixture into the pot with simmering beans.

3. Stir gently to blend, reduce heat to low, then cover and cook for another 20 minutes or until the beans are tender. Serve soup in bowls and garnish.

SERVING SUGGESTIONS: Good served alongside a fresh salad and *tostones*, or your favorite *neo-frituras*.

STOCK
Caldo

Stock (*caldo*) is basically a flavored base that is made from the rich extracts of the soluble parts of a particular meat, fish, poultry, and even vegetables. The stock's function is imperative in the building of many dishes because it provides the accent, integrity, and intensity of flavors to the finished product, particularly soups, sauces, and gravies.

In this book I use the stock that we refer to as *caldo* in brothy dishes, such as the seafood *asopaos*, and in the highly flavorful rice dishes, such as *Arroz con Pollo*, the *Paella*, and the *guisados* variety (meats and beans, stewed dishes). The following beef, ham, chicken, and fish stocks or broths are specifically prepared to be used with the recipes in this book, either as a substitute for water or as an element to intensify the flavor of a sauce, as a moisture replenishing agent, and as a base for soups.

The stocks are easy to prepare and can be made ahead as a way to salvage and take advantage of fresh leftovers such as meat scraps and bones, then stored in the freezer for an indefinite amount of time. Be sure to skim off the fat solids that form on the top after exposure to the cold. Clear stock is that which has been strained, and the content of most fat and carcass, or bone debris, has been removed.

Beef Stock

Caldo de Res

MAKES 1 QUART

Use this stock in recipes calling for clear broth.

4   *pounds of soup bones (beef or veal, neck bones, head bones, shanks, tail, feet, back rib bones, meat scraps previously cooked or raw)*

5   *garlic cloves, cracked*

1   *teaspoon coarse rock salt*

1   *teaspoon cracked black peppercorns*

5   *sprigs of fresh cilantro*

1   *sprig of fresh oregano (approximately 4 inches long)*

1   *fresh sage leaf*

2   *bay leaves*

1   *celery rib*

1   *small yellow onion, peeled*

1/2   *green bell pepper, seeded*

4   *quarts boiling water*

1. Combine all of the ingredients in a 6-quart stockpot and add 1 quart of water. Set on top of stove over low-to-medium heat, cover pot, and allow stock to simmer until the liquid has been reduced by 80 percent. Then stir the contents of the pot and add 2 quarts of water. Continue to simmer until liquid is reduce by 50 percent. Stir and add 1 quart of boiling water, and continue to simmer until the liquid has been reduced by 50 percent. The amount of time to make the *caldo* will vary from 2 to 3 hours.

2. Once the *caldo* is done, allow to cool, then line a strainer with cheesecloth and filter the stock into another pot or large bowl. The debris trapped in the cheesecloth can be returned to the stockpot with additional water and be fortified with more herbs and spices, for a second extraction.

Ham Stock

Caldo de Hueso de Jamón

MAKES 1 QUART

The use of ham as a flavoring element is imperative to the basic Puerto Rican *sofrito*. Salt-cured ham, because of its intense flavor, is the most commonly used stock. Puerto Ricans call it *hueso de jamón* or "ham bone," but oddly enough, it is mostly flesh with little or no bone present.

There are, however, the *nudillos*, which is commonly known in the States as smoked-cured ham hocks, that I find to be an excellent source of intense flavor, without the extra salt.

Whenever I want to dramatically enhance the face and flavor of a particular pea or bean, rice, or leaf vegetable dish, I will automatically turn to the smoke-cured ham stock for the desired results.

Use this stock in recipes calling for ham stock.

4   *ham hocks, cracked (4 to 6 ounces each)*
5   *whole garlic cloves*
1/2 *teaspoon whole cumin seeds*
1   *teaspoon black peppercorns*
3   *spice cloves*
4   *green onions*
2   *sprigs of cilantro*
2   *bay leaves*
4   *quarts of boiling water*

1. Prepare the same way as the beef stock.

Chicken Stock

Caldo de Pollo

MAKES 1 QUART

Use in the preparation of most poultry dishes calling for chicken broth.

4 *pounds of combined chicken parts such as backs, wings,*
 necks, legs, thighs, gizzards.
5 *garlic cloves, cracked*
1 *teaspoon crushed rock salt*
1 *teaspoon whole peppercorns*
1/4 *teaspoon saffron threads*
1/2 *tablespoon whole cumin seeds*
3 *sprigs of fresh cilantro*
1 *sprig of fresh oregano*
1/2 *medium green bell pepper, chopped*
2 *bay leaves*
1 *medium yellow onion, cut into quarters*
4 *quarts of boiling water*

1. Prepare the same way as the beef stock.

Fish Head Stock

Caldo de Pescado

MAKES 1 QUART

For recipes calling for fish head stock, I always use a freshly made batch, not one that has been prepared ahead and/or frozen.

2 *pounds of fish head split into 4 (snapper, perch, or bass)*
2 *quarts water*
1 *medium yellow onion, cut into quarters*
1/2 *medium green bell pepper*
2 *celery ribs, sliced*
1 *large carrot, peeled and diced*
5 *whole garlic cloves*
1 *teaspoon crushed rock salt*
1 *teaspoon cracked black peppercorns*
5 *sprigs fresh cilantro*
1 *teaspoon lime juice*

1. Place all the ingredients in a pot and bring to a boil. Reduce heat and simmer until the meat falls off the head (approximately 1 to 1½ hours).

2. Strain stock using a fine sieve or tight mesh wire strainer.

Rice

Arroz

Where here can I find
like in my creole land
a plate of chicken and rice,
a cup of good coffee?

VIRGILIO DÁVILA

When a person maintains a high profile, we say he or she is like the *arroz blanco* (white rice) found everywhere. This analogy best describes the popularity of rice in the typical Puerto Rican kitchen where it is the number one staple, and the dish on which most meals are based.

Rice made its way from Malaysia to West Africa to Spain, and was introduced by the Spanish colonists to the New World. The development of a rice-based cuisine was also influenced by African slaves in Puerto Rico and throughout the Caribbean.

Preparing an exquisite rice dish depends on the "personality" of the rice grain and the cooking method employed. Short-grain and medium-grain rice will provide greater, gradual absorbency of the liquids and flavor. They also require longer cooking time. The long-grain rice requires less moisture and less cooking time, and will provide a fluffier texture, whether served plain or mixed with spices, meats, or seafood.

In Puerto Rico, two types of rice are used. Medium-grain rice is best for brothy rice dishes (*asopaos*) and for desserts, like the holiday favorite *Arroz con Dulce*. The long-grain rice is used for the drier mixed rice dishes, such as *Arroz con Pollo*, *Arroz con Gandules*, Black Rice, and Yellow Rice. The technique of preparing rice varies slightly from recipe to recipe as we go from preparing a basic White Rice dish to a more complex dish like the *Paella* or *Arroz con Pollo*.

Any good quality, raw, unbleached rice can be used in these recipes. I use Valencia, Sello Rojo, Mahatma, and Carolina. These products are available in most supermarkets and Latino produce stores. And I always use a cast-iron kettle because it conducts the heat evenly.

Once you become proficient in cooking rice, you will discover that it is not just a side dish of starch, but a universal, exotic nutrient, and revered by most rice consuming cultures.

White Rice
Arroz Blanco
SERVES 4

The following recipe is for basic white rice the Puerto Rican way. The three important requirements for making good, plain rice are: buy long-grain rice, start with cold water, and use a cast-iron kettle. The total process takes about 24 minutes.

One traditional method used in the Puerto Rican kitchen, was the sautéing of the rice first in a mixture of salted pork fatback that had been diced and fried with chopped garlic until a hot, melted, seasoned fat mixture was created. After water was added and the rice was almost done, the cook dipped the bottom of the cooking spoon into the grease, and coated the top layer of rice until the rice grains took on a translucent texture, thought to be synonymous with perfect rice. Mushy rice was never tolerated!

Although this technique always guaranteed a flavorful and grainy rice dish, it also increased the fat content, making it less healthy by today's standards. In this recipe, I have replaced animal fat with vegetable oils, which are lighter and lower in cholesterol.

Glazing the rice with the vegetable oil prior to adding the water—as you will experience—is the key making loose, fluffy rice. The glaze slows down the absorbent quality of the grains, allowing the rice to cook until tender as the water turns to vapor and rises with pressure. Keeping the kettle uncovered during this initial stage will allow excess moisture to escape and slow down the cooking time.

During the cooking process, the essence of the rice dish is absorbed in the *pegao*—the thin layer of rice that sticks to the bottom and sides of the kettle. The word *pegao* comes from the Spanish word *pegado*, which means "stuck." In a Puerto Rican home the *pegao* is a delicacy and considered a treat. It is a compliment to the cook when a dinner guest asks for the *pegao*. The cook then scrapes the pot and fashions out a ball or two of the flavorful, crispy-textured rice, and presents it with great fanfare. For the children, the *pegao* is used as an incentive to coax them to help mother wash the dinner dishes. Try it!

2   cups long-grain white rice

4   cups cold water

3   tablespoons vegetable oil

1/2 teaspoon pulverized rock salt

1. Place the rice in a colander and rinse it under cold running water. This will eliminate any talcum residue that is sometimes used at rice mills to protect the rice while in storage. Eliminating the talcum will prevent the rice from becoming pasty during the initial cooking phase.

2. In a preheated kettle over low-to-medium heat, pour in the oil. Stir in the rice making sure that the rice becomes completely glazed. Immediately add the cold water and salt. Stir, scraping the bottom and sides of the kettle.

3. Bring the rice to a boil and allow it to cook down until small bubbling craters begin to appear. Set the heat on low and cover the kettle. Cook for approximately 12 minutes.

4. Uncover and fold the rice from the bottom up. Continue cooking for 9 more minutes or until the water is almost fully absorbed. Then remove from heat and uncover for a few seconds to allow the vapor and excess moisture to escape. The rice should be soft and grainy, not mushy or pasty. To ensure that the rice maintains a grainy texture, insert a dinner fork through the center and gently fluff up the rice, breaking up any firm mass that may have formed during the cooking process. Do not disturb the *pegao* until all of the rice has been dished out.

Rice with Crabmeat
Arroz con Jueyes
SERVES 4

When Robert and I went to lunch at a local streetside cafe, I ordered *Arroz con Jueyes*. I expected a mound of fresh crabmeat with some rice on the side—but I was surprised when the two were served mixed together. I was delighted to taste this rice dish, especially with pinto beans and a salad served on the side. Since the crabmeat is flaked into pieces and shapes that look similar to the rice, the total dish is one in which the crab enhances the rice, and vice versa. The herbs and spices that come forth act like a soft veil, enhancing the flavor of the rice while balancing the intensity of the seafood. Here is Robert's version of this wonderful dish.

1/3 cup olive oil

5 garlic cloves, minced

1/3 cup finely chopped yellow onion

1/2 cup chopped fresh tomato

2 tablespoons chopped fresh cilantro

1/2 teaspoon cumin

2 teaspoons fresh oregano chopped (1 teaspoon dry)

1/4 teaspoon saffron threads

1 teaspoon paprika

1/3 teaspoon white pepper

1/3 teaspoon cayenne pepper

1/2 teaspoon pulverized rock salt

1 tablespoon lemon juice

3/4 pound crabmeat

2 cups boiling water

1/3 cup white wine

1 medium green bell pepper, broiled, cut into 6 strips

1 medium red bell pepper, broiled, cut into 6 strips

1. In a preheated kettle, over low heat, combine olive oil, garlic, onion, tomato, cilantro, cumin, oregano, saffron, paprika, white pepper, cayenne pepper, salt, and lemon juice. Sauté until onions become soft. Add crab and sauté very lightly, for 2 or 3 minutes. Add rice and gently stir until rice is completely glazed, then add the boiling water. Use of preboiled water accelerates the cooking time of the rice while at the same time protecting the delicate meat from overcooking and dehydration.

2. Cover pot and cook over medium heat for 10 minutes. Uncover; fold mixture from bottom to top. Sprinkle the wine over the rice. Place strips of broiled bell peppers on top of rice. Cover and cook for another 6 minutes or until rice is done. Be sure to test that rice is soft and fluffy. Serve immediately while it is still steaming hot.

SERVING SUGGESTIONS: Serve with stewed pinto beans on the side, *tostones*, and Avocado Salad with *mojo* dressing (a must!) and your favorite wine. For dessert, Coconut Flan and Spanish Coffee.

VARIATIONS: For Rice with Lobster, substitute 4 lobster tails for the crabmeat, cut into 5 sections each. For Rice with Shrimp, substitute 20 medium-sized shrimps for the crabmeat, peeled and deveined.

Rice with Codfish

Arroz con Bacalao

SERVES 4

Arroz con Bacalao is one of the oldest and most socially controversial dishes in the Puerto Rican kitchen today. I have heard many sad stories about poverty and near starvation during World War II, when food supplies were limited and one of the few affordable items was *bacalao* (codfish). A *penca* (slab) of *bacalao* went a long way in most homes. The dry, salted codfish was sold with bones and gills, and used in its entirety. The flesh was removed and saved for other meals. The carcass was boiled in water with herbs and spices and turned into a strained flavorful stock for use as a base for soups, rice dishes, and fritters. Because no *bacalao* was actually in the prepared rice dish, it was ironically referred to as *mira bacalao* (see the codfish). But the intense flavor of the seafood remained in the dish, and the vision of the codfish flesh lived in the minds of hungry people.

"We were so poor," some folks will say, "that the only thing we had to eat was a *cola de bacalao* (the tail of the dry codfish)." For many Puerto Ricans, these memories of an impoverished life still make them shun the idea of serving *Arroz con Bacalao* while others glorify it, serving the dish proudly as a reaffirmation of faith and survival. I prefer the latter attitude about *bacalao* and have created this recipe with that in mind.

3/4 pound dry codfish fillet

1 quart plus 3 1/2 cups cold tap water

1 lemon cut in half

1/3 cup olive oil

5 cloves garlic, minced

1 teaspoon minced fresh gingerroot

1/3 cup finely chopped green onion

2 tablespoons finely chopped red bell pepper

2 tablespoons finely chopped green bell pepper

1 tomato, cored, seeded, and finely chopped

2 teaspoons chopped fresh oregano (or 1 teaspoon dry, crushed)

1 tablespoon chopped fresh cilantro

1/4 teaspoon saffron threads

2 teaspoons paprika

1/3 teaspoon cayenne pepper

1/3 cup sherry

2 1/2 cups long-grain rice

Garnish: 1 large red bell pepper, broiled, seeded, and julienned

1. Prepare codfish by cutting it into one-inch squares. Place in a stockpot with 1 quart of water and lemon. Bring to a boil. Drain the water and discard the lemon. Rinse the codfish under cold running water. Taste a piece of the codfish; if it is still very salty, run it through cold water again until most of the salty taste is gone. Allow the codfish to sit in cold water until ready to use. Then strain it prior to folding into the rice.

2. In a preheated kettle over low-to-medium heat, combine olive oil, garlic, ginger, green onion, red and green bell peppers, tomato, oregano, cilantro, saffron, paprika, and cayenne pepper. Sauté for 2 minutes. Stir in the sherry.

3. Add the rice, mix until the grains are coated and tinted orange. Add 3 1/2 cups of water and stir. Make sure that you scrape the bottom of the kettle and the rice is floating. Then fold in the codfish and bring the rice mixture to a boil. Allow to cook down until bubbling craters appear on the surface. Then set the heat on low,

cover and cook for 9 minutes. Gently fold the rice from the bottom up. Cover kettle and finish cooking for another 10 minutes or until rice is fluffy.

4. Make sure the rice is soft and fluffy, not mushy, then turn off heat. Uncover for approximately 2 minutes to allow excess moisture to escape.

5. When serving, be sure to distribute the codfish evenly in proportion to the rice being served. Garnish with strips of broiled peppers.

SERVING SUGGESTIONS: This is an excellent dish with New Puerto Rican Style Simmered Beans using either the black or red beans, broiled ripe plantain slices and Avocado Salad on a bed of watercress. Your favorite chilled wine or cold beer is imperative!

Yellow Rice
Arroz Amarillo
SERVES 4

Yellow Rice, or *Arroz Amarillo*, is widely referred to by most Puerto Ricans as Spanish Rice, and is one of the most popular rice dishes offered by the Puerto Rican kitchen. This dish can always be prepared and served as an alternative to white rice.

Yellow Rice is dynamic whether served by emphasizing the *sofrito*, saffron, or stock with which it is prepared, or the smoke-cured ham or other meats that may be added in variations that follow this recipe. The intensity or the subtleties of the highlighted flavors can be controlled—the amounts suggested in all my recipes serve as a point of reference and can be modified according to each individual's taste and preference.

Served as a special dish or as part of an ordinary dinner, Yellow Rice will impart a dramatic feeling by the sight and smell of its saffron and paprika. The addition of smoke-cured ham or chorizo enhances its appeal.

    4 *tablespoons vegetable oil*
    2 *cloves garlic, minced*
    2 *teaspoons paprika*
  1/4 *teaspoon saffron threads*

$1/4$ teaspoon cayenne pepper

$1/3$ cup tomato, peeled, seeded, and chopped

$1/4$ teaspoon pulverized rock salt

1   tablespoon chopped yellow onion

1   tablespoon finely chopped yellow bell pepper

2   cups long-grain rice

$2^1/2$ cups water, at room temperature

     Garnish: 1 red bell pepper, roasted and cut into 8 strips

1. Prepare the saffron by soaking the threads in $1/2$ teaspoon of warm water for about 2 minutes. Do not strain, use as is. (See instructions for preparing saffron in "Tools, Techniques, & Ingredients" chapter.)

2. In a preheated kettle over low-to-medium heat, combine oil, garlic, paprika, saffron, cayenne pepper, tomato, salt, onion, and yellow bell pepper. Stir until mixture turns slightly orange, then add the rice and stir until it is totally glazed. Add water and stir, scrapping the bottom of the kettle to ensure that no rice grains are sticking to the bottom. Bring liquid to a fast boil, set the heat on low, cover pot, and allow to cook until most of the moisture has evaporated, approximately 10 minutes.

3. Uncover and fold the rice from the bottom up. Do not stir, or the rice may turn pasty. Cover and continue cooking for another 7 to 9 minutes or until done, the rice should be yellow, soft, and grainy. Remove from heat.

4. Garnish with strips of red roasted peppers. Serve as part of the main course.

SERVING SUGGESTIONS: Serve with Puerto Rican Style Simmered Beans— a red bean or black bean is best. Serve Avocado Salad or Avocado Chayote Salad or Avocado-Watercress Salad on the side. The Chayote Salad is especially refreshing if the rice is made spicy. To accompany, there is nothing like chilled *Sangría* or *Limonada*.

VARIATIONS: For a delightful variation with a country, smoky taste, make *Arroz con Jamón*. Combine the following with the other ingredients prior to adding rice:

1/4 *pound smoke-cured ham, cut into* 1/2-*inch cubes*

2 *tablespoons of raisins*

2 *tablespoons dry sherry*

For Spicy (*Picante*) Rice and Sausage, combine the following with the above ingredients prior to adding rice:

1/4 *pound of Spanish dry chorizo or Italian pepperoni or linguica,*
     sliced into 1/2-*inch lengths*

1 *hot chili pepper, seeded, and chopped*

2 *tablespoons dry sherry*

   For a milder variation, *omit the chili pepper.*

For an exotic perfume touch to Yellow Rice, increase the amount of saffron to 1/2 teaspoon, add 1/4 teaspoon of curry powder and 1 pinch of ground cloves.

Rice with Pigeon Peas

Arroz con Gandules

SERVES 6

For a Puerto Rican, Christmas is not complete if one does not indulge in a plate of *Arroz con Gandules*. On *Noche Buena* (Christmas Eve), families and friends, dressed in their finest attire, all carrying gifts, food, and typical island instruments, converge at a designated home and prepare for *La Navidad* (Christmas). Bearing the *cuatro* (The Island's original four-string guitar that evolved into a ten-string instrument), *güiros* and *maracas*, percussion instruments fashioned out of dry gourds, the musicians assemble and gather together a chorus of family and friends to take their songs and music throughout the neighborhood.

While all this is taking place, the preparation of the food is going on in the background. Although the *pasteles* have probably been premade and the roasted pig (*lechon asado*) may no longer be turning on the spit, the *Arroz con Gandules* is prepared on the spot as one of the main entrees of the Christmas feast. After enjoying the banquet, the music begins again and couples take to the dance floor. By 11:30 P.M., the neighbors begin to pour out of their homes onto the street, and everyone heads toward the church where *misa de gallo* (Christmas mass) is heard. After returning home, the Christmas holidays are officially started, and they do not end until after January 5th, Three Kings' Day.

I was born on *Noche Buena* and my first contact with food was with *Arroz con Gandules*. My mother tells that she was not about to pass up the celebration and the *Arroz con Gandules* merely because she just had given birth. So she enjoyed her Christmas banquet with her second-born child, and I enjoyed my very first *Navidad*.

Fresh gandules are available in December and can be purchased at most Latino fresh-produce markets, especially in Puerto Rican communities. The packaged variety, whether dry, frozen, or canned, is available all year round at almost any well-stocked supermarket in the United States. When using the frozen variety, thaw out prior to using. The canned variety comes precooked and packed in salt water. Discard the solution and rinse the *gandules* in cold water prior to using, and make sure that when using this variety, you fold them in at the very last minute. This prevents the *gandules* from breaking down as a result of double-cooking.

1/3   *cup olive oil*

 6   *garlic cloves, minced*

 2   *teaspoons chopped fresh oregano (1 teaspoon dry)*

 4   *green onions, chopped*

1/2   *green bell pepper, finely chopped*

 2   *medium tomatoes, finely chopped*

 4   *sprigs fresh cilantro, coarsely chopped*

1/4   *teaspoon black pepper*

1/4   *teaspoon pulverized rock salt*

 1   *tablespoon paprika*

1/4   *pound smoke-cured ham, diced*

 3   *cups long-grain rice*

 4   *cups clear pork stock (see recipe in "Soups" chapter)*

 1   *pound fresh gandules (or 1 can of pigeon peas or use Gandules Guisado;*

for fresh or dry gandules, see recipe in "Beans" chapter)

2 *red bell peppers, broiled and each cut into 6 wedges*

1. In preheated kettle over low-to-medium heat, combine olive oil, garlic, oregano, green onions, green bell pepper, tomatoes, cilantro, black pepper, salt, paprika, and ham. Sauté until tomatoes liquefy.

2. Add rice and stir until rice is glazed. Add the clear pork stock. Scrape the bottom of the kettle to ensure that the rice is not sticking, then add the pigeon peas. Increase heat to high and bring mixture to a quick boil. Reset heat on medium and cook down until liquid is absorbed by the rice, approximately 10 minutes. Fold the rice from the bottom up. Set heat to low, cover pot, and continue to cook until rice is done, approximately 7½ minutes.

3. Fold in broiled red pepper wedges. Serve immediately so that you may best enjoy the full flavor of the *Arroz con Gandules*.

SERVING SUGGESTIONS: Enjoy it with roast pork, broiled pork chops, or broiled lamb chops swimming in a fresh mint and roasted garlic marinade (see "Sauces" chapter), and either a crisp green salad or a simple Avocado Salad.

Rice with Corn
Arroz con Maiz
SERVES 4 TO 6

Another one of my favorite dishes of the *arroz junto* varieties (mixed rice dishes) is the old classic, *Arroz con Maiz* (Rice with Corn). The interesting characteristic of this dish is the mixing of two principal grains to create a perfect blend.

1/3 *cup olive oil*

4 *garlic cloves, minced*

1 *tablespoon chopped shallots*

2 *teaspoons chopped fresh oregano leaves (1 teaspoon dry)*

2 *teaspoons chopped fresh cilantro*

1/4 teaspoon cayenne pepper

1/2 teaspoon pulverized rock salt

1/3 cup finely chopped yellow bell pepper

1/3 cup peeled, chopped tomato

1/4 teaspoon saffron threads

1/3 teaspoon ground cumin

2 teaspoons paprika

2 cups long-grain rice, rinsed

2 cups of corn kernels

1 1/2 cups water

1 cup chicken stock (see recipe in "Soups" chapter)

Garnish: 1 large red bell pepper, roasted and cut into 8 strips

1. To make the rice, in a preheated kettle over low-to-medium heat combine 1/3 cup olive oil, shallots, yellow bell pepper, tomatoes, saffron, cumin, and paprika. Sauté slowly, stirring until the tomatoes break down.

2. Stir in the rice, making sure that the rice is completely glazed. Incorporate the corn kernels, water, and the chicken stock, and bring the mixture to a boil. Cook down until bubbling craters begin to appear. Set the heat on low and cover the kettle.

3. Cook for approximately 10 minutes, uncover, then turn the rice by folding from the bottom up. Place a layer of roasted red peppers on top of the rice and continue cooking for 7 minutes. Remove from heat and transfer to a serving platter.

SERVING SUGGESTIONS: Serve with Rum Glazed Ripe Plantains, and a salad such as Avocado Salad with *mojo* dressing, or even just fresh avocado slices. This rice dish is also an excellent stuffing base for chicken or cornish hens.

Rice with Chicken

Arroz con Pollo

SERVES 4

Chicken with rice or rice with chicken. Either way you say it, it is correct. The end product is a succulent dish that is quick and easy to prepare, nutritious, and flavorful. As with most chicken and rice dishes, saffron is the key to turning a common one-plate dinner into a dish with exotic overtones.

I enjoy creating intense flavor and aroma without sacrificing the texture of the rice grains and the chicken. I want the rice to be grainy and bursting with the flavor of the chicken and the aromas of the herbs and spices that cling to the chicken. I also want the meat portions to be intact and whole, not dry or falling apart from over exposure to dry heat or steam pressure.

Traditionally, the one-step cooking method is used to make *Arroz con Pollo*. Pre-made *sofrito* is combined with the chicken, rice, and water and then cooked down until done. But another method uses two steps: partially cook the rice mixture in a kettle on top of the stove until most of the moisture has evaporated, transfer it to a baking pan glazed with olive oil, and finish the cooking process in the oven. Yet another method is a three-step one. First, the chicken is seared in a skillet. Then a rich tomato sauce is made and combined with the rice. The rice is placed in a deep baking pan and layered with the braised chicken, fresh peas and carrots, and spinach leaves soaked in chicken stock. The dish is then cooked slowly in the oven. All of these methods are still used and should be experimented with according to the boldness and creativity of the chef!

1/3 *cup white wine*

1/3 *cup beer*

5 *garlic cloves, minced*

2 *tablespoons chopped fresh cilantro*

2 *teaspoons chopped fresh oregano leaves (1 teaspoon dry)*

1/3 *teaspoon cayenne pepper*

1/2 *teaspoon crushed rock salt*

1   chicken, approximately 4 pounds (quartered and skinless)
2/3   cup olive oil
2   tablespoons chopped shallots
1/3   cup finely chopped yellow bell pepper
1/3   cup peeled chopped tomato
1/2   teaspoon saffron threads
1/3   teaspoon ground cumin
1   tablespoon paprika
2   cups long-grain rice, rinsed
2 1/2   cups chicken stock (see recipe in "Soups" chapter)

Garnish: 1 large red bell pepper, broiled, cut into 8 strips,
1/2 cup cooked peas, 1/2 cup cooked fresh diced carrots

1. Prepare saffron in water according to instructions in "Tools, Techniques & Ingredients" chapter. Set aside.

2. In a deep bowl, combine wine, beer, garlic, cilantro, oregano, cayenne pepper, and salt. Blend with a wire whisk or spoon. Add the chicken parts and toss vigorously. Cover, refrigerate, and allow to marinate for at least 1 hour.

3. Preheat skillet and set burner on low heat. Add 1/3 cup olive oil, coating the entire surface of the skillet (save the remainder of the olive oil). Remove chicken parts from the marinade and place in the skillet. Arrange so that all parts fit without crowding. Slowly braise the chicken on all sides using a set of tongs to turn. Do not allow chicken parts to stick to the bottom of the skillet; use a spatula to pry the chicken loose. Baste the chicken with leftover marinade and continue cooking until chicken is fully cooked, about 20 to 30 minutes. Then remove skillet from the heat and set aside.

4. To make the rice: In a preheated kettle over low-to-medium heat, combine 1/3 cup olive oil, shallots, yellow bell pepper, tomato, saffron, cumin, and paprika. Sauté slowly, stirring until the tomatoes break down.

5. Stir in the rice, making sure it is completely glazed. Add the chicken stock, bring mixture to a boil and cook down until bubbling craters begin to appear. Set the heat on low and cover the pot.

6. Cook approximately 10 minutes, then turn the rice by folding from the bottom up. Place a layer of broiled red peppers on top of the rice and arrange the chicken parts on top of the peppers and cover. Continue cooking for 7 minutes. Remove from heat and transfer the *Arroz con Pollo* to a serving platter. Garnish with peas, carrots, and remaining broiled pepper strips.

SERVING SUGGESTIONS: Enhance this dish by serving it with red beans or pinto beans, Rum Glazed Ripe Plantains, and a salad such as Avocado Salad with garlic dressing, or just fresh avocado slices.

Black Rice
Arroz Negro

SERVES 4

Black Rice, *Arroz Negro*, is yet another one of the many delectable dishes in the wide range of Puerto Rican cuisine that is virtually unknown outside of Puerto Rican communities. Not to be confused with the Cuban dish known as "gray rice,"—a rice made dark gray by mixing it with the stock of black beans—Black Rice gets its name because the rice is mixed with the black ink from the sacks of the calamari (also known as squid) slices which are also served with the dish.

Black Rice is very popular in Barcelona and all along the Mediterranean coast of Spain. It is treated with the same respect as a *Paella*, and the cooking technique is the same. However, as with other brothy rice dishes inherited from Spain, such as *Paella*, Black Rice followed the same path of transformation in the Puerto Rican kitchen. It went from a "wet" dish to one that is fluffier, contains less moisture, and is grainy in texture, which holds up very well when either short-grain, medium-grain, or long-grain rice is used.

In this recipe, I use Valencia medium-grain rice. The power of absorption is far greater than with the long-grain, and the end result is a fluffy rice, coated and bursting with the intense flavor of the sea.

Unfortunately most calamari sold at fish stores in the United States is cleaned, processed, and sold without the ink sacks. Some seafood wholesalers, however, will carry small prepackaged amounts. Other retailers may let you special order unprocessed calamari and other "exotic" items. For the sake of convenience, I suggest the option of combining fresh calamari with a prepackaged Spanish import of squid in its ink, which I think is very good, and will not adversely affect the finished dish. The imported variety can be found in most Latino markets and large supermarkets. Be sure to ask for the product that contains the most ink.

  1 *pound of calamari (squid)*
  1/3 *cup olive oil*
  5 *garlic cloves, minced*
  1/3 *cup finely chopped yellow onion*
  2 *habanero peppers, finely chopped*
  1/2 *cup chopped tomato*
  2 *teaspoons chopped fresh oregano (1 teaspoon dry)*
  2 *tablespoons coarsely chopped fresh cilantro*
  1/3 *teaspoon ground black peppercorns*
  1/3 *teaspoon cayenne pepper*
  1/2 *teaspoon pulverized rock salt*
  1/3 *cup dry sherry*
  2 1/2 *cups medium-grain rice, rinsed*
  4 *ounces of squid ink; if none available, then use 2 cans of*
     imported Spanish squid in its ink (3 1/2 ounces each)
  2 *cups clear fish head stock (see "Soups" chapter) at room temperature*
  1/3 *cup boiling water*
  1 *large red bell pepper, broiled, cut into 8 strips*

1. Slice calamari bodies into 1/2-inch rings and keep tentacles whole. If using the imported squid, open the tins in which they are packed and transfer the contents to a glass bowl. Allow the squid to "breathe" for a few minutes prior to mixing. This will eliminate most of the aftertaste associated with pre-packaged foods.

2. In a preheated kettle over low-to-medium heat, combine olive oil, garlic, onion, *habanero* peppers, tomato, oregano, cilantro, black pepper, cayenne pepper, and salt. Add the fresh calamari and sauté lightly.

3. Add dry sherry and stir in rice and ink, or if you are using canned squid, the canned squid and its ink. Add fish head stock and boiling water. Gently scrape the bottom of the kettle to make sure there is no rice sticking to the pot.

4. Bring the rice mixture to a quick boil, then reduce to medium heat. Cook down until most of the liquid has been absorbed by the rice. Set heat to low, cover kettle, and continue cooking for 10 minutes. Uncover and fold rice from the bottom up. Then layer the broiled pepper strips on top of rice, cover, and finish cooking for another 6 minutes or until rice is fluffy. Serve immediately, while the rice is steaming hot.

SERVING SUGGESTIONS: Serve this rice dish with Stewed Red Beans in Wine Sauce, green salad or Avocado Salad or Avocado and Chayote Salad, and Breadfruit *Tostones* topped with garlic *mojo*.

Paella

SERVES 4

Probably Spain's most famous exported rice dish, *Paella*, evolved from a simple combination of rice, vegetables, garden snails, and codfish, to a complex and exquisite rice dish that includes saffron, shellfish, fowl, sausage, and pork. Years ago, during several visits to Spain, I spent most of my eating time sampling *Paellas* from different restaurants in Barcelona, Palmas de Majorca, Jerez de la Frontera, Valencia, and Madrid. Every *Paella* that I sampled was unique, each bursting with its own intricate, regional flavors and textures.

In Barcelona, right off the main strip *La Rambla*, and not too far from the *boqueria* (the marketplace), I found a kiosk that sold *tapas* and wine. I was greeted by the owner, Federico, a well-mannered and jovial individual who instantly reminded me very much of the great Sancho Panza [Don Quixote's sidekick]. So eager was he to make me feel welcome that as soon as I asked who made the best *Paellas* in Barcelona, he quickly disappeared behind the curtain that separated the front counter area from the back of the store and reappeared with Josefina, his wife. "She makes the best *Paella* in this *Bendita Tierra* (Holy Land)!," he exclaimed.

After a few rounds of great wines, *tapas*, and merrymaking, we all agreed that Josefina would make a *Paella* and I would return the following evening for dinner. I handed Federico the equivalent of thirty U.S. dollars in Spanish *pesetas* to go toward the purchase of the ingredients for the *Paella*, and we bid each other farewell until the next day.

The *Paella* I ate the following day was just as promised—the best I had ever tasted. Perhaps it had to do with the fact that the meal was not a commercially prepared dinner but rather homemade—enjoyed and shared with a family of strangers who instantly became an extension of my own family. The *Paella* had been prepared in the traditional way, cooked outside over a *lena* (an intense fire fueled by fruit tree logs). Fresh seafood and a variety of sausages, chicken, and slightly braised chunks of country-cured ham, all came together in a seafood-flavored brothy rice, garnished with roasted red bell peppers, fresh Spanish olives, and topped with grated, aged cheese. *Sangría* was in abundance, and for dessert we ate whole Spanish peaches in a cinnamon-clove spiced brandy sauce served alongside a light almond custard.

I had been under the impression that the *Paella* got its name from the pan in which it is cooked and served. Federico, however, insisted that his version was the actual explanation. A certain king, he told me, had become obsessed with one of the palace courtesans and wanted to seduce her. Thinking love letters, poetry, and gifts to be all too common, the King sought the advice of one of the royal chef's apprentices who did not have social rank or the qualities of a handsome romancer, yet seemed always to be sought after by various "ladies in waiting."

"Is in the food!," exclaimed the apprentice when asked his secret. "I really don't know why, but whenever I mix the *marisco* (seafood) with the rice and other ingredients, especially during the nights when the moon is full, some of the ladies find their way into the kitchen to thank me personally for such an excellent dinner."

"You will teach me how to cook this dish!" replied the King.

After a couple of weeks experimenting in the kitchen, the King was ready to make his conquest. He acquired the finest ingredients and the most superb wines, and planned to woo his desired lady after serving her his magical, aphrodisiac supper. He set the date for an evening when the moon would be at its fullest. He secretly summoned her to his chamber under false pretenses. The King draped the royal chamber in alluring textures of silk, satin, and velvet, and filled the air with the enchanting aromas of his culinary experimentations. Throwing open the balcony doors, he saw the soft light of the moon shining on the murmuring waves of the Mediterranean. The night was calm and perfect.

"Ah," he sighed to himself, "*para ella!* (for her)." The rest, as Federico said, was history. After that great night, the King proclaimed that his dish would henceforth be known as *Pa* (ra) *ella*. In tribute to my encounter with Federico and Josefina in Barcelona, twenty-five years ago, I have created my own version of the *Paella*.

My *Paella* is meant to be moist, however, the amount of moisture will vary with the taste preference of the cook and the overall mood of the diners. In my recipe, I allow for the amount of moisture that the rice will absorb without becoming pasty or waterlogged. Whenever I want a grainy *Paella*, I use long-grain rice and water instead of stock. When I experiment, I always start with the ratio of liquid to rice which is almost 1½ to 1. Then add or take away, and cook for a longer or shorter time, depending on the grain to be used.

Although a bit more expensive to prepare than other dishes, it is well worth it. *Paella* is a splendid and romantic late-night dinner to enjoy in the intimacy of one's home on New Year's Eve or any other special occasion.

 2 *cups fish head stock (see "Soups" chapter)*
 2 *teaspoons minced fresh horseradish*
 2 *teaspoons minced fresh mint*
 2 *teaspoons lime juice*
 4 *4-ounce lobster tails (butterflied)*
 8 *medium shrimp, peeled and deveined*
 4 *crab claws, cracked*
 8 *clams in the shell, thoroughly washed and scrubbed*
 8 *mussels in the shell, thoroughly washed and scrubbed*
 1/3 *cup olive oil*
 6 *garlic cloves, minced*
 12 *pork baby back ribs*
 2 *Spanish sausages, each cut into 4 sections*
 1/3 *cup thinly sliced shallots*

2 chicken breasts, skinless, deboned, and cut into 1-inch cubes

1/2 pound lean smoke-cured ham, cut into 1-inch cubes

1 cup dry sherry

2 habanero peppers, seeded and minced

1 cup diced fresh tomato

2 teaspoons chopped fresh oregano

2 tablespoons chopped fresh cilantro

2 teaspoons paprika

1/4 teaspoon cayenne pepper

2 teaspoons chopped fresh sage (1 teaspoon dry, crushed leaves)

8 large black pitted olives cut in halves

1 teaspoon saffron threads, processed according to instructions in "Tools, Techniques, & Ingredients" chapter

2 cups medium-grain rice, rinsed

1 cup chicken stock

1 large red bell pepper, broiled, seeded, and sliced into 8 strips

Optional: 4 tablespoons grated romano cheese

1. To prepare the initial phase of the *Paella*, combine in a kettle, fish head stock, horseradish, mint, and lime juice. Bring to a quick boil. Turn heat off, then add to the stock the lobster tails, shrimps, crab claws, clams, and mussels. Cover and allow the shellfish to sweat until ready to assemble.

2. In a preheated deep skillet (or a *paella* pan) over low-to-medium heat, add olive oil, garlic, baby back ribs, Spanish sausage, and shallots. Cook slowly, stir and turn until the ribs and sausages are seared.

3. Make room in the center of the skillet, then add the chicken cubes, ham cubes and sauté. Incorporate the ribs and sausage, then add half of the dry sherry to deglaze the skillet. In a circular motion, add the *habanero* peppers, tomato, oregano, cilantro, paprika, cayenne pepper, sage, olives, and saffron.

Add the remainder of the dry sherry. Shake the skillet back and forth to make sure nothing sticks to the bottom. Sauté until tomatoes reach a liquid state.

4. Spread the rice evenly, covering the entire surface of the skillet or *paella* pan. Then fold so that most of the rice is on the bottom and glazed. Quickly add the chicken stock. Carefully shake the pan while using a spatula to scrape the bottom of the pan. Then add 1 cup of the fish head stock and cook down for about 6 minutes.

5. Carefully start assembling the steamed shellfish on top of the rice mixture (press the portions down so as to partially bury them in the rice). Then, applying a whirling motion, starting from the inside wall of the pan, add the remainder of the fish head stock. Layer the strips of broiled peppers on top, cover, and cook down for approximately 15 minutes. Test the rice for doneness, turn off the heat, and transfer *Paella* to the immediate serving area or dining table. Serve directly from the pan. Romano cheese sprinkled on the *Paella* is optional.

SERVING SUGGESTIONS: Paella is a magnificent one-plate meal, but it can be enhanced by an Avocado Salad, or slices of fresh avocado and fresh tomatoes, garnished with wedges of lemon or lime. My family and I always celebrate the New Year with this meal. *Paella* itself should be celebrated with a robust red wine, a champagne, or my *Sangría*. *Paella* also deserves an elegant dessert such as *Flan de Vanilla*. Serve flan with a cup of Puerto Rican coffee or Spanish Coffee with Brandy.

Beans

Habichuelas

> *We drank hot cocoa and talked about*
> *summertime. Momma talked about*
> *Puerto Rico and how great it was, and*
> *how she'd like to go back one day, and*
> *how it was warm all the time there*
> *and no matter how poor you were over*
> *there, you could always live on green*
> *bananas, bacalao, and rice and beans.*
>
> PIRI THOMAS

Beans are by far the number two item of a typical Puerto Rican meal, rice being number one. Put rice and beans together and you have a supple and balanced meal because of the high nutritional value of the beans. Together they are said to form a perfect protein. In fact, the term *el matrimonio* or "the perfect marriage" is often used to describe this food duo on The Island. Beans are also referred to as "poor people's meat."

Although a variety of beans already existed when Columbus and his followers arrived in Puerto Rico, more were brought to The Island by the Spanish conquistadors in the early part of the sixteenth century. The warm and humid climate, the right amount of rainfall, and the fertile soil were ideal for planting and harvesting beans all year round. Beans also became an important trading commodity, both in the new world and the old, and they still are. Huge armies were fed beans then, and huge armies are fed beans now.

Each variety of bean has its own flavor and textural characteristics that greatly complement accompanying rice dishes. But whatever the color, flavor, or texture of the beans, they have always provided a way for us to have a varied diet without buying expensive meats. By varying special ingredients in the beans, or combining them with one of many rice dishes, it can feel like eating an entirely different meal every night. To us, the thought of eating beans and rice does not conjure up visions of poverty, but instead, memories of luscious eating and a whole array of possible menus.

NEW PUERTO RICAN STYLE
SIMMERED BEANS
Habichuelas Puertorriqueñas

Beans are universal, and while it's true they are not exclusive to the Puerto Rican diet, I have yet to find another cuisine where the method of preparing, cooking, combining, and serving of beans, can compare to that of the Puerto Rican kitchen. Although in most Latin American countries, beans are referred to as *frijoles*, the Puerto Rican name for beans is *habichuelas*. *Frijoles* to us are black-eyed peas. We identify beans by their color and characteristics such as dried red beans or fresh white beans. On The Island and in the States, fresh picked beans are most often found at farmers' markets.

For the purpose of introducing the beans, and the stewing method of Puerto Rican style bean cookery (*habichuelas guisadas*), I have selected the most popular grains (*granos*) of the Puerto Rican kitchen.

The red beans, pinto beans, and *gandules* (pigeon peas) will invariably be of the dry variety that requires prewashing and reconstitution by soaking of the beans overnight. The beans are then made soft prior to cooking. Although this technique is effective in cutting down the cooking time, I find the beans lose color density and the beans' outer shell weakens causing the beans to fall apart during the cooking phase. Also a slight fermentation sets in, which may be responsible for creating the dreadful gas associated with bean eating.

In the interest of good eating, I have modified this approach to preparing and stewing the perfect bean dish. I have gone from the traditional one-step cooking method (where all the combined ingredients are confined in a kettle and cooked down) to a slightly more complex and organized one that will allow the cook to have absolute control in the initial phase of the preparation, and the freedom to be creative in the final cooking phase of the bean dish.

The key factor in turning out great beans that perfectly balance a particular rice dish, is to select the bean that would make the rice dish more attractive. One must take into consideration the color and texture of both the beans and the rice. A plain white rice dish will go with any stewed bean but will usually require a complementary serving of a meat, salad, or *tostones* to produce a simple, yet exciting, one-plate dinner. A yellow rice or a mixed rice (such as *Arroz con Bacalao*), which is loaded with textures and bursting with different flavors and aromas, will stand up on its own. But add stewed red beans on the side and you dramatically enhance the nutritional and aesthetic value of the dish, and eliminate the need for other side dishes.

For most Puerto Ricans, a meal of beans and rice is not just a plate of food, but rather the culinary expression of the Puerto Rican cultural experience. After you have learned to cook and eat rice and beans the Puerto Rican way, you will have enormous insight into daily life on *La Isla!*

Basic Bean Recipe

SERVES 6 +

Here is my basic bean recipe that can be made and served as is. It is also the recipe to be used when cooked or simmered beans are called for in the following recipes.

By using the simmering technique (cooking slowly) in the restricted confinement of a covered pot, the texture of the beans are kept intact (whole and firm). The intense flavors of the fresh herbs and spices interacting with the bean stock is preserved and not diluted when replenishing the water level that may be lost through evaporation. The end result is a superb composition of whole beans held together by a natural stock bursting with the rich fresh flavors of the herbs and spices.

 1 *pound dry beans*
 3 *quarts water and 1 quart hot water*
 5 *garlic cloves, minced*
 1 *whole medium yellow onion, peeled*
 1/2 *green bell pepper, seeded*
 2 *bay leaves*

2 sprigs fresh cilantro

1 teaspoon vinegar

1 teaspoon crushed rock salt

1/2 teaspoon ground white pepper

1 cracked ham hock (approximately 1/4 pound)

1. Place dry beans in a colander and wash under running water for approximately 1 minute. Look for and remove any foreign particles such as small twigs, pebbles, or perforated *granos*.

2. Once beans are cleaned, transfer them to a kettle and add 3 quarts of water and all the listed ingredients. Bring to a quick boil over high heat, then reset heat to low. Cover and simmer the beans for approximately 30 minutes to ensure uniform cooking and proper texture. The liquid level must always be maintained at approximately 1 inch over the simmering beans. The beans will absorb most of the liquid but some is lost through evaporation. With the additional 1 quart of hot water standing by, replenish the liquid lost in the cook-down process by adding 1 to 2 cups at a time when needed. We don't want to dilute the flavor-rich stock of the beans by adding too much water. Test the beans for consistency. They should be firm on the outside and creamy inside. Make the test by squeezing a bean or two between the fingers.

3. Once the beans are done, remove any part of the onion, garlic cloves, and bell pepper that may not have broken down. Also remove the ham hocks and the bay leaves.

4. If beans are to be used immediately, follow the instructions for the related recipe, otherwise transfer the beans with stock to a cold container and allow to cool. Cover and refrigerate for future use. The beans will keep for at least 3 days in the refrigerator and will keep for an indefinite amount of time when frozen.

SERVING SUGGESTIONS: Serve with any favorite rice and a salad on the side. Open a cold drink and toast *el matrimonio!*

Pinto Beans

Habichuelas Rositas

SERVES 6

The pinto bean, perhaps the most universal of the dried variety, is my favorite choice when I'm confronted with a moment of indecision about what kind of bean to enjoy with a particular meal. It will complement all rice dishes.

This bean has a slightly thinner skin than the smaller red bean and absorbs more moisture when reconstituting. This sponge-like behavior in the cooking process, and the resilient quality of the skin, allows the bean maximum expansion capacity, providing a greater yield per serving and a creamier and more flavorful texture. These particular qualities make the pinto bean ideal for creating new bean dishes.

I like this recipe. I trap the beans in a sauce flavored with fresh carrot and tomato puree, and a bit of pineapple juice. The result is a mildly piquant taste with a subtle sweet fragrance of pineapple rising from within the beans.

1/3 cup olive oil

5 garlic cloves, minced

1/3 cup chopped yellow onion

1 tablespoon chopped green bell pepper

1 tablespoon chopped red bell pepper

1 teaspoon minced fresh ginger

3 serrano chili peppers, minced

2 teaspoons chopped fresh cilantro

2 teaspoons chopped fresh oregano (1 teaspoon dry)

1 teaspoon white wine vinegar

1 cup pineapple juice

1/2 cup pureed cooked carrots

1/2 cup tomato puree

1 pound simmered pinto beans with stock
(see Basic Bean Recipe on page 156)

1. In a preheated kettle, combine olive oil, garlic, onion, green and red bell peppers, ginger, chili pepper, cilantro, and oregano. Sauté until most of the oil has been absorbed.

2. Stir in vinegar and pineapple juice, bring to a sizzle, then stir in the pureed carrots and the tomato puree. Blend and allow to cook down to a thick paste.

3. Slowly break down the paste with the bean stock until you achieve a rich, thick sauce. Lower the heat and add the beans, folding gently to blend. Let the beans simmer for approximately 12 minutes. Add salt to taste, remove from heat and serve.

SERVING SUGGESTIONS: Absolutely superb with *Arroz con Pollo!*

Red Beans Stewed in Wine Sauce
Habichuelas Rojas Guisadas en Vino Tinto

SERVES 6

When a Puerto Rican thinks of "mom's cooking," he or she thinks of the way mother served stewed red beans with rice. As a great lover of beans, I can appreciate them cooked in almost any manner, and as a chef, I am always creating new ways of preparing these wonderful legumes. In this new dish, as with other stewed bean dishes to follow, I make use of precooked or pureed vegetables, such as squash, carrots, turnips, and sweet potatoes. I control the consistency of the sauce without altering the taste of the beans. Using yellow vegetables, I supplement the nutritional value of the beans without adding the additional starch found in the tubers.

Incorporating diced tubers, such as *malanga* (giant-sized taro), *yautía* (taro), and *yuca* (cassava), is a culinary custom in traditional Puerto Rican home cooking. The glutinous property of these tubers mixes with the natural stock of the beans, creating a perfect emulsifier that holds the beans together. Although the result is terrific, the naturally nutty flavor of the bean tends to become subordinated to the intense flavor of the starchy tubers.

In my new style of Puerto Rican bean cookery, I offer a method where the combined properties of the vegetables act as natural emulsifiers and sweeteners. And the sum of all these ingredients interacting and blending together renders an exquisite new way to enjoy the bean at its best.

1/4 *pound banana squash*

1/3 *cup olive oil*

  5 *garlic cloves, minced*

  5 *shallots, thinly sliced*

1/3 *cup chopped red bell pepper*

  2 *tablespoons chopped fresh cilantro*

  1 *teaspoon chopped fresh parsley*

  2 *teaspoons chopped fresh oregano (1 teaspoon dried)*

1/2 *cup lean diced ham*

  4 *medium tomatoes, peeled (use the charred method to peel tomatoes)*

  1 *cup dry red table wine*

  1 *pound simmered red beans with stock (see Basic Bean Recipe)*

1/4 *teaspoon pulverized rock salt*

1/4 *teaspoon ground white pepper*

1. Peel the banana squash and simmer in enough water to cover the squash until fully cooked. Discard water and mash the squash with a fork or blender while it is still hot. Set the puree aside.

2. In a preheated kettle on low heat, combine olive oil, garlic, shallots, red bell pepper, cilantro, parsley, oregano, and ham. Sauté slowly, until most of the oil has been absorbed. Stir in tomatoes and squash puree and bring to a sizzle.

3. Stir in the wine and allow to cook down to a thick paste consistency. Slowly break down the paste with the bean stock until achieving a rich sauce. Add salt and pepper to taste.

4. Lower the heat, then gently fold in the beans and blend without damaging the beans. Simmer for approximately 12 minutes.

SERVING SUGGESTIONS: Serve with White or Yellow Rice. This is also good alongside Avocado Salad or Avocado Salad with Chayotes.

White Beans with Squash and Mint

Habichuelas Blancas con Calabaza y Menta

SERVES 6

The white bean is very popular in stews and soups because of its delicate quality and natural, sweet hazelnut-like flavor. The white bean will interact well with just about any combination of herbs, spices, and textures. It will be wonderful when prepared in different mediums, such as *picante* in a chili sauce or *dulce*, sweetened with molasses. White beans frequently appear in the tasty traditional Puerto Rican *asopaos* and *guisados*.

In this recipe, I introduce the dried variety of white beans, and lace them with chopped green onions, cilantro, mint, olive oil, and white wine vinegar. Through the combination of these ingredients I am able to simulate the fresh taste and aroma of the authentic fresh bean dish.

This dish was born in order to satisfy a longing for the garden fresh beans I enjoyed as a child in Puerto Rico. The delicate and flavorful fresh white beans are a rarity, therefore very expensive, even at the marketplaces in Puerto Rico. Such occasions usually call for inviting special guests to dinner to share in the flavorful cooked bounty.

1 *pound simmered white beans (see Basic Bean Recipe)*

2 *Spanish sausages (chorizos), sliced into 1/2-inch pieces*

3 *garlic cloves, minced*

2 *tablespoons finely chopped shallots*

1/3 *cup finely chopped red bell pepper*

3 *medium tomatoes, peeled and finely chopped*

2 *teaspoons chopped fresh oregano (1 teaspoon dried)*

1/4 *pound banana squash*

1/4 *cup extra virgin olive oil*

2 *teaspoons white wine vinegar*

2 *tablespoons chopped fresh mint*

2 *tablespoons chopped green onions*

2 *tablespoons chopped fresh cilantro*

1/4 *teaspoon pulverized rock salt*

1/4 *teaspoon white ground pepper*

1. Using a sieve, strain the beans and reserve the stock. Then transfer the beans to a mixing bowl and set aside.

2. In a preheated kettle or deep skillet on low-to-medium heat, sauté sliced sausages until natural juices begin to appear. Stir in garlic, shallots, and red bell pepper. Sauté for approximately 2 minutes, then blend in tomatoes, oregano, and 2 cups of the bean stock. Stir to blend.

3. Cook down until a heavy sauce is formed, then add the squash and remainder of the bean stock. Stir to blend and simmer until squash is soft. Then incorporate the beans into the sauce, cover, and continue to simmer until the beans are piping hot. Remove from heat and serve.

4. While the beans are simmering in the pot, combine olive oil, vinegar, mint, green onion, cilantro, salt, and pepper in a container or glass jar with a lid, and shake vigorously. Lace each individual bean serving with the dressing, or place it near the bean pot at the dining table, to be sprinkled on top of the beans for an instant burst of freshness.

SERVING SUGGESTIONS: These beans are good with any number of rice dishes, such as White Rice, Black Rice, or *Arroz con Pollo*.

Stewed Pigeon Peas
Gandules Guisados
SERVES 6

The most popular legume in Puerto Rico is the *gandul*, known as the pigeon pea, and is not really a bean at all. Often called our "national bean," it is believed to have been brought to the island by Moorish soldiers attached to the Spanish brigades. The *gandul's* origin is African, and the Arabic meaning of its name is supposedly "laziness" or "lazy one," due to the plant's propensity to lean and rest against any nearby solid object or, if nothing is available, against itself. The *gandul* plant is from the hemp family and will grow to a height of 6 to 8 feet by 4 to 5 feet wide.

The plant's popularity is due to its versatility. It promotes shade because of its shrub-like structure. When planted close together, it acts as a natural fence and deterrent against intruders. It makes excellent kindling wood for cooking and roasting. The *gandul* is a high-yield legume that provides Puerto Ricans with an abundance of delicious "meat."

The *gandules* can be cooked in rice, with rice, or in stews, soups, and gumbos. It is similar to the green pea in that while growing it is green and tender. When it matures and is ready to be harvested, the color changes from pure green to a dark maroon color. It is as full as a pea but slightly flat. The texture is glossy on the outside and the pulp is solid and creamy. When cooked, the *gandules* remains whole, firm, and intact, and will not fall apart.

1   pound dried gandules
3   quarts water
1/2   teaspoon salt
1/4   teaspoon ground black pepper
2   whole garlic cloves, peeled
1/2   onion, chopped
1   smoke-cured ham hock, cracked in half
1 1/2   cups Red Sofrito (see "Sauces" chapter)

1. Rinse *gandules*, then combine in a stockpot with water, salt, black pepper, garlic, onion, and ham hock. Soak for 1 hour.

2. Place over high heat and bring to a boil. Lower heat to medium-low and let simmer for 30 minutes.

3. Add the *sofrito*, stir, and let simmer for another 30 minutes. By this time the sauce should have cooked down to approximately 1/2-inch above the *gandules*. Stir gently and remove from heat.

SERVING SUGGESTIONS: Serve piping hot alongside White Rice, with *pasteles* or baked chicken, and a watercress, avocado, and tomato salad.

Tubers & Vine-Grown Vegetables

Viandas & Verduras

> *And sadly the jibarito goes*
> *thinking this way,*
> *talking this way,*
> *crying this way*
> *down the road.*
> *What will be the fate of Borinquen,*
> *my dear God!*
>
> RAFAEL HERNANDEZ

Viandas are Puerto Rican vegetables. Also known as *verduras*, derived from the Spanish word for green, *verde*, this group includes tuberous vegetables such as *yuca* (cassava), *batatas* (sweet potatoes), *papas* (potatoes), *yautía* and *malanga* (taro roots), *ñame* (yam), as well as vine-ripened vegetables like *calabaza* (squash), chayote, squash, corn, okra, eggplant, and the *mapén* (breadfruit), a large fruit grown on trees and eaten mainly as a vegetable.

Eating a meal of *vianda* and roasted pork is thought of as country eating, the manner of eating enjoyed daily by the Puerto Rican farmer. Living and working in the countryside, the *jíbaro* had immediate access to fresh-grown vegetables and fruit, and the livestock they raised.

The *jíbaro* has now become a symbol of Puerto Rico's past—a time that possessed a seemingly more carefree lifestyle. Although it can be argued that The Island's present political status as a Commonwealth has raised the living standards of the population, this progress has replaced agricultural self-sufficiency with dependence on the United States. The calm, bucolic life of a farm-based economy has been transformed into the fast pace found in all industrialized nations. The *jíbaro* is still referred to nostalgically in poetry and song as someone who, on disappearing completely, will mean that The Island has been totally disconnected from its past.

I frequently think of the days when I lived the life of a *jíbaro*, visiting my relatives up in the mountains of Maragüez. I awoke at the crack of dawn to the sounds of roosters crowing and the enticing smell of fresh roasted coffee brewing. Every morning was the same and yet every morning was unique. Some days I spent half the morning in the *cerros* (rolling hills), foraging and digging up *ñames*, *yautías*, and *batatas*, and cutting down green bananas. On other days, my uncle and I gathered freshly grown oranges and limes, or sought out secret spots where we could pick berries or wild herbs. We filled up an old burlap bag with our treasures and hiked up and down country roads back toward his house. Every now and then my uncle stopped to point his *machete* to the *cerro* and said in a sad and prophetic tone, "It won't be long before all this is completely gone." He was referring to a new public works project that was underway. The land was expropriated and the entire area was being converted to a reservoir that would provide water and hydroelectric power to the municipality of Ponce. The *jíbaro* and his way of life has since become almost extinct, but not so the legacy of simple living and the enjoyment of preparing simple, earthy foods with the fresh flavors and aromas of generations past.

People in Puerto Rico and other Caribbean islands include the region's tubers and vine-ripened vegetables as essential parts of their diets. Cookbooks from the Caribbean reveal a wide variety of methods for cooking and enjoying cassava, sweet potatoes, okra, chayote, corn, squash, and other vegetables. Some vegetables are found more readily than others in Puerto Rican communities. In fact, the influx of immigrants from the Caribbean and Central America has given rise to numerous local produce markets that import fresh food items from the Caribbean Basin, as well as the existence of sections in large supermarket chains carrying "specialty items."

It was and still is comforting to me to see tubers and plantains in markets where I shop. My experience growing up in New York City during the first transitional year

after moving from The Island was made less traumatic because of weekend visits with my family to the *marketa* in the *barrio* (Spanish Harlem) and the Essex Street Market on New York's lower East Side. As long as I was there, among the familiar sounds and smells of home, I felt happy. My brother Mike and I, nostalgic for our Island home, would spend most of our afternoons, and all our weekends, at the marketplace selling brown paper shopping bags. Our fantasy was to make enough money to go back to The Island. It was ten years before either of us returned to Puerto Rico.

Sometimes fruits and vegetables from another culture may be difficult for outsiders to identify, or to feel confident about successfully preparing. Rather than passing up an opportunity to indulge in a new culinary adventure, I suggest to my friends that they simply ask the produce vendors to identify the names and origins of the food items that interest them and suggest ways to prepare, cook, and serve them. Most fresh produce retailers welcome the opportunity to share their knowledge of food with customers. It used to be that tubers were exclusive to small Latino or Asian produce stands, but the great demographic changes throughout most of the United States have influenced some larger supermarket chains to stock many of these products. I suggest you take a little adventure and purchase a Puerto Rican vegetable, then follow my directions for superb Puerto Rican country cooking, serving, and eating.

TUBERS

Tubers, or root vegetables, are what a Puerto Rican will think of when asked what is a typical Island vegetable. In fact, I'll bet that other islanders from the Caribbean feel the same—a vegetable to us is not always green. It can be brown or slightly reddish on the outside and white, sienna, or even a very light purple when cooked. It is a shame that more of our northern neighbors do not know about these earthy treasures.

Tubers are quite simple to cook. Once one has dealt with the challenge of recognizing them in a market, purchasing them, and bringing them home, the next task is to peel off their rather hard and crusty skins. This can readily be accomplished with a sharp knife that is also used to cut the body of the skinned tuber when the recipe calls for cutting the tuber into chunks before cooking. (See instructions in various recipes.) I like to cut the tubers into approximately 2-inch chunks.

Once peeled, the tubers are boiled in lightly salted water. They can be served plain, with a sauce like a garlic *mojo* or as part of a more complex dinner plate, served with Stewed Codfish (*Bacalao Guisado*).

The Log of Christopher Columbus, by Robert H. Fuson. Copyright 1987. Published by International Marine Publishing. Reprinted with permission of McGraw-Hill, Inc.

SWEET POTATOES
Batatas

One of the most recognizable tubers are sweet potatoes—*batatas* we call them. Sweet potatoes are tuberous roots from a tropical vine related to the morning glory, with differently shaped leaves and purplish flowers. Although indigenous to the tropics, they are also commercially cultivated in warm regions of the United States and in other tropical climates throughout the world. Although many people think that sweet potatoes are related to yams, they are actually from a different plant family than yams, which were brought to the Caribbean from Africa. Yams, of course, are also commonly found in the United States, and may be easily substituted in this recipe. For the Tainos living on the island of Puerto Rico, cultivating sweet potatoes was a substantive part of life, as was raising cassava (*yuca*), both of which were raised in large mounds of rich soil called *conucos*.

Batatas continue to have their rightful place in the Caribbean kitchen, their preparation taking on different characteristics with each passing generation of cooks, including the more recent culinary eclectics. From a simple root served boiled and peeled and cut into chunks, to a mashed fresh vegetable appropriate for babies to eat, and onto superb finished dishes, the sweet potato can be used in almost every meal. Throughout the Caribbean, Puerto Rico, and the other islands, the sweet potato is used in desserts—especially cakes, pastries and pastes. The sweet potato is a truly international vegetable.

The sweet potato is smooth and sensitive; it is warm, filling, flavorful, colorful, and most importantly, nutritious. It is easy to prepare, is suited to any cooking medium, and is available at most fresh produce stores and supermarkets all year round. The sweet potato is inexpensive and keeps for a prolonged period of time when properly stored.

Basic Sweet Potato Recipe and Preparation

To prepare the *batatas* for a recipe calling for cooked batatas or to simply serve simmered *batatas* as an accompanying food item to balance a meal, choose medium-sized *batatas*, scrub well, cut into 3 sections, and place in a stockpot with water (water level should be 3 to 4 inches over the sweet potatoes). Add 2 whole cloves, 2 sticks of cinnamon, and a pinch of salt. Bring to a quick boil, then lower heat. Simmer until *batatas* are done, approximately 30 minutes. Test by inserting a fork in the center. The fork should slide in with ease. Once done, remove from heat, discard the water, and remove the skin (optional). Proceed with the serving instructions from your choice of the following recipes.

Baked Batatas with Sour Cream

The spices in these sweet potatoes complement the natural sweetness of the tubers. The brown sugar, cinnamon, and other spices make the sweet potatoes come "alive." Please note that you will need to multiply the amounts of the ingredients by the number of servings you wish.

Preheat oven to 375°

   1 *sweet potato*

   2 *teaspoons soft butter*

   1/2 *teaspoon fresh lemon juice*

   1/4 *teaspoon ground cinnamon*

   1/4 *teaspoon ground ginger*

   1/8 *teaspoon ground nutmeg*

   1 *teaspoon light brown sugar*

   1 *8-inch square, foil wrapper*

   2 *teaspoons chilled sour cream*

   Garnish: *1 sprig fresh mint*

1. Choose small to medium, unblemished sweet potatoes, wash and scrub well with a vegetable brush, cut 8-inch squares of aluminum foil wrappers, place one *batata* in the center of foil. Using a dinner fork (hold on a slant) make a honeycomb pattern of perforations ⅛-inch deep along the length and on all sides of the *batata*. Set aside.

2. In bowl combine and blend, soft butter, lemon juice, cinnamon, ginger, nutmeg, and brown sugar. Using a pastry brush, coat the sweet potato heavily on all sides. Tightly seal the wrapper on all sides by folding in envelope fashion (do not crush the foil). Place on a baking sheet and bake for 1 hour.

3. To serve, carefully open wrapper and invert onto the center of a serving dish. Make a superficial well in the center of the sweet potato by pressing down with a spoon, fill with sour cream, accent lightly with a sprinkle of ground cinnamon, and garnish with a sprig of mint.

Oven Roasted Batatas

1 SERVING PER PERSON

Taste these sweet potatoes as a lush accompaniment to a dish like Ponce Chicken or Sugar Cane and Ginger Glazed Ham. Please note that you will need to multiply the amounts of the ingredients by the number of servings you wish.

   1 *sweet potato*
   2 *teaspoons soft butter*
   1 *teaspoon fresh lime juice*
   2 *teaspoons Spanish brandy*

2 *teaspoons powdered sugar*

$^{1}/_{8}$ *teaspoon pure almond extract*

Garnish: *orange wheels, fresh mint sprigs*

1. Wash and scrub small *batatas* well, (do not dry) and cut in half lengthwise. Set a cake cooling rack on a sheet pan, arrange sweet potatoes skin side down on the rack.

2. In a bowl combine and blend, butter, lime juice, brandy, powdered sugar, and almond extract. Using a pastry brush, apply a light coat of the brandy butter spread on the *batata* halves and place the assembled rack under the broiler at the lowest point possible. Sear for 6 minutes, slide out from under broiler, and brush on another coat of brandy butter spread. Continue to broil for approximately 3 minutes or until batter appears slightly charred. Slide rack out and turn sweet potato skin side up, coat skin heavily with brandy butter spread and return to broiling position for approximately 6 more minutes or until skin is slightly charred.

3. Remove from broiler, turn over, and apply a final light coat of the brandy butter spread. Serve skin side down.

Tamarind and Rum Glazed Batatas

SERVES 4

In this recipe, the tamarind's unique flavor in combination with the sugar and spices plays nicely against the rum and gingerroot flavors.

Preheat oven to 400°

3 *medium batatas*

3 *quarts water*

$^{1}/_{2}$ *teaspoon baking soda*

3 *cinnamon sticks*

3   *whole cloves*

3   *star anise seeds*

$1/2$ *ounce fresh gingerroot*

$1/2$ *cup melted butter*

1   *cup pureed tamarind pulp (see Tamarind Sauce recipe on page 301)*

1   *cup dark brown sugar*

$2/3$ *cup unsweetened pineapple juice*

$1/3$ *cup dark Puerto Rican rum*

Garnish: *mint sprigs, orange, cherries, pineapple slivers*

1. Peel *batatas* using a vegetable peeler. Cut each one into 3 wheels. Dissolve the baking soda in the stockpot with the water. Place the sweet potatoes in the solution, set the pot over high heat, bring to a quick boil, lower heat, and add the cinnamon sticks, cloves, star anise, and gingerroot. Allow to simmer for 15 minutes.

2. While *batatas* are simmering, combine in a saucepan, the pureed tamarind pulp, brown sugar, and pineapple juice. Place over medium heat and stir. Bring to a boil. Lower heat and stir in the rum. Remove from heat and set aside. If the glazing sauce becomes too thick, use approximately $1/3$ cup of the spice stock from the *batatas* and slowly break down the sauce.

3. Remove the sweet potatoes from the heat, strain the liquid, and remove the spices. Carefully so as not to break the *batatas*, arrange the wheels in a deep baking pan (leave approximately $1/2$-inch space between each wheel), and pour the melted butter over each piece, using all the butter.

4. Place the pan in the oven for 10 minutes. Rock the pan back and forth to ensure that the *batatas* are not sticking to the bottom of the pan. Then evenly spread the tamarind rum sauce over them, lower the temperature to 325°, and continue baking for 15 minutes. Remove from oven and transfer to a serving tray or assemble on individual plates.

A garnish of mint sprigs, orange, fresh cherries and fresh pineapple slivers, makes a lovely presentation!

YAUTÍA

The *yautía* is a member of the taro root family. It is the size of a potato, but more pear-shaped, with a brown fuzzy outer skin. Inside, the vegetable flesh is white and very slippery, and when cooked, the texture transforms into a delicate custard. There is also a purple *yautía* (we call it *mora*) which is just slightly firmer and less sensitive than the white variety. The third type is the yellow *yautía*, very rare and expensive, and not to be found outside of The Island.

The *yautía* is almost always part of a *serenata* (see Puerto Rican Vegetable Serenade) or a side dish with *escabeche* (see Kingfish *en Escabeche*) and is widely used in a great variety of ways on The Island. It is perhaps one of the most natural thickeners of soups, stocks, stews, and beans, and is also one of the main ingredients in the dough of Puerto Rican *pasteles*. On other Caribbean islands, the *yautía* is frequently used, and on some of the French and English-speaking islands the leaves of the plant are eaten in a soup and called callaloo (in French, *calalou*).

The *yautía* can be peeled with the use of a sharp paring knife (a vegetable peeler will not work on the tough outer skin) and placed in hot boiling water with a pinch of salt and simmered for approximately 20 to 30 minutes. Test with a fork the same as with the *batatas*. Once done, remove from heat and transfer the *yautías*, using a slotted vegetable spoon, to a glass tray containing cool water. Handle the vegetable as little as possible to keep it from crumbling.

Marinated Yautías

For a marinated dish, cube the cooked *yautía* and follow the instructions in the Green Bananas *Escabeche* recipe (or the method described in the "Tools, Techniques, & Ingredients" chapter).

Yautías with Onions and Roasted Peppers
Yautías con Cebollas y Pimientos Asados

SERVES 4

8 cooked *yautías*

1 bunch watercress

1/2 cup olive oil

6 garlic cloves, chopped

1 medium yellow onion, sliced

2 green onions, chopped

juice of 1 lime

1 red bell pepper, roasted and cut into 1/2-inch rings

1 green bell pepper, roasted and cut into 1/2-inch rings

1 yellow bell pepper, roasted and cut into 1/2-inch rings

1. Cut *yautías* in half, lay out a mat of watercress on a glass serving tray, arrange the *yautías* on top of the watercress. Set aside.

2. Preheat a skillet and add half of the olive oil (reserve the rest). Add the garlic, onion slices, and green onions. Sauté until yellow onions become translucent. Drizzle the lime juice on top and remove from heat.

3. Fold in the pepper rings. Drizzle the remainder of the olive oil on top, shake the skillet to distribute the moisture. Then pour the contents of the skillet on top of the *yautías*, making sure that all the portions are blanketed.

Baby Food

Place one *yautía* into a blender with a dash of honey and 6 ounces of milk and liquefy. Transfer the formula to a baby bottle, and your child will be sound asleep before the bottle is empty. For spoon feeding, puree the *yautía* with carrots and spinach.

Mashed Yautías

SERVES 4

6 *cooked yautías*

1 *tablespoon olive oil*

1 *teaspoon salted butter*

4 *garlic cloves, minced*

1 *tablespoon minced shallots*

1 *teaspoon white wine vinegar*

1 *chili pepper, minced*

2 *teaspoons chopped fresh cilantro*

2 *tablespoons sour cream*

6 *strips of broiled bacon, chopped*

   Garnish: *2 teaspoons chopped chives*

1. Place the cooked *yautías* in a mixing bowl and cover to contain the heat. Keep in a warm place.

2. In a preheated skillet, combine the olive oil, butter, garlic, shallots, vinegar, and chili pepper. Sauté lightly. Remove from heat, fold in cilantro, sour cream, and bacon. Pour the mixture over the hot *yautías* and mash with a potato masher, making certain that all the ingredients are nicely blended. Transfer to a serving bowl and garnish with chopped chives.

SERVING SUGGESTIONS: Use this dish as a potato substitute. *Yautías* are superb with roast chicken or pork chops—the complexity of flavors and aromas will make such combination dishes a natural, and requires no help from sauces or gravies. However, a bit of drizzle over the top from the natural juices of the meat to be served will further enhance the performance of the *yautía*.

MALANGA

The *malanga* is also a taro root. It is a large, round tuber with brown outer skin and an underlining purple tissue. The inside is white with purple specks. When the *malanga* is peeled, it will feel very slippery, and when cooked, it will turn purple in color. It can be boiled, fried, or baked. In the Hawaiian Islands, this taro root is prepared as a paste known as *poi*. Traditionally, in Puerto Rico, the *malanga* has been boiled and served as a side dish with a little bit of olive oil and sautéed onions or as part of a combination *vianda* dish.

To cook the *malanga*, cut the vegetable into wedges approximately 3 inches thick and boil the same way you would *yautía*. Follow the same instructions as those for the *yautía*, including the variations.

Grilled Malanga

On The Island we often serve *malanga* as a breakfast or lunch side dish: slice thin wheels of *malanga*, then beat 2 eggs. Dunk the wheels in the egg batter, then grill on a hot skillet. Serve alongside sausage or bacon.

ÑAME

The *ñame* is available in most Latino fresh produce stores, but if the produce market is on the mainland, this giant tuber could be called by any number of names. The Spanish translation of the word *ñame* is yam, yet this vegetable is unlike what Americans call a yam, which is typically a smaller tuber that looks rather like a sweet potato. The confusion about the name has probably existed since the 1500s, when yams began to be exported to the New World from Africa, along with the slave trade. At the same time, tubers from the New World were coming into kitchens in the Old World.

Having said this, we suggest that you ask for the vegetable by its Spanish name at a Latino produce market and see what the vendor directs you to. Here's what to look for: the *ñame* is probably, in size, the "king" of the tubers. The outer skin is brown and coarsely textured, while the inside is very porous and contains a lot of moisture. The *ñame* grows to enormous size in a hand-like pattern, with "fingers" weighing no less than 2 pounds each. The texture can be coarse and loose, or smooth and tight when cooked. This variation in texture is predicated on the freshness of the tuber. Once it has been dug out of the ground and exposed to the surface environment, the *ñame* slowly begins to lose its moisture and creamy consistency. To select a (true) yam, ask to see a cross-cut sample. Or, if not available, simply dig your thumbnail into the skin and scratch off a sliver. The *ñame* should "bleed" a milky white, sticky liquid immediately. The perfect *ñame* should have a pure, coarse white center bursting with moisture and not have any fibers. Dry and fibrous is unacceptable.

To cook the *ñame*, cut it into portions 3- to 4-inches thick if it is of the wide (hand) section, or into 2- or 3-inch wheels if it is of the finger section. Then peel each portion with a paring knife. Cook and handle the *ñame* in the same way you would the *yautía*. The sponge-like characteristic of the *ñame* makes the item an excellent boat for natural juices, sauces, and gravies. It is a superb base for stuffing and an excellent natural thickening agent for soups and stews.

Ñame with Codfish and Olive Oil

SERVES 4

4 *portions of cooked ñame*
2 *hard-boiled eggs, cut into 4 wedges*
1/4 *teaspoon cayenne pepper*
1/2 *pound charbroiled codfish*
1/3 *cup olive oil*
1 *tablespoon balsamic vinegar*
1 *small red onion, sliced julienne*
4 *large pimiento-stuffed Spanish table olives, cut into halves*
2 *teaspoons Spanish capers*
2 *teaspoons chopped fresh mint*

   Garnish: *watercress, avocado slices, tomato wheels*

1. Arrange the *ñame* portions on the center of a serving platter. Layer with egg wedges and sprinkle with cayenne pepper.

2. In mixing bowl, flake the charbroiled codfish. Add olive oil, vinegar, onion, olives, and capers, and blend together. Spread the mixture evenly over the eggs and *ñame*, sprinkle with chopped mint. Garnish with watercress sprigs, avocado slices, and tomato wheels.

VARIATIONS: Instead of codfish, use smoked herring, broiled shrimps or lobster, cooked crabmeat, octopus, or squid.

Ñame in *Escabeche*: See Pickled Green Bananas recipe (this chapter) and substitute *ñame* for bananas.

CASSAVA
Yuca

Cassava—*yuca*—has always been an important part of the Puerto Rican diet. In pre-Colombian days, when the island was known as Borinquen and inhabited by Taino Indians, cassava was the primary crop, grown in large mounds of rich soil known as *conucos*. Probably found in all the Caribbean islands even before the conquests by the Old World, *yuca* was served as a bread called *casabe* after it was shaped into a loaf and baked over a fire. The *casabe* is an unleavened bread whose cracker-like characteristics may remind the eater of matzoh bread. It remains a staple to this day throughout the tropics.

In the more contemporary world, *yuca* is fashioned into dumplings for soup, bread, chips, fries, or cakes, or served with a main course as a vegetable. In Puerto Rico, *yuca* is served as a vegetable alone or as part of a *Serenata*, and also grated and used in batters for meat pies and *pasteles*. It is found in the United States mainly in the form of tapioca.

Yuca is also called *manioc*, and its name is often confused with that of a cactus plant called yucca. The *yuca*, cassava, is a long, dark-brown colored tuber 8 to 10 inches long. This root vegetable has a white interior that's somewhat fibrous. The *yuca* has been described from time to time as a rather insipid, starchy, and unfriendly tuber. Happily, it undergoes a remarkable transformation during cooking and becomes a delightful, creamy-textured, and naturally sweet vegetable.

Boiled Cassava

Yuca

SERVES 4

The essence of this tuber can best be appreciated when it is prepared and served in a simple, uncomplicated way. On The Island, it is often fixed for lunch by boiling and serving with a drizzle of olive oil, a piece of salted codfish, slice of onion, and a wedge of avocado.

> 3 *pounds of yuca*
> 4 *quarts water*
> 1 *teaspoon salt*

1. Peel the *yucas* by trimming the ends and dividing them into 3-inch sections. Using a paring knife, make 4 vertical incisions on the bark, one on each side. Using a knife with a rounded point (a butter knife works well), peel the bark by inserting the knife at an angle and pushing back against it. Repeat the process until the *yuca* is completely peeled. *Yucas* should be all white with no pink or gray spots showing after peeling. If the *yuca* shows spots with gray fibrous strands after peeling, cut away the affected area and use only the solid white portions.

2. Cross cut the *yucas* and place in a stockpot with the water and salt. Bring to a quick boil, then lower heat and simmer for approximately 35 minutes. Once done, carefully strain the water and serve the *yuca* sections while steaming hot.

3. To serve: assemble the portions on the center of a dinner plate. Flake broiled salted codfish (see Stewed Codfish on page 269) on top, place thin slices of raw red onion rings on top, arrange 3 thin slices of avocado on top, and 3 thin slices of tomato. Drizzle olive oil and vinegar (enough to dress) over the mound and serve. Garnish with a sprig of watercress.

Yuca in Lemon Garlic Marinade

Yuca en Mojo de Ajo y Limón

SERVES 4

Marinated *yuca* is boiled *yuca* prepared with a mixture of fresh oregano, mint, and garlic, held together in olive oil and fresh lemon juice.

3   pounds boiled yuca, prepared according to preceding recipe
8   garlic cloves, peeled
2   teaspoons rock salt
1/3   cup fresh lemon juice
1   tablespoon chopped fresh oregano
1   tablespoon chopped fresh mint
1/3   cup freshly squeezed lemon juice
1/3   cup olive oil
1/3   cup stuffed Spanish table olives, cut in halves
1   tablespoon Spanish capers

Arrange the boiled *yuca* portions in a deep platter or serving tray and cover to keep hot. Combine the garlic and salt in the belly of a mortar, and pound to a coarse paste, break down with the lemon juice. Stir in the oregano, mint, and olive oil. Once all the ingredients are blended, pour over the boiled *yuca*, sprinkle olives and capers over the *yuca*, and cover. This dish can be served either steaming hot, at room temperature, or even as a chilled dish.

SERVING SUGGESTIONS: Serve with any seafood salad, roasted meat, poultry, or fish.

CASSAVA PIES
Yuca Pasteles y Yuca Empanadas

Hail the native meat pie wrapped
in banana leaves!

Juan Avilés

The *yuca* is cooked, served, and enjoyed in many ways, from a simple boiled dish to complex cooked dishes like *pasteles* and *empanadas*. The interesting aspect of these two particular dishes is that the processing of the *yuca* and its components—dough, fillings, and wrappings—are the same, but the end result is two completely different and distinct flavored, elegant dishes.

The differing textures and tastes of these dishes has to do with how the *yuca* responds to different cooking mediums and heat intensities. When we assemble the *empanada* and expose it to open flames of the broiler, its outer texture becomes tight and crusty, and it is laced with the smoky taste and aroma of the charred banana leaf wrapper, which seals in a moist and succulently-flavored meat filling.

When we take this same item, place it in a pot of boiling water, and cook it for 1 hour, the end result is a delicate pie of creamy texture enveloping a center bursting with the country fresh flavors of chunks of pork and spices, along with raisins and garbanzo beans. These are the beloved *pasteles*, treasured as much for their precious flavors as for the tender care and patience required to make them.

Broiled Yuca Pies & Boiled Yuca Pies

Empanadas & Pasteles

MAKES APPROXIMATELY 8 *EMPANADAS* OR *PASTELES.*

FOR EMPANADAS

- 4 pounds yuca (cassava), fresh or frozen
- 2 teaspoons pulverized rock salt
- 1/4 teaspoon cayenne pepper
- 2 tablespoons olive oil
- 2 teaspoons paprika
- 1/2 cup coconut milk
- 1 whole egg
- 2 cups filling (see filling recipes)

1. To peel the *yucas*: trim the ends and divide the *yucas* in half. Using a paring knife, make 4 vertical incisions on the bark, one on each side; then using a knife with a rounded point, peel the bark by inserting the knife at an angle and pushing back against it. Repeat the process until the *yuca* is completely peeled. *Yucas* should be all white with no pink or gray spots showing after peeling. If the *yuca* exhibits spots with gray fibrous strands, cut away the affected area and use only the solid white portions. After you have finished peeling, allow the tubers to soak in a bowl of cold water until ready to grate.

2. To grate *yuca*: use a heavy duty manual grater on the fine-texture side or a food processor with the grating attachment. *Yuca* will need to be finely grated to a mealy consistency. When using the frozen variety of *yuca*, allow to thaw before grating. Squeeze out extra moisture caused by freezing.

3. Next, strain the grated *yuca* by spreading a linen cloth inside a colander and placing the grated *yuca* in the center of the cloth. Close the cloth, holding up the four ends and twist with a circular motion until most of the moisture has been removed. Transfer *yuca* meal to a mixing bowl. Add salt, cayenne pepper, olive oil, paprika, coconut milk, and egg. Using your hand and fingers, work all the ingredients together, until a thick batter is achieved.

4. To assemble the *empanadas* you will need a stack of banana leaves. Trim the leaves into 8 inch by 8 inch pieces. Fill a deep square pan halfway with hot water. Using both hands, carefully pick up one leaf by the top corners and submerge it into the hot water until the leaf becomes wilted. Lay the leaf flat on an absorbent cloth or paper towels and pat dry. Repeat the process until the batch is completed. Handle the leaves gently to protect from tearing.

5. Preheat oven to 375°. Set up your work station with wilted banana leaves, followed by the *yuca* batter, and *empanada* filling.

6. To assemble the pie lay out 1 banana leaf (longest side), scoop out ½ cup of batter onto the center of the banana leaf, then using a spatula or the flat part of a serving spoon, spread the batter to form a smooth square approximately 5 inches by 5 inches.

7. Scoop out ⅓ cup of the filling and spread to layer the surface of the batter. Carefully hold the banana leaf by the lower corners and fold over evenly, crease a 1-inch margin on the left and righthand side of the wrap, fold margins inward and hold in position.

8. Finish securing the *empanada* by folding the upper part of the wrap forward envelope fashion. Place the pie on a flat sheet pan with the flap down. Allow a ½-inch space between each *empanada*. Continue the process until the batch is completed.

9. Cover the sheet pan with aluminum foil and place inside the oven. Bake for 20 minutes. Reset the oven to broil. Remove the foil, and place the sheet pan under the broiler for 5 minutes. Then slide the sheet pan out and carefully flip over the empanadas, slide it back under the broiler for another 5 minutes, or until most of the banana leaves become charred. Remove from broiler and serve.

10. To serve: place one pie on a serving plate, carefully fold back the leaf, and trim with scissors to expose the empanada. Serve on banana leaf or invert onto a dinner plate.

SERVING SUGGESTIONS: Serve as part of the main course with rice and beans.

    8 *sheets of 8¹/2 inch by 11 inch cooking parchment*

    8 *strands of cooking cord (butcher's string), each 30-inches long*

1. Follow steps 1 through 8 above.

2. Spread out one cooking parchment. Place the pie in the center of the parchment, fold in the same manner as when wrapping in banana leaf. Secure by tying with one strand of cooking cord. Repeat until batch is completed.

3. Fill a large stockpot with water and bring to a quick boil. Reset burner to medium heat. Add 2 teaspoons of salt to the water, then carefully place the *pasteles* in the boiling water. Cook approximately 45 minutes to 1 hour. Remove from heat.

4. To serve: hold a dish and carefully take the *pasteles* out of the pot as needed. Using cooking shears, snip the cord off. Open the cooking parchment and slide the banana leaf package onto the waiting dish. Using the cooking shears, cut away the top part of the leaf to expose the *pasteles*. Serve immediately.

SERVING SUGGESTIONS: Serve with Rice and *Gandules* or with slices of crusty bread.

Beef Filling for Yuca Pasteles or Empanadas

MAKES APPROXIMATELY 8 FILLINGS

  ¹/3 *cup Spanish olive oil*

    4 *garlic cloves, minced*

    1 *teaspoon minced fresh gingerroot*

    1 *pound chopped sirloin*

    2 *teaspoons chopped fresh oregano (1 teaspoon dried)*

    3 *small chili peppers, minced*

  ¹/3 *cup raisins*

  ¹/2 *teaspoon pulverized rock salt*

$1/3$ cup sherry

3 green onions, chopped

1 tablespoon chopped fresh cilantro

1 medium tomato, chopped

$1/2$ medium red bell pepper, chopped

$1/2$ medium green bell pepper, chopped

8 green Spanish olives, pitted and sliced

$1/3$ cup Spanish capers

1. In a preheated skillet on low-to-medium heat, add olive oil, garlic, ginger, ground sirloin, oregano, chili pepper, raisins, and salt. Stir until beef turns brown. Stir in burgundy and onions. Cook down for 2 minutes. Remove from heat and allow to cool, then fold in the cilantro, tomato, red and green peppers, olives, and capers.

2. Use as per recipe instructions.

Pork Filling for Yuca Pasteles or Empanadas

MAKES APPROXIMATELY 8 FILLINGS

$1/3$ cup Spanish olive oil

3 minced garlic cloves

$1 1/2$ pounds pork butt (trim excess fat), cubed into $1/2$-inch pieces

1 teaspoon pulverized rock salt

$1/2$ teaspoon fresh gingerroot, minced

2 small red chili peppers, seeded and minced

2 teaspoons fresh oregano, chopped (1 teaspoon dried)

$1/3$ cup raisins

3 green onions, chopped

$1/3$ cup Spanish brandy

2 medium tomatoes, chopped

1/2 cup diced red bell pepper

1/2 cup diced green bell pepper

8 ripe pitted Spanish olives, cut into halves

1/3 cup capers

1 tablespoon chopped fresh cilantro

1. Preheat skillet on low-to-medium heat. Add olive oil, garlic, diced pork, salt, ginger, chili peppers, and oregano. Sauté until meat turns white. Add raisins and onions, stir in brandy. Set heat to low, cover and finish cooking. Remove from heat when pork is fully cooked and tender. Allow to cool, then fold in the remaining ingredients.

2. Use as per recipe instructions.

GREEN BANANAS

Oh, how beautiful is my hut
and how happy is my palm grove
and how cool is my plaintain field
on the small banks of the river.

Luis Lloréns Torres

We like to cook green bananas and serve them along with various tubers. These are eating bananas, chosen for their greenness and not allowed to ripen.

I always cook green bananas separately because they are firm and full of resin that can taste bitter if not neutralized during the cooking process; this happens if it is undercooked. The banana becomes tender and creamy once it is properly cooked, but it will break down and become a mass of puree if overcooked.

The following steps are essential for cooking the perfect banana: Make sure that the bananas are crispy green, with no hint of yellow and no blemishes on the outer skin. Cut off the tips at both ends. Cup the banana with your left hand and using the point of a paring knife, very carefully make a straight incision from one end to the other. Rinse the bananas under running water to eliminate any foreign matter. Place them in a stockpot. Add water to approximately 4 inches above the bananas. Add 2 teaspoons of crushed rock salt. Place pot over high heat, bring to a quick boil, and lower heat. Add 1 cup of milk and simmer. Halfway into the cooking time, the milk solids will combine with the resin (neutralizing the bitterness) and accumulate on the top forming a dense white layer. At this point, start skimming and discarding immediately. If you wait too long, it will rise and spill all over the place.

The bananas should be done in 30 to 40 minutes, or when the skin opens up and the creamy flesh is exposed. To test for doneness, stick the tips of a fork through the middle of the exposed flesh and gently twist to the right. If the banana is done, it will break in half with no effort.

If it is not done, it will feel crunchy or mealy. The tendency for tubers and bananas is that the bottom layers will always cook faster since they are the closest to the heat source. Therefore, I recommend that halfway into the approximate cooking time rotate the top and bottom layers. The water level should be kept as high as the pot will allow without boiling over. Once done, remove from heat and discard the water. Then quickly place under cold running water, refill the pot with water (use tongs to execute the following movement), and separate the bananas from the skin. Set aside until ready to use (take care not to break the bananas). Discard the skin. Or, you can have a deep square pan, half-filled with cool clear water, standing by. Immediately after discarding the hot water, remove the skin from the bananas and place the peeled bananas into the square pan.

Use this process whenever a recipe calls for (boiled) cooked green bananas, such as the Pickled Green Banana (*Escabeche*). The boiled green banana makes an excellent accompaniment to seafood and pork dishes.

Pickled Green Bananas

SERVES 4

8   cooked green bananas

1/2   cup olive oil

6   garlic cloves, thinly sliced

1/3   cup sliced shallots

1/3   cup white wine vinegar

2   tablespoons fresh lime juice

1   teaspoon crushed rock salt

2   teaspoons cracked black peppercorn

4   green onions, chopped

1/2   cup ripe pitted olives

1/3   cup capers

3   whole bay leaves

2   tablespoons chopped fresh cilantro

1   medium red bell pepper, roasted and diced

1   medium green bell pepper, roasted and diced

1. Allow the green bananas to chill in a cold bath (add ice to the pan with cool water). Once bananas are chilled, drain the water. Cut the bananas in approximately ¾-inch long cylinders and place them (mound fashion) in a deep glass pan. Set aside.

2. In a preheated skillet combine half the olive oil (reserve the rest), garlic, shallots, half the white vinegar, half the lime juice, salt, and peppercorn. Sauté for 2 minutes. Remove from heat. Stir in the remainder of the olive oil, vinegar, and lemon juice. Fold in green onions, olive, capers, bay leaves, cilantro, and red and green peppers.

3. Immediately pour mixture over the mound of bananas and fold to incorporate all the ingredients. Rock the pan gently back and forth to level the mound. Cover and refrigerate overnight or at least 6 hours. Then set out at room temperature a half hour before serving.

SERVING SUGGESTIONS: To serve as an appetizer or side dish, assemble on a crisp bed of lettuce. Or simply lay out on a serving platter, garnish with lemon and lime wedges. For further complexity, add slivers of smoked herring, or broiled shrimps, or flat anchovies.

Puerto Rican Vegetable Serenade
Serenata
SERVES 6

This one-plate dinner is a very typical meal throughout The Island. Its origins are in the countryside. The combination of textures, colors, and the distinct flavors of these vegetables gave rise to its name, *serenata* (serenade). The tubers and plantains found in the serenade have formed the dietary basis of the island's inhabitants, from the pre-Columbian Tainos to the *jíbaros*, and the modern city dwellers.

Serenata is composed of chunks of tubers—*yuca, yautía, malanga,* sweet potatoes along with thick slices of both green bananas and plantains. The dish is typically served alongside a mound of *bacalao*, salted codfish that has been stewed (see "Stewed Codfish" recipe on page 269).

Traditionally, these vegetables are cooked by simmering them together. Employing the one-pot cooking method facilitated the task of cooking for and feeding a huge family. But because of the variable texture, color, and flavor of each individual item, I prefer to cook them separately. This prevents the undercooking of some items and the over-cooking of others. The vegetables in the *serenata* combine to form a melodic combination of fresh, earthy, and sometimes subtle flavors. If not all the vegetables that I suggest are available to you, don't be afraid to cook up those that you do have. We used to have a version of *serenata* when we went to an informal *come y vete* ("eat and go") restaurant near Old San Juan. This place served a delectable, juicy, and spit-roasted chicken with a dish of mixed tubers on the side. It became one of our favorite eating spots.

6 *green bananas, cooked separately*

3 *yautías, cut in half*

1 *medium malanga, peeled and cut into 6 sections*

2 medium yucas, peeled and cut into thirds

1½ pounds ñame, peeled and cut into 6 sections

  2 yellow plantains, skin intact and each cut into 3 sections

  3 small sweet potatoes, scrubbed clean, skin intact, and cut into halves

  1 breadfruit, peeled, cored, and cut into 6 wedges

1½ pounds of calabaza (squash), skin intact and cut into 6 pieces

1. Follow preparation and cooking instructions for each of the *viandas* that you have.
   A *serenata* does not need to contain every one of these items.

SERVING SUGGESTIONS: It is delectable served with a garlic sauce (see *Salsa de Ajo* recipe on page 295). We serve this dish alongside Stewed Codfish (*Bacalao Gusiado*)—which completes the *Serenata*.

Chayote Gondola

SERVES 6

Pork and other meat-stuffed chayotes are part of the typical Puerto Rican kitchen. But I have created the following dish to please some of my vegetarian friends. Chayotes are in abundance during late fall. They are inexpensive and easy to prepare.

Preheat oven to 375°

  4 large chayotes

½ cup fresh diced carrots

½ cup fresh sweet peas

⅓ cup diced red bell pepper

⅓ cup sliced mushrooms

  1 cup grated cheddar cheese (mild)

  1 tablespoon olive oil

1 tablespoon butter

2 tablespoons lime juice

2 teaspoons sliced shallots

2 garlic cloves, minced

2 teaspoons chopped fresh parsley

1/4 teaspoon pulverized rock salt

1/8 teaspoon cayenne pepper

1/2 cup fresh whole wheat bread crumbs

2 teaspoons chopped fresh oregano

1/4 teaspoon chopped sage

1/4 teaspoon chopped rosemary

1. Cut chayotes in half (the long way), then place the portions in a stockpot, skin side down. Add water to approximately 2 inches above the chayotes. Add a pinch of salt and bring water to a quick boil. Cover the pot, lower the heat, and simmer for 30 minutes.

2. Drain the water and transfer chayotes to a sheet pan. Soak a clean kitchen towel in ice cold water, wring out, and place the dampened towel over the chayote. Once the chayotes are cool to the touch, carefully carve out the center core and discard. Very carefully, so as not to damage the skin (hold the knife at an angle) slide the paring knife between the shell (approximately 1/8-inch from the base) and the inside flesh, and run the knife all the way around. Then run a spoon, in carving fashion, straight down the center to finish separating the flesh from the shell. Do the same with the other shells. Arrange the empty shells on a well-buttered, glazed baking pan skin side down.

3. Dice the flesh and place in a mixing bowl. Fold in the carrots, peas, pepper, mushrooms, and half the cheddar cheese (reserve the rest). Set aside.

4. In a preheated skillet combine olive oil, butter, lime juice, shallots, garlic, parsley, salt, and cayenne pepper. Sauté lightly. Remove from heat. Using a rubber spatula or wooden spoon, fold mixture into the vegetables.

5. Divide the mixed vegetables into equal parts and spoon into the shells. Pack tightly. Divide the reserved grated cheese into equal parts and layer on the tops. Combine and mix the bread crumbs, oregano, sage, and rosemary. Sprinkle all the bread crumbs on top of the cheese layer. Place in preheated oven for 15 minutes, or until molten cheese starts to trickle down from the top and sides. Serve on the side to balance any meal or as a main vegetarian dish.

(To make fresh bread crumbs freeze 8 to 10 slices of fresh whole wheat bread and mince while still frozen, then add the herbs, and sprinkle before totally thawing out.)

SQUASH
Calabaza

Calabaza, Spanish for gourd, grows on trees and its uses range from musical instruments to liquid containers and eating utensils. Some gourds were also exploited for their medicinal properties.

However, the eating variety of the *calabaza* grows on vines, and is a squash, but has always been called a *calabaza* because of its gourd-like characteristics (hard outer skin and hollow center). This vegetable is very delicate and flavorful when cooked, and handles well whether boiled, baked, broiled, fried, or grilled. The *calabaza* is probably the number one natural thickening agent in most brothy dishes, and can also act as the base for superb desserts.

Puerto Rican *calabazas* are very light, and are not generally available in the United States. When none are available, the banana squash or the butternut squash are excellent substitutes.

To prepare: simply slice and core, remove the seeds and loose fibers. Then cut into 3-inch cubes. Arrange portions with skin side down in a kettle, and add water to approximately 2 inches above the squash portions. Cover and simmer for approximately 15 minutes. To test for doneness, insert a fork down the center of a cube. It should feel like piercing soft butter. Remove from skillet very carefully (use a flat spatula or a slotted vegetable spoon), and transfer to a dry container. Then proceed with instructions as per individual recipe calling for cooked squash.

Squash Pudding
Budín de Calabaza

SERVES 6 TO 8

Preheat oven to 375°

1/2 pound peeled squash

4 cups water

2 sticks of cinnamon

1/2 ounce fresh gingerroot, peeled

3 spice cloves

2 cups diced french bread (1/2-inch cubes)

1/3 cup raisins

1/4 teaspoon grated lemon peel

1/8 teaspoon cayenne pepper

1 tablespoon melted butter

3 whole eggs

1 tablespoon light brown sugar

1/3 cup coconut milk

1. Dice the squash into 1-inch cubes. Set aside.

2. Combine water, cinnamon, ginger, and cloves in a stockpot, bring to a quick boil, lower heat and add the diced squash. Cover the pot and simmer for 10 minutes or until squash is tender.

3. Strain the liquid. Remove the spices and transfer the cubes to a mixing bowl, and coarsely mash the squash. Set aside. In a separate bowl, incorporate (using your hands) the diced bread, raisins, lemon peel, cayenne pepper, and butter. Set aside.

4. In a blender on low speed, cream eggs with sugar. While the blender is still running, add the coconut milk and blend for 30 seconds. Add the cream into the bread and whip to form a batter. Then incorporate the mashed squash. Pour the batter into a well-greased round cake pan.

5. Place a deep baking pan in the oven, large enough to accommodate the cake pan containing the pudding. Place the cake pan inside the deep baking pan and add enough hot water to come halfway up sides of the cake pan. Bake in a preheated 375° oven for 1 hour. Remove from oven and allow to cool for a few minutes. Cut into wedges.

Baked Squash

SERVES 4

Preheat oven to 350°

    8 *cubes of cooked squash*
    4 *tablespoons light brown sugar*
  $1/2$ *teaspoon ground ginger*
    2 *teaspoons ground cinnamon*
  $1/2$ *teaspoon ground nutmeg*
    1 *tablespoon brandy*
  $1/2$ *cup melted butter*

1. Arrange the squash cubes in a deep baking pan side by side. Combine and mix, sugar, ginger, cinnamon, and nutmeg. Divide the mixture into 8 equal parts, and pat each squash cube with the mixture.

2. Combine and blend brandy and melted butter. Drizzle (use a pastry brush) over the entire surface of the sugar-coated squash cubes.

3. Place in preheated oven for 40 minutes. Remove from oven and serve piping hot. Use a spatula to serve portions, two portions per serving.

SERVING SUGGESTIONS: Serve along with any white meat dish or fowl.

CORN
Maiz

Corn, it seems, has been around since the beginning of time. It has always occupied a significant part of the basic diet of my family. My mother would frequently surprise us with a new dish where corn was the primary ingredient.

For breakfast, we always had a choice of hot corn bread, corn bread sticks (*surullos*), corn fritters, coconut corn pie, hot corn meal punch, or sweet corn chowder.

For dinner we had *guanimes*, corn "tamales," served with stewed codfish on the side; *funche*, seasoned cornmeal (*polenta*), served with stewed beans on the side; or *marota*, an island of *funche* immersed in a flavorful fish or chicken broth. Whether it was in a dough, batter, kernels, or on the cob, fried, boiled, baked, or broiled, corn would always find its way into one of our daily meals.

My mother always planted seven rows of corn, and each separate row was dedicated to her particular spiritual deity and spiritual guides. During the time when the corn was ready for picking, we would build a *fogata* (sacred fire) made from dry fruit branches, wear our seven strings of beads, and throw the first seven ears of corn into the fire as part of an offering to the deities. Then we would pick and shuck the corn, make gift packages, and share it with family and friends.

The number of cooked corn dishes are infinite. I have limited myself here to the ways that my family and I enjoy cooking and eating corn at home.

Corn on the Cob
Poached in Coconut Milk

SERVES 4

2   *cups water*

4   *cinnamon sticks*

4   *spice cloves*

2   *tablespoons light brown sugar*

1   *cup coconut milk*

2   *tablespoons cornstarch*

4   *ears of corn, cut in halves*

1. Combine water, cinnamon sticks, cloves, and sugar in a saucepan. Bring to a quick boil. Lower the heat and allow to simmer for 10 minutes, strain stock into a soup pot. Place pot in a double boiler over medium heat.

2. Dissolve the cornstarch in the coconut milk, making sure there are no lumps. Add the coconut milk (stirring slowly) into the spice stock, until a light cream is achieved. Add the corn and rotate to coat on all sides. Cover and let simmer for approximately 6 to 8 minutes.

SERVING SUGGESTIONS: Serve hot as a vegetable, side dish or snack.

VARIATIONS: To make sweeter, pungent, or spicy hot, add more sugar or sprinkle with ginger or cayenne pepper.

Corn Confetti
Papelillos

SERVES 4

This dish was prepared to salvage irregular corn that either did not mature or was blemished in places. The inedible portions would be cut away and discarded while the salvaged pieces would be used for stews, soups, or combined with other ingredients to form salads and mixed vegetables dishes. One of my favorites was the *papelillo*, which translates into flyers (leaflets). The *papelillo* was an instant mass media communication tool used to disseminate information. (What was then called propaganda.) It was a thrill for us to see the planes and blimps drop their payload, which momentarily covered the sky, blocking the sunlight with torrential paper rain. Everyone would scramble onto the open areas hoping to snatch a flyer before it touched the ground.

One day my mother was foraging in the patio, and when I asked her what we were having for dinner, she replied *papelillo*. (I thought I heard her say *pastelillos*). Up until that time, we had no name for the following dish. I have, of course, modified it in name and ingredients but not in spirit. The essence is still there.

2 *cups clear chicken stock*
16 *baby corn ears*
16 *snow peas (clip the ends)*
4 *baby carrots*
1 *tablespoon olive oil*
1 *tablespoon butter*
1 *tablespoon sliced shallots*
1 *teaspoon white wine vinegar*
1/3 *cup sliced almonds*
1 *tablespoon raisins*
2 *teaspoons capers*
2 *tablespoons diced red bell pepper*
2 *tablespoons diced bell pepper*
1/3 *cup dry sherry*

1. Bring the chicken stock to a quick boil and remove from heat. Add the corn, peas, and carrots. Cover and set aside. In a deep preheated skillet over low-to-medium heat, add olive oil, butter, shallots, and vinegar. Sauté lightly. Add the almond and raisins, and sauté for 1 minute more. Fold in capers and diced peppers. Deglaze skillet with dry sherry. Sweep mixture into a pile to one side of the skillet. Then, using a slotted vegetable spoon, transfer vegetables from stockpot to skillet. Spread the almond-raisin mixture over the vegetables and rock the skillet to distribute the moisture; drizzle some chicken stock over the vegetables if needed. Serve piping hot.

Char Broiled Corn on the Cob
Maiz al Carbón

Peel back the entire mass of husk to expose the kernels, remove the silk strands, coat the whole corn with Garlic Sauce (see the "Sauces" chapter). Pull the skin forward to seal the corn. Place the cob over hot coals, rotating every few minutes until most of the outer skin is burned away and the corn is slightly charred inside.

SERVING SUGGESTIONS: Serve as is or baste with barbecue sauce.

Corn Guanimes

Guanimes de Maíz

SERVES 4

Guanimes are corn pies that look somewhat like Mexican tamales, fashioned out of a seasoned corn mash batter, wrapped in banana leaves, and boiled. Due to the labor-intensive aspect of this original home version, which entails grating the fresh corn and processing the mash to make a dough-like batter, I have substituted, in the interest of time and practicality, commercially packaged cornmeal for fresh corn to render a contemporary version of this wonderful dish.

In the case where there are no banana leaves available, cooking parchment, lined with green wilted cabbage leaves, will do the job as well. Submerge the outer cabbage leaves in hot water for 30 seconds, pat dry and press down to flatten.

2	*cups yellow cornmeal*
2¹/₂	*cups clear stock (fish head or chicken)*
4	*tablespoons olive oil*
1	*teaspoon garlic paste*
¹/₄	*teaspoon ground oregano*
¹/₄	*teaspoon ground cumin*
¹/₄	*teaspoon ground coriander*
1¹/₂	*teaspoons paprika*
¹/₈	*teaspoon cayenne pepper*
¹/₄	*teaspoon pulverized rock salt*
1	*cup coconut milk*
8	*banana leaf wraps, 8 by 10 inches*
8	*cooking parchments, 10 by 12 inches*
8	*strands of cooking string, 24 inches each*

1. In a mixing bowl, combine and mix the corn meal and clear stock to form a batter. Set aside until the liquid has been totally absorbed by the corn meal.

2. In a preheated kettle over low heat, combine 3 tablespoons olive oil (reserve the rest), garlic paste, oregano, cumin, coriander, paprika, and salt, stir to blend. Then incorporate the cornmeal batter, stir until the batter starts to become stiff. Remove from direct heat. Stir in the coconut milk and continue to stir to eliminate any lumps. Batter should be thick, moist, and spreadable (not dry or lumpy).

3. Lay out a sheet of cooking parchment, then lay out a sheet of banana leaf wrap on top of the parchment (if available). Using a pastry brush, apply a light surface coat of reserved olive oil to wrapper, then scoop out $1/2$ cup of batter onto the center of the wrapper. Using a spatula, spread the batter in pancake fashion approximately 4 inches in diameter.

4. Fold the wrapper by holding between your thumbs and forefingers the two corners closest to you and folding over to align the edges. Hold the wrapper with one hand while using the cutting edge of your other hand to pack the center. Make another horizontal fold in a handkerchief-like fashion. Make a crease on the left side and fold the left flap in. Make a crease on the right side and fold the right flap in. Then secure the package by tying with cooking string.

5. Fill a stockpot with 8 quarts of water, bring water to a quick boil, then lower heat. Carefully, one by one, place the *guanimes* into the pot. Cook for 1 hour.

6. To serve: place one *guanime* on a serving plate. Using a knife or kitchen shears, cut away the cord and remove *guanime* from paper wrap.

SERVING SUGGESTIONS: Serve with Stewed Codfish (see *Bacalao Guisado* recipe on page 269).

BREADFRUIT
Mapén

Breadfruit is one of those delicate and delicious, typically misunderstood and underestimated, exotic fruits that are eaten like vegetables, and that can produce wonders in anyone's kitchen. It is a very fragile fruit and will not wait long to be consumed. Once it is cut down from its tree, it will ripen and ferment quickly, going from starch to sugar to alcohol in a couple of days. To preserve it, I recommend peeling, coring, and slicing, and placing it in a plastic bag for freezing. For desserts, the best time to use it is when the sugar level is at its peak. That's when the outer skin becomes resilient. It does everything the potato does and goes one step beyond, becoming a possible dessert. I have included a recipe for *Flan de Mapén* (Breadfruit Flan) in the Desserts chapter of this book.

The breadfruit is round, approximately 5 to 8 inches in diameter, with a green, rough-textured outer skin. It slightly resembles a cantaloupe. It does not look like bread when it is hanging from a high branch of the breadfruit tree, but rather the flesh resembles bread after it has been baked. Breadfruits have their origin in Ceylon, Polynesia, and Africa. Supposedly, they were brought to the Caribbean by Captain Bligh in 1792. In Puerto Rico, we have two varieties of breadfruit: the *mapén*, which yields the breadlike flesh, and the *panapén*, which produces *pepitas de pana* (the seed of the breadfruit or chestnuts).

Although I have not seen breadfruit on the west coast, we do get glimpses of the fruit on the east coast—mainly in New York City and Florida, during the winter months. Chestnuts, however, are widely available for roasting.

To peel the breadfruit: first slice off the stem at the base to make it flat. Then cut into wedges, 3 inches thick. Remove the pulp and seeds (run the paring knife under the base of the pulp to slice it off). Discard the pulp and peel each wedge. To cook, submerge the wedges in a pot with water, add a pinch of salt, bring to a boil, and then simmer for approximately 20 minutes. Handle the same as *yautía*. Use in recipes calling for boiled (cooked) breadfruit.

Breadfruit Stuffing

Preheat oven to 350°

1	cooked breadfruit
1/3	cup brandy
1/3	cup raisins
1/3	cup olive oil
6	minced garlic cloves
1/2	cup chopped green onions
1/3	cup chopped celery
1/3	cup chopped green peppers
2	teaspoons chopped fresh sage
1	teaspoon chopped fresh oregano
1	teaspoon chopped fresh thyme
1	teaspoon pulverized rock salt
1/4	teaspoon cayenne pepper
1/3	cup sliced almonds
8	broiled bacon strips
3	broiled sausages

1. Spread the cooked breadfruit wedges in a bowl. Using a dough cutter, coarsely mash the breadfruit. Set aside.

2. Combine raisins and brandy in a bowl, and allow the raisins to soak until they become puffy.

3. In a preheated skillet, combine the olive oil, garlic, onions, celery, green pepper, oregano, thyme, salt, cayenne pepper, and almonds. Sauté for 2 minutes. Remove from heat and fold into the mashed breadfruit.

4. Chop the bacon strips and thinly slice the sausages. Fold into the breadfruit. Fold in the brandy-soaked raisins, including the liquid.

5. Using a 2-ounce ice cream scoop, scoop stuffing onto a baking pan. Cover with foil and bake at 350° for 30 minutes. Remove from oven and serve on the side.

6. For stuffing fowl, pork chops and other meats, assemble the stuffing balls on the plate and place meat directly on top. Or stuff the fowl immediately after folding all the ingredients together, then bake according to instructions.

Breadfruit Tostones

Preheat oven to 375°

1 *breadfruit*
10 *garlic cloves, peeled*
1 *teaspoon rock salt crystals*
2/3 *cup olive oil*

1. Peel and core the breadfruit and divide into wedges. Then divide the wedges into cubes approximately 2-inches long and spread onto a baking sheet.

2. Combine the garlic and salt crystals into a mortar and pound to a paste consistency. Add the olive oil. Using a pastry brush, coat all the breadfruit cubes on all sides (including the baking sheet).

3. Place inside a preheated oven for approximately 20 minutes, then remove from oven. Place the sheet pan on top of a flat surface and with a potato masher, press down (halfway) on each cube to flatten. Brush another coat of garlic-infused oil and return to oven for another 10 minutes.

4. To serve: Remove to serving platter and serve hot alongside any meat dish, soup or salad.

PLANTAINS
Plátanos

Although the *plátano* is related to the banana, the size, color, texture, and starchy characteristic puts the *plátano* into a league of its own. The common banana goes through two quick stages of change: green and ripe. This limits the potential use of the banana in a hot medium. The *plátano*, however, starts from the green stage, and every stage of the ripening process allows the cook to employ different mediums to exploit the *plátano's* unique variety of texture and flavor. It can be simply boiled, or be part of a complex dish like *Mofongo al Pilón*. The *plátano*, once a food staple for the Arawaks, Caribs, and Tainos over 500 years ago, is still a very important food source and trading commodity, and enriches the economic base for many Latin American and Caribbean countries.

Plantains are a familiar sight and can be purchased at most large supermarket chains in the United States. Unlike the banana bunch, the *plátanos* are displayed and sold individually (by the pound). Unless one has an immediate need to serve a ripe *plátano* dish, the ideal ones to purchase are the green variety, which can then ripen at home. During the ripening process, plantains go from very green to soft yellow, then a dark orange yellow, and finally a deep brown or black.

When the *plátano* is on the green side, the outer skin is firm and crisp, and the inner flesh is solid, with a bone-colored velvety texture, starchy, and not sweet, and with a high content of staining resin. (During the Forties and Fifties when immigration from The Island to the mainland was most prevalent, the popular phrase to indicate a newcomer was to say that he or she "still has the stain of the *plátano*.")

As it moves from green to yellow, the high content of resin disappears, the starch diminishes, the sugar gets progressively higher, and the texture of the inner flesh becomes silky and resilient with an intense yellow, almost orange color.

Each stage provides the *plátano* with a new identity, i.e. *verde* (green), *amarillo* (yellow), and *maduro* (ripe), and each identity will determine the way in which the *plátano* is to be used. I have limited myself to presenting at least one sample of each category as a starting point for becoming familiar with the versatile vegetable.

Basic Steps for Peeling a Plátano Verde (Green Plantain)

1. First cut the tip at both ends, then holding the plantain in the left hand, insert the tip of a paring knife to pierce the skin approximately ⅛ inch deep.

2. Carefully, and with an even stroke, slide the tip of the knife down to make a superficial incision from end to end. Then give the plantain a ⅓ rotation to the right, and make another incision. Repeat the action (another rotation and another incision).

3. To separate the outer skin, hold the plantain in front of you, then insert and position the tip of the blade on the bottom end of the first incision. Then holding the blade at approximately a 45 degree angle, press outward to the right following the motion upward, prying the skin open until the skin becomes detached from the flesh of the plantain.

4. Once the plantain is peeled, carefully scrape off the green fibers that may still be attached to the flesh. Place the plantains in a bowl, cover with water, and add a teaspoon of salt. The salt water solution will neutralize the resin and heavy starch content, and will render a lighter cooked product. Refrigerate and use according to recipe. Plantains can stay in water for a couple of days.

Initially, the task may seem like a project, but after the first experience you will have developed the dexterity necessary to peel *plátanos* the same way Caribbean natives have been doing for over 500 years.

Basic Steps for Peeling an Amarillo (Yellow Plantain)

1. Simply cut the tips off at both ends and make one straight incision, then with the tip of your thumb, pry the skin back and the flesh will pop out.

2. Do not place in water for more than 10 minutes.

Basic Steps for Peeling Maduros
(Ripe Black Plantains)

1. The skin will be very thin and stick to the delicate mass. To peel: very carefully cut off the tips and make a very light incision, then remove the skin with the tips of your fingers. Should the skin become stubbornly attached in certain spots use the tip of the knife and slice off the tissue, then continue to separate the skin. The *maduros* will be very moist and sweet. Once peeled, set aside and use according to recipe instructions.

2. To keep from falling apart, do not submerge the *maduros* in water, and handle as little as possible.

Simmered Plantains
SERVES 6

The green plantain's versatile characteristics and reliability make it the most favored vegetable in the Puerto Rican kitchen. It is inexpensive, nutritious, and easy to prepare. The three most convenient ways to use them are in *tostones* (fried chips), *mofongo* (fried and pounded in a mortar), and *herbido* (boiled). Each of these processes serve to balance a main course, entrée, soup, salad, or brothy dish (*asopaos*).

In the following recipes, I use the simmered *plátano* as a main dish and also as a start-up base for dishes which have been traditionally deep-fat fried.

> 3 green plantains, peeled (see method)
> 1 teaspoon crushed rock salt
> 4 quarts of water

1. Cut peeled plantains in half through the middle. Then cut the halves lengthwise.

2. Put all the portions into a stockpot with water and add salt. Place pot over high heat, bring to a quick boil, lower heat to medium, and simmer the plantain slices for approximately 25 minutes or until cooked tender. (When done, the plantain

will change to a mustard color.) Test for tenderness by inserting a fork into the center of the thickest part; it should slide in with little or no effort.

3. When done, remove from heat. To serve: use a set of round-tipped tongs or a slotted vegetable spoon carefully, so as not to break the plantain slices, and remove them from the pot. Serve steaming hot and sprinkle garlic *Mojo* on top. It is a superb boat for all sauces, gravies, and natural meat juices, and can be served with any meat or seafood. It's wonderful with crab dishes and any type of salad.

4. To obtain a delightfully integrated dish, the *plátanos* should be arranged to form an open circle or assembled in symmetrical patterns and the entrée (*mestura*) should be placed in the center of the plate and spill over the sides of the plantains.

SERVING SUGGESTIONS: My favorite accompanying dishes are Stewed Codfish and Avocado Salad.

Tostones

SERVES 4

Tostones are quite common throughout the Caribbean, and can best be described as the Puerto Rican counterpart of French fries. But they are not to be confused with the commercially packaged variety sold in cellophane bags called plantain chips (*platanutres*). Although both are required to be deep-fried, the difference is comparable to that of French fried potatoes and potato chips.

Tostones are traditionally cooked on the spot and served immediately as an accompaniment to most hot or cold dishes, substituting for rice, bread, or potatoes. Traditionally, they are partially cooked in hot, deep fat or oil, then placed in between two layers of the plantain skin and flattened. Then they are submerged in a solution of salted water and re-dipped into the hot grease to complete the cooking cycle. The result is a superb plantain chip, crisp on the outside with a creamy and chewy texture on the inside—like a perfect cookie. However, in my attempt to eliminate the excessive grease from deep frying, I have modified the traditional method by using my technique of boiling and broiling. The end result is delicious and healthy.

3 *green plantains*

3 *quarts of water*

2 *teaspoons crushed rock salt*

4 *tablespoons garlic sauce (see recipe for Garlic Sauce, page 295)*

1. Peel the plantains (save the skin). Place the plantains on a flat surface with the arched side of the plantain facing left. Hold them in to prevent from sliding off and, using an all purpose kitchen knife, cut ¾-inch thick diagonal slices. You do this by positioning the edge of the knife at the corner tip of the plantain and pressing downward. Always reposition the knife to obtain uniform slices. One plantain will usually yield six to seven slices.

2. Place the slices in a colander and rinse under cool running water. Then transfer to a stockpot with the water. Add salt and place pot over high heat. Bring to a quick boil, reset the heat to low, simmer until the slices are done, approximately 15 minutes or when soft in the center. Test by inserting a fork. When done, carefully drain the water and keep covered. Have standing by, the plantain skins, the garlic sauce, and an olive-oil glazed sheet pan (for broiling).

3. The skins are used to flatten the cooked slices. You need one skin for the bottom and one for the top. Using a pastry brush, apply a light coat of olive oil to the inside of each skin to be used. Place one plantain slice in the center of the bottom skin, then place the second skin on top of that slice, making a sandwich. With the heel of your palm on the spot where the slice is located, carefully flatten down with an even steady pressure.

4. Once flattened, remove from skins. Arrange on sheet pan. Repeat steps until the batch has been completed.

5. Dip a pastry brush in the garlic sauce and coat the *tostones*. Place the sheet pan under the broiler until *tostones* start to sizzle, then remove from broiler. Using a spatula, flip the *tostones*, coat with garlic sauce, and place back under the broiler for another minute. Remove from broiler, apply another coat of garlic sauce, and serve hot.

SERVING SUGGESTIONS: Serve as a side dish for all seafood, meat, and poultry dishes, soups and salads, and as a party treat with your favorite dip.

Mofongo al Pilón

SERVES 4

There is no better way to serve and enjoy *mofongo* other than the traditional one straight from the *pilón*. The *pilón* is the mortar, and the mortar is used in this delightful plantain dish as a preparing and serving medium. What makes it exciting is the quick rush of intense aromas that come up through the center and engulf the senses, exceeded only by the burst of flavors that entice the palate.

The classic Puerto Rican way of cooking *mofongo* is to deep fry the plantain, usually in melted pork fat obtained from the *empella* (the pure fat deposits from the loin of the pork). The residue of crispy fried pieces that are left over once the fat has been melted down, are then incorporated with the plantain and the herbs and spices in the belly of the mortar, and blended by pounding. Then the *mofongo* is made into a ball and served directly in the mortar with fried meat and/or broth on the side.

Many household kitchens may not be equipped with more than one mortar and pestle, if any. Therefore, I suggest the use of banana leaf wrappers as an alternate method. The wrap of the banana leaves will seal the heat and contain the *mofongo* in its natural cloth, preventing the loss of moisture, flavors, and aromas of the herbs and spices, while at the same time intensifying the essence of the plantain. The *mofongo* should be served piping hot.

> 4 *simmered green plantains (see page 211)*
> 3/4 *cup Garlic Sauce (see page 295)*
> 1 *hot red chili pepper (fresh or dry), chopped*
> 1/4 *teaspoon sage*
> 1/2 *teaspoon fresh mint, chopped*
> 2 *teaspoons fresh cilantro, chopped*
> 8 *broiled chopped bacon slices*
> 4 *processed banana leaves (see "Tools, Techniques, & Ingredients" chapter)*
> 4 *strands of kitchen cord, 12 inches each*

1. To prepare the *mofongo*, lay out the sliced, simmered plantains on a cookie sheet. Using a pastry or basting brush dipped in the garlic *mojo*, apply a light coat over

the slices, then place the cookie sheet under the broiler until plantains are slightly charred. Remove from broiler, flip the plantains and repeat the movement. Once slightly charred on both sides, remove from the broiler and reset the oven to warm.

2. To the *Mojo* Sauce, add the chopped chili pepper, sage, mint, and cilantro, and blend with a fork.

3. Place in the mortar 2 pieces of plantain, sprinkle in 1 teaspoon of Garlic Sauce, 1/2-teaspoon of chopped bacon and mash down with the pestle. Add 2 more slices of plantain, 1 teaspoon of *Mojo* Sauce and 1/2-teaspoon of chopped bacon and mash down until the ingredients have fused to form a tight ball inside the mortar. Slide a butter knife around the inside edge to pry loose the *mofongo*, then turn the mortar upside down on top of a banana leaf and tap the side of the mortar to release the *mofongo* ball. It should drop nicely onto the banana leaf. Sprinkle approximately 1/2-teaspoon of *Mojo* Sauce on top of the *mofongo*, then using both hands collect all the flaps of the banana leaf to form a neck. Slowly twist with a wringing motion (carefully so as not to tear the leaf) until the shape of the ball appears outlined against the leaf. Keep the wrap tight and secure it with a piece of kitchen cord.

4. Line a deep pan with approximately 1/4 inch of hot water. Place the wrapped *mofongo* in the pan and place the pan into the oven. This method will keep the *mofongo* steaming hot until ready to serve.

5. Make sure that there are no flaws on the banana wrappers. Should there be a flaw, wrap a sheet of aluminum foil around the banana wrapper and proceed with instructions.

6. Repeat the process. Work with speed.

7. Once completed, the *mofongo* can be served as a side dish. Allow the guest to open the wrap at the dinner table and relive the culinary experience of the ancient Taínos.

SERVING SUGGESTIONS: Serve as appetizer or main course with any meat, poultry, or seafood. Serve with broth and salads.

VARIATIONS: Can also be fashioned into meatballs and served as canapés. Keep covered to prevent from drying out, and maintain hot in a double boiler.

Plantain Puffs
Bolitas de Plátano

MAKES 12 PLANTAIN PUFFS

Bolitas de Plátano are integrated in soups and stews for added texture, flavor, and as a light thickening agent. They are most commonly used in pigeon pea (*gandules*) dishes, especially *Gandules Guisados*. Although they may require a bit of extra work, the end result will make your effort worthwhile. They are also an excellent item at a vegetarian's table as a substitute for meatballs.

2   *peeled green plantains*
1   *teaspoon crushed rock salt*
6   *garlic cloves, pounded to a paste*
1/4   *teaspoon cayenne pepper*
1/4   *teaspoon ground cumin*
1/2   *teaspoon paprika*

1. Place the peeled, whole plantains in a bowl with 1 quart of water. Add salt and soak for approximately 30 minutes. Strain the water.

2. Using a hand grater on the smooth-textured side, grate the plantain into a flat pan to catch the meal. Make a mound with the meal and add the garlic paste, then sprinkle the cayenne pepper, cumin, and paprika. Mix well using a wooden spoon. Shape dough into a 2-inch thick cylinder and divide into 12 equal portions. Shape each portion into a tight ball, and set aside to be used as per recipe.

3. The puffs will always be added last. Bring the liquid to a quick boil, reset to simmer, then add the puffs. To keep the puffs from breaking or falling apart, handle each puff with a spoon.

Green Plantain Croutons

SERVES 6

One of the best things that ever happened to leftover bread was croutons. And the best thing that happened to croutons is that we can make them out of green plantains. At home we had garlic soup that my mother called Bread Soup. Although the dish is an excellent one, the pieces of bread croutons ultimately suffer a textural breakdown, becoming soggy and sponge-like, with scattered flakes floating to the top of the bowl, immensely detracting from appetizing eye appeal.

I realized that I wanted to enjoy my garlic soup differently, so after experimenting with different bread textures and seasonings without much success, I decided I needed an alternative to the bread croutons. We already had the *mofongo*, so it was just a matter of coming up with a new cooking method to use the plantain as a bread substitute in the garlic soup.

The size of the crouton squares will be determined by the function of the croutons. For broth, I prefer sections the size of the bottom of the bowl. For consommés, 1/2-inch squares. For salads, I like 1-inch squares assembled, leaning on the side of the bowl or coarsely crumbled for texture toppings in lieu of bacon crisps.

Preheat oven to 375°

2	*simmered green plantains*
1	*tablespoon soft butter*
6	*garlic cloves, peeled*
1	*teaspoon pulverized rock salt*
1/4	*teaspoon black peppercorns*
1/4	*teaspoon ground cumin*
1	*sprig fresh thyme*
1	*sprig fresh sage*
1	*sprig fresh dill*
1	*teaspoon paprika*
1	*tablespoon olive oil*
1	*raw egg beaten*
2	*tablespoons flour*

1. Simmer the plantains until they are very soft in the center, strain the water, add the butter. Proceed to mash coarsely with a potato masher (do not whip). Cover and set aside.

2. In the belly of a mortar combine and pound to a paste, the garlic cloves, salt, peppercorns, cumin, thyme, sage, dill, and paprika. Then break down with olive oil. Stir to mix, using a spoon to incorporate the beaten egg.

3. Pour the sauce over the mashed plantains and blend. Sprinkle the flour on top and mix well. Spread the dough onto a glazed cookie sheet and mold into a tight square, approximately ¼-inch thick. Smooth the top by sliding a spatula across the surface as though applying frosting on a cake.

4. Place the sheet pan in a preheated oven for 35 minutes. Remove from oven and gently rock the pan back and forth, then slide the *torta* onto a cutting board. The *torta* should be able to slide off with no problem. If the *torta* sticks, pry it loose by sliding a spatula along the bottom. Then using a long sharp blade, divide the *torta* into squares.

VARIATIONS: As in most of my recipes, the suggested amounts of condiments are a comfortable starting point which can be intensified or made more complex by increasing the measurement of the particular herb or spice to be highlighted. However, the modification must take place in the blending (fusing) phase of the ingredients (mortar or food processor).

Sweet Ripened Plantains
Maduros

Maduros, or sweet ripened plantains, are the last phase of the plantain's ripening process. The color of the outer skin turns black and the flesh inside a deep yellowish-orange, and the moisture, acid, and sugar content are at their highest level. The plantain has become very delicate and somewhat fragile at this point. In the following methods of cooking, we take advantage of the natural fruit structure of the plantain and employ it in simple, delicious side dishes to accompany most courses at mealtime.

Grilled Maduros

Due to the delicate nature of the *maduros*, the cooking time is very short (approximately 1 minute on each side). Therefore, I recommend cooking one plantain at a time (six or seven slices). The amount of ingredients that I suggest is for one serving and should be multiplied by the quantity of the plantains to be prepared.

1 *sweet ripened plantain*
1 *tablespoon melted butter*
$^1/_8$ *teaspoon ground nutmeg*
$^1/_2$ *teaspoon ground cinnamon*

1. Gently peel the plantain by cutting off the tips and making a light incision down the center, and pry the skin back. Do not lift the flesh, let it rest in the skin.

2. Cut diagonal slices approximately 1½-inch thick. Preheat a skillet on low-to-medium heat. Spread clarified butter on the skillet. Arrange the plantain slices in the skillet. Combine nutmeg and cinnamon. Sprinkle on top of each slice and sauté approximately 1 minute. Turn and sprinkle the remainder of the mixture on top of the slices. Continue to sauté for another minute or until a golden brown color is achieved on both sides. The texture should be crisp and slightly charred.

SERVING SUGGESTIONS: Serve hot. Great for breakfast with ham and eggs. And as a side dish with any meal.

Broiled Whole Maduros

4 *sweet ripened plantains*
2 *tablespoons soft butter*
1 *tablespoon brown sugar*
1/4 *teaspoon ground ginger*
1/4 *teaspoon ground nutmeg*
1 *tablespoon lime juice*

1. Peel off outer skin and arrange on a broiling pan, leaving approximately 1/2-inch between each plantain. Score each one and set aside.

2. In a bowl, combine and blend soft butter, sugar, ginger, and nutmeg. Break down with lime juice. Using a pastry brush, coat all the plantains.

3. Place under broiler for approximately 2 minutes on each side or until all sides are golden brown and slightly charred. Remove from broiler and arrange on a serving platter. Garnish, and serve hot.

SERVING SUGGESTIONS: Excellent with any chicken or pork dish.

VARIATIONS: Outdoor grilling: Make one incision on the outer skin, push the skin back, and score the flesh. Brush the sauce on, close the skin, and place the whole plantain on top of the grill. Rotate sides to obtain uniform cooking. Serve on the charred skin or transfer to banana leaves (if available).

Foil cooking: Substitute the outer skin with a sheet of aluminum foil, seal tightly, and place in a well of hot coals for approximately 10 minutes. Use tongs to retrieve the *maduro*-packed foil, allow to cool off, then serve as is. Exercise caution when opening the wrap as it may contain pressurized hot vapors.

Whole Maduros in Orange Brandy Sauce

SERVES 4

4 peeled, sweet ripened plantains

3 tablespoons melted butter

1/2 teaspoon orange zest

1/2 cup water

4 whole cloves

2 cinnamon sticks

1/2 ounce crushed fresh ginger

4 star anise

2/3 cup fresh orange juice

1/2 cup brown sugar

1/3 cup Spanish brandy

Garnish: orange wheels, mint sprigs

1. Arrange the plantains in a deep skillet, make 3 diagonal line cuts on the surface of each. Coat each with the melted butter, sprinkle the orange zest on top of each. Place the skillet over low heat and allow the plantains to brown slowly on all sides.

2. While they are browning, combine in a saucepan water, cloves, cinnamon sticks, ginger, and star anise. Bring to a quick boil. Lower heat and simmer. Allow to cook down by half. Then remove the ginger, cinnamon, and star anise.

3. Add the orange juice, sugar, and brandy. Bring to a quick boil and simmer until reduced by one-quarter.

4. Add the sauce to the *maduros* and reset the heat to medium. Rock the pan back and forth to ensure proper distribution of the liquid. Cover skillet and continue cooking down by 50 percent, or until the sauce thickens. Remove from heat and transfer to a cool glass pan.

SERVING SUGGESTIONS: Serve on the side with any meal at room temperature or slightly chilled. For a great dessert, top with whipped cream accented with sprinkled cinnamon.

EGGPLANT
Berenjena

Eggplant is another one of those wonderfully universal vegetables that defies gastronomic boundaries. It is both an herb and a fruit; the plant is considered an herb and its fruit is eaten as a vegetable. The eggplant produces the purple fruits which are dressed in the flavors and textures that uniquely represent the specific culture serving it. In the Puerto Rican kitchen, the *berenjena* is traditionally prepared and served with *Bacalao Guisado* (stewed codfish) or *Carne de Cerdo* (pork meat). Both dishes are served along with White Rice and Boiled Green Bananas, or with a combination of tubers.

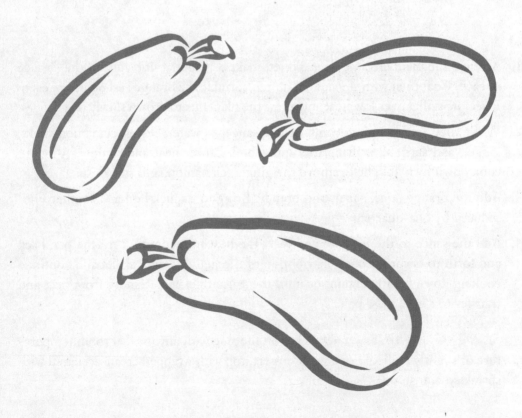

Eggplant with Codfish

Berenjena con Bacalao

SERVES 4

2 medium eggplants
1/2 pound salted codfish
1/3 cup olive oil
8 garlic cloves, minced
1/3 cup diced yellow onions
1/3 cup diced green bell pepper
1/3 cup diced red bell pepper
2 teaspoons fresh chopped oregano (1 teaspoon dry)
1 teaspoon fresh chopped sage (1/2 teaspoon dry)
1/4 teaspoon ground cumin
1/4 tablespoon cracked black peppercorns
1/3 cup dry sherry
2 tablespoons capers
2 cups tomato puree
1 tablespoon chopped fresh cilantro

1. Cut off the base of the stems and peel the eggplants with a vegetable peeler. Cut into cubes approximately 2-inches thick and place in a colander. Cover with a damp kitchen towel and set aside.

2. Cut the codfish into 1-inch squares and place in a stock pot with 3 quarts of water. Bring the codfish to a quick boil, then simmer for 5 minutes. Remove from burner. Holding the colander containing the eggplant over the sink, slowly strain the codfish through the cloth-covered colander. Pick up the cloth with the trapped codfish and twirl it to form a bag. Remove the colander from the sink and set aside.

3. Place the codfish bag under cold running water for 1 minute. Carefully, so as not to break up the codfish, press and twirl the bag to extract most of the moisture, then open the bag and combine the codfish with the eggplant in the colander and set aside.

4. In a preheated deep skillet over low-to-medium heat combine olive oil, garlic, onions, and green and red peppers. Sauté until onions become translucent, stir in oregano, sage, cumin, dry sherry, and capers. Rock the skillet for uniform distribution of the herbs and spices, then add the eggplant and codfish mixture and sauté for 2 minutes.

5. Spread the tomato puree evenly over the eggplant, cover and finish cooking for approximately 12 minutes. Turn once with a spatula for uniform cooking. When done, remove from heat source and sprinkle with fresh chopped cilantro. Serve piping hot.

Eggplant with Goat Cheese and Serrano Ham

Berenjena con Queso de Cabra y Jamón Serrano

SERVES 4 TO 8

There was a time on The Island when home refrigeration and the use of electrical appliances was limited and accessible only to a few, due primarily to the unaffordable cost of the appliances and the lack of generators needed to service most households, especially in rural areas. Perishable items and dairy products were purchased on an "as needed" basis. Most people would make the trip to the plaza or marketplace between four and six A.M. to purchase fresh produce before sunrise.

Early selection of the produce did not always guarantee a spoil-free product if kept out too long on a hot day. Milk was always a problem, and to take advantage of curdled milk, my mother would make *dulce de leche* (milk candy) and house cheese. She would find many uses for the cheese in hot cooked dishes, salads, desserts, spreads, and snacks.

For cooking, she would use goat milk cheese because it had a strong bite, and held up well to her seasonings and condiments. My mother's special goat milk cheese dish was a ham and cheese hot sandwich called *emparedado de papas*. It was made with whole potato slices, wrapped in an egg batter and cooked on a hot wrought iron *plancha* (grill). It was my memory of this dish that inspired me to create the following eggplant dish. Although the *Serrano* ham I use is a Spanish import to The Island, and perhaps unavailable in some parts of the United States, Black Forest ham will work just as well.

1 large eggplant

4 eggs

1/3 cup milk

1/2 cup flour

1/2 cup cracker meal

1/2 teaspoon pulverized rock salt

2 teaspoons paprika

1/4 teaspoon ground black pepper

1 teaspoon garlic powder

1/3 cup olive oil

2 tablespoons melted butter

1 cup tomato puree

1 tablespoon Madeira wine

2 spice cloves

1 teaspoon light brown sugar

2 whole bay leaves

1/3 cup raisins

1/3 cup brandy

6 ounces goat cheese

1/3 cup chopped green onions

1/3 cup chopped red bell peppers

1 teaspoon chopped fresh oregano

1 teaspoon chopped fresh cilantro

1 teaspoon chopped fresh parsley

1/2 teaspoon chopped fresh sage

1/2 teaspoon chopped fresh rosemary

1 tablespoon pine nuts

6 ounces thinly sliced Black Forest ham

16 spinach leaves, washed and patted dry

1. Cut the eggplant into 8 equal wheels. Begin the cut from the widest end of the eggplant to obtain uniform sizing. Carefully butterfly the wheels and set aside.

2. In a large mixing bowl combine eggs and milk and beat with a fork, or wire whisk to form a batter. Refrigerate until ready to use.

3. In a deep pan, combine and mix together: flour, cracker meal, salt, black pepper, paprika, and garlic powder, and set aside. In a deep skillet, combine olive oil and melted butter and set on top of burner, standing by.

4. In a sauce pan, combine tomato puree, Madeira, spice cloves, brown sugar, and bay leaves. Set aside. In a bowl, combine raisins and brandy, and allow to soak until ready to use.

5. In a mixing bowl, combine and fold to incorporate, the goat cheese, green onions, red bell peppers, oregano, cilantro, parsley, sage, rosemary, pine nuts, and brandy soaked raisins.

6. Set up an assembly work area starting with sliced eggplant, cheese mixture, sliced ham, egg batter, and flour cracker meal mixture. To assemble, divide the cheese mixture into 8 equal portions. Place one portion on 2 slices of ham and stuff the package into the inside of the butterflied eggplant slice. Press down slightly to pack. Repeat until all slices are completed.

7. Carefully holding shut the stuffed eggplant, dunk it in the egg batter (let the excess batter drip back into the bowl), then place the "sandwich" in the flour cracker meal mixture and dredge. Make sure that all sides are coated with the powder; shake loose excess powder and place on a wax paper lined sheet pan. Repeat process until batch is completed.

8. Preheat the skillet containing the oil and butter. Using a spatula, slide the breaded eggplant portions into the skillet and bronze on both sides. Remove from skillet and transfer to a baking pan, and cover with foil. Place baking pan in a preheated oven at 375° for 15 minutes. Place saucepan in a double boiler to simmer tomato puree and stir to blend. Remove saucepan from heat source, remove the foil from the baking pan in the oven, slide pan out of the oven and ladle a portion of sauce over each sandwich and allow to continue baking uncovered for an additional 7 minutes.

9. To serve, remove from oven and serve on a mat of spinach leaves. Place 1 or 2 sandwiches on the center of 4 or 5 leaves. Great at any meal. Omit the ham for vegetarians.

Pasteles de Masa

MAKES 12 *PASTELES*

Pasteles are my culinary metaphor
of family,
of a people,
an intrinsic combination
of earthy roots
enveloped in a green field of hope,
securely fastened
with common fibers
of firm determination.
Pasteles is plural,
to mean many.
Many hearts,
many hands,
many ingredients
to make
many Pasteles,
to feed many people,
many times.

ROBERT ROSADO

There is no appropriate translation for *pasteles*—there is too much about them to properly translate. *Pasteles* are the central food item on which the traditional Noche Buena (Christmas Eve) dish is based. They are served and balanced with *Arroz con Gandules* (Rice with Pigeon Peas), and spit roasted pig.

Having been born on this very special and eventful day, the *pasteles* have a very profound meaning for me. On every one of my childhood birthdays I would receive a specially made *pastel* filled with flavorful, succulent pieces of pork and extra raisins in lieu of a regular birthday cake with plump pimiento-stuffed table olives adorning the surface of the pastel in place of lit candles.

As I became older, the number of olives increased, and so did the size of the *pastel* and the size of the pot in which they were cooked. This birthday tradition, which my mother and I have come to cherish, still continues to this day. But there has been a slight modification however. She now makes one pastel for each year of my life. Every Christmas Eve I can count on receiving a parcel from my mother containing my traditional, delicious birthday gift.

PASTELES ARE PREPARED AND ASSEMBLED IN FOUR STAGES.

1. Prepping and cooking the filling.
2. Prepping and flavoring the *masa* (batter).
3. Prepping the banana leaves and parchment wrappers.
4. Making the *pasteles*.

1	*pound lean pork meat, diced to $1/2$ inch*
4	*cups water*
2	*teaspoons pulverized rock salt*
2	*bay leaves*
3	*whole garlic cloves, peeled*
1	*cup red sofrito (see recipe in "Sauces" chapter)*
$1/2$	*pound smoke-cured ham, dice to $1/2$ inch*
$1/2$	*cup cooked chick peas*
$1/2$	*cup raisins*
8	*green bananas, peeled*
1	*pound small taro roots, peeled*
1	*pound baking potatoes, peeled*
1	*pound banana squash, peeled*
$1/3$	*cup warm light cream (or half-and-half)*
1	*tablespoon paprika*
$1/2$	*cup olive oil*
12	*banana leaves*
12	*sheets cooking parchments, $8^{1/2}$ inch by 11 inch*
12	*strands of kitchen twine 30 inches long (butcher string)*

1. To make the pork filling: In a kettle, combine diced pork, water, salt, garlic cloves, and bay leaves, and place over medium heat. Cook until the liquid is reduced by half, then skim from the top and remove 1 cup of the stock and reserve. Remove the whole garlic cloves and bay leaves and discard.

2. Reset the heat to low and stir in the *sofrito*. Fold in the diced ham, chick peas, and raisins. Cover and continue cooking for approximately 30 minutes. Uncover the kettle, fold the ingredients, and remove from heat and set aside.

3. To make the *masa* (batter), this specific step is traditionally executed using a hand-held heavy duty grater on the fine side. Because of the large amount of batter needed to make enough *pasteles* for family and friends, every member of the family recruited friends to actively participate in the preparation and assembly line. Everyone takes turns peeling and grating the enormous amount of green bananas and tubers needed to mass produce a couple of hundred *pasteles*. However, for the purpose of this recipe, I have limited the amount to 1 dozen *pasteles*.

4. The cook has the option to use a manual grater on the fine side or a food processor set up with the chopping attachment for prepping the batter. Grate the bananas, taro root, potatoes, and squash to a fine mealy consistency. Place all the ingredients in a deep bowl, and then using your hands, mix them together. Feel for the presence of any small chunks in the batter; if any are found remove and discard. Then using a wooden spoon, stir in 1/3 cup of the reserved stock (save remainder) and 1/3 cup warm cream. Continue stirring until the batter is tight and spreadable. Run the clean flat bottom part of the spoon across the surface of the batter; the spoon should glide with no batter clinging to it and the batter should have a smooth silky surface. If needed, use the remaining stock, adding small trickles while constantly stirring to achieve the desired consistency. Once done set aside. It is all right to refrigerate at this point, by covering batter with a tight seal. The surface of the the batter will start to turn slightly dark. Do not panic—this is just a chemical reaction to the environment.

5. Prior to assembling the *pasteles*, stir the batter well and allow to sit at room temperature to reincorporate the mixture.

6. To assemble the *pasteles*, set up the work area first. You will need a stack of banana leaves. Trim the leaves to 8 inches by 8 inches. Fill a deep square pan halfway up with hot water. Then using both hands, carefully pick up one leaf by the top corners and submerge it in the hot water until the leaf becomes wilted. Lay the leaf

flat on top of an absorbent cloth or paper towel, and pat dry. Repeat the process until the batch is completed. Handle the leaves gently to protect from tearing.

7. Set up your work station with the stack of cooking parchment, wilted banana leaves, a bowl containing the olive oil and paprika emulsion, followed by the batter, pork filling, and cord strands.

8. To assemble the *pasteles*, lay out 1 cooking parchment and 1 banana leaf on top of the parchment (longest side). Scoop out ½ cup of batter onto the center of the banana leaf. Using a spatula or the flat part of a serving spoon, spread the batter to form a smooth square approximately 5 inches by 5 inches.

9. Next scoop out ⅓ cup of the filling and spread to layer the surface of the batter. Carefully hold the parchment and banana leaf together by the lower corners and fold over evenly, away from your body, followed by a second and third fold to form a rectangular shape approximately 3 inches wide.

10. Crease a 1-inch margin on the left- and right-hand side of the wrap, fold margins inward toward the center, and hold in position securely by folding the upper part of the wrap forward, envelope fashion. Finish securing the *pastele* by tying with one strand of cooking cord. Repeat until batch is completed.

11. Fill a large stockpot with water and bring to a quick boil. Reset burner to medium heat. Add 2 teaspoons of salt to the water, then carefully place the *pasteles* in the boiling water. Cook for approximately 45 minutes to 1 hour. Remove from heat.

12. To serve, carefully take the *pasteles* out of the pot (as needed) and place on a dish. Using cooking shears, snip off the cord. Open the cooking parchment and slide the banana leaf package onto the waiting dish. Using the cooking shears, cut away the top part of the leaf to expose the *pasteles*. Serve immediately.

SERVING SUGGESTIONS: Serve a one-plate dinner with *Arroz con Gandules*, spit roasted pork, or fresh ham. Or serve with crusty bread and salad. I serve them for breakfast, lunch, dinner, snacks—every chance I get, straight out of the pot!

Meat

Carne

Pre-Colombian Puerto Rico was devoid of any livestock, with the exception of a variety of small wild dogs and iguanas. The discovery and colonization of The Island by the Spanish settlers soon changed that. Every imaginable species of domesticated livestock was exported to Borinquen from Spain and the Mediterranean region. Cattle, goats, sheeps, pigs, rabbits, and every variety of fowl, found their way to The Island, most turned loose to roam freely and feed in open ranges. With the passing of time, some adapted to the environment and some did not. Those that did adapt were capable of surviving in many terrains, from the salty coastal plains to the high rocky slopes and mountain regions of the interior.

These new breeds of animals earned the name *del pais*, meaning "from the island of Puerto Rico." Their quality was uncontroverted. They were sold live, directly to butchers like my father. When shopping for cattle, he always took me to a particular farm in the country where I learned to select, inspect, and transport the cattle. It was during this time that I also learned to select and raise pigs and chickens.

My father was a butcher by profession during an era where this work was not a job, but a demanding lifetime career. The success of the individual was relative to his personal commitment and his dedication to serving his community. This attitude required the individual to be knowledgeable so that he could impart his knowledge to his customers. "You always need to know more about why and how things are done," my father used to say to me, "or people will not take you seriously. I sell excellent meat, but I must also sell the different ways in which meat can be prepared and served, so that it may be enjoyed each and every time. I want my friends and neighbors to come back and feel happy about buying my meat."

In this chapter, I share some of my father's suggestions and approaches to the preparation, cooking and serving of beef, pork, and goat—meat dishes that have been traditionally enjoyed in Puerto Rican homes.

PORK
Cerdo

For a Puerto Rican, the smell of roasted pork evokes memories of the countryside, and of drives or walks down winding roads to family gatherings where a pig was roasting on a spit. Roasted pork cooking brings to mind the chants of the *jíbaros* filling the morning air, *"ai lo le lo lai, lo le lo lai"* as they herded their livestock up and down the gentle slopes of hillsides to grazing pastures and waterholes.

Pigs were the most popular livestock because they were relatively inexpensive to breed and maintain. For many families, pigs were a commodity that could provide cash when needed through the sale of fresh meat or by-products. The list of possible uses for pigs, other than pork meat, may very well sound unappealing, or even harsh to big city dwellers north of Puerto Rico, or to modern, health-conscious individuals. *Morcilla*, a spicy sausage made from the guts and blood of the pig, or *chicharon volao* (cracklings), *gandinga* (innards cooked in a hot spicy sauce), *cuchifritos* (fried pigs ears, stomach lining and bladder, topped with a hot spicy sauce and served with boiled bananas), fried brains with eggs, stuffed tongue—all of these found their way into the Puerto Rican diet ever since pigs were raised on The Island.

No special event, such as Christmas dinner or a wedding banquet, would be complete without a freshly roasted pig. Served as pork chops (*chuletas*), or diced and used as part of a stuffing for *pasteles*—the uses for pork on The Island are almost too numerous to mention. All are served on a daily basis at restaurants in Puerto Rican communities in the states too, especially on the Eastern seaboard at food establishments called *cuchifritos*.

Cuchifrito is considered a "fast food" and is enjoyed by many "New Yoricans" during lunch hour. It is also served at parties as *hors d'oeuvres* especially during the Christmas holidays when the hot innards of the pig are eaten as a prelude to the main feast, the *lechon asao en vara*—spit-roasted pig.

Because of the exotic nature of these dishes and the negative health attitudes toward consuming animal innards, I have excluded most of these dishes from this "healthier" book. I offer instead, recipes which I find much more appealing to the contemporary palate and more appropriate for a healthy lifestyle. Delicious taste need not be sacrificed, however, as there are both traditional and new "prepping" and cooking techniques that allow for maximum success in these pork dishes.

The key to a succulent and delectable Puerto Rican style pork is in the *adobo* (see "Sauces" chapter). *Adobo* is the marinating technique applied to most meat for flavor and tenderizing during the preparation phase.

The size of the cut of meat (when it is not a whole pig), the amount and type of ingredients and the length of curing—sometimes called sweating time—is crucial. Most important is the texture of the *adobo*, which will be required to remain intact as it penetrates the meat layers and delivers the intense flavors of herbs and spices deep down to the bone throughout the entire cooking process. The use of a mortar and pestle to coarsely crush and mix the herbs and spices is a very effective method for controlling the texture of the *adobo*, and for minimizing the loss of natural flavors and aromas.

Roast Leg of Pork
Pernil Asado

SERVES 10 TO 12, WITH LEFTOVER PORK FOR SANDWICHES

The *pernil* is either the front or hind leg of the pig. The front leg (*pernil delantero*), is the most popular—ideal for roasting and carving. It is referred to as fresh ham. For other pork dishes that require combining with other ingredients, such as rice and pork, or *pasteles*, or soups, or appetizers, the hind leg portion is used (*pernil trasero*). This part of the pork meat is darker and slightly tougher, with a larger network of membranes, muscle tissues and bones. It will require more cleaning, as well as prolonged use of intensive heat, than will the front or top part of the pig. The *trasero*, however, is very flavorful and will behave very well diced, chopped or ground, when interacting with other ingredients.

Most front leg *pernils* are over 10 pounds and the weight that I suggest in this recipe is approximately 15 pounds to feed ten eaters and have some left over for sandwiches and ham bone stock. For the following recipe the use of a mortar and pestle is essential (see "Tools, Techniques and Ingredients" chapter).

    1   leg of pork (approximately 15 pounds)
   20   garlic cloves, peeled
  1/4   cup rock salt
  1/3   cup black peppercorns
    1   tablespoon coriander seeds
    1   tablespoon oregano (1/2 tablespoon dried)
    2   teaspoons cumin
    2   teaspoons sage
  1/4   cup achiote seeds (annatto seed)
  1/2   cup olive oil

1. Place the *pernil* in a deep roasting pan, skin side up. Using a damp kitchen towel, wipe the meat clean on all sides, then use a sharp boning knife to cut the excess fat from top, sides and bottom of the leg. Make long diagonal cuts to score the entire surface, approximately 1/4-inch deep.

2. Turn the leg with the skin side down, and insert the boning knife at about a 45 degree angle to a depth of approximately 1½ inches. Make overlapping incisions about 3 inches apart, starting from the widest part of the leg and working your way down to the shank or handle of the leg.

3. For the following step a large mortar and pestle is needed. Should the mortar be too small to accommodate all the ingredients, divide the amounts proportionally and repeat the step. Transfer the processed portion into a glass bowl. Combine in the mortar: garlic, rock salt, black pepper, coriander, oregano, cumin, sage, and press to crack and crush hard ingredients. Then pound lightly to mix all the ingredients inside the well, making a coarse but integrated paste. Using your fingers, take small amounts of the paste and coat the inside of the 1½-inch holes, then flip the leg over and take the remaining paste and rub it thoroughly and vigorously into the entire surface of the leg.

4. Combine the *achiote* and olive oil in a stainless steel or cast iron saucepan, and simmer over low-to-medium heat until oil starts to turn deep yellow or light orange. Remove from heat, stir, and set aside for cooling. When cool, run the mixture through a fine mesh sieve, reserving the oil in a glass bowl, and discard the brown seeds.

5. Use a pastry or basting brush to apply a heavy coat of the yellow oil on the entire *pernil*. Cover with a lid that does not come in contact with the meat and refrigerate overnight or at least 12 hours.

6. To roast, set the oven at 375° for 15 minutes; reset to 350°, then place the pan without the lid into the oven and cook for 35 minutes per pound or until reaching an internal temperature of 185°.

7. To minimize the grease, I recommend changing the pan halfway into the cooking time and adding 3 cups of water to the new pan. Continually baste the roast with the stock until done.

8. The success of the *pernil* is predicated on the flavor, aroma, and moisture of the meat, and crispiness of the skin, which we call *cuerito*. Like the *pegao* of the *arroz* (rice), asking for the *cuerito tostao*, is the ultimate compliment to the cook.

SERVING SUGGESTIONS: Serve with your favorite rice or dish of tubers. *Serenata* (Puerto Rican Vegetable Serenade) is a great accompaniment—a true countryside dish. An avocado salad or slices of avocado with a garlic *mojo* will greatly enhance this pork dish. Anything with juices and intense flavors like garlic will go quite nicely. For dessert, try a New Puerto Rican Fruit Salad, or the more traditional *Arroz con Dulce*. Here you will enjoy the best of traditional Puerto Rican cuisine.

Sugar Cane &
Ginger Glazed Pork Leg
Pernil en Melao de Cana con Jengibre

SERVES 10 TO 12

Christopher Columbus brought the sugar cane from the Canary Islands on his second voyage to the New World in 1493. Early in the sixteenth century, slaves were brought to The Island to cultivate the cane and process the sugar for making rum.

The great demand for sugar in the United States and Europe in the middle of the nineteenth century brought wealth to many in the Caribbean Islands who cultivated the cane as a cash crop. But the profits took too high a price in human life and dignity. The plantation system of commercial agriculture demanded the total exploitation of slave workers in order to be profitable and efficient. This meant working the slaves from 3 A.M. to 9 P.M., with few or no rest periods. In many cases, chewing the sugar cane was the only way to appease hunger.

This was too cruel a system for a civilized society that was on the threshold of self discovery as a people and as a culture. Protests from the burgeoning Creole class brought about significant social and political pressures which eventually led to the abolishment of slavery and the demise of the plantation system in Puerto Rico.

The abundance of sugar cane made it possible to expand the gastronomic dimensions for domestic and commercial uses of sugar. From the *turron* or the *melao*—the crystallized sugar and the first agent in the production of rum—to the refined brown and light sugars for cooked dishes, desserts and beverages, each step in the process of sugar production yielded its own distinct characteristics and uses.

The city of Ponce was one of the major sugar and sugar by-products producers in The Island, and for most *ponceños*, sugar and *melao de cana* (molasses) was a way of life. At my family's home in Ponce we had a small hand-operated cane presser with which we worked wonders. Whenever we wanted a cane soft drink, we would peel and slice the cane, put it through the presser, extract the natural juice, add water, and come up with the drink we call *Guarapo de Cana*.

My father used to make *agua ardiente*, which was a cane wine, produced from the fermentation of the molasses placed inside dry coconut shells and buried under the ground for curing. This closely approximated bootlegging! My mother would use the cane extract for desserts, sauces, curing meats, and finishing glazes in meats and vegetables.

One of my favorite cooked dishes is the following fresh ham recipe, which can be enjoyed hot or cold, as a main dish, or in sandwiches. Sugar cane is not always available, and so this recipe calls for brown sugar. I first use the dark brown sugar, combined with fresh herbs and spices, as a condiment, then second, as a glazing agent for color and texture with rum and fresh gingerroot.

 1 *shoulder pork leg (approximately 15 pounds)*
10 *garlic cloves, peeled*
 1 *tablespoon black peppercorns*
 1 *tablespoon pulverized rock salt*
 2 *sticks of cinnamon*
 5 *laurel leaves*
 1 *tablespoon white vinegar*
 1 *pound light brown sugar*
 3 *cups pork stock*
1/4 *cup fresh gingerroot, finely chopped*
1/4 *cup dark Puerto Rican rum*
 1 *cup dry sherry*

1. Place the fresh ham on a flat surface. Using a damp kitchen towel, wipe the ham clean. Use a sharp boning knife and peel the skin off three-quarters of the way down. Then score the ham approximately 1/4-inch deep.

2. Place the ham vertically, with shank side up in a 20-quart stockpot and fill three-quarters of the way up with water.

Add garlic, peppercorns, rock salt, cinnamon sticks, laurel leaves, white vinegar, and ½ pound of brown sugar (reserve the rest of the sugar). Place the pot on the burner and bring stock to a quick boil, then lower heat to medium and simmer for 1 hour.

3. Carefully remove ham from stockpot and transfer to a deep roasting pan, scored side up. Stir the stock, then strain 3 cups of it into a saucepan. Add the remainder of the brown sugar and stir to dissolve. Place over low heat, then add gingerroot, dark rum, and sherry. Bring to a quick boil, stir, and remove from heat.

4. To roast, preheat oven at 350° for 10 minutes. Then, using a ladle, spread one-third of the ginger-rum sauce uniformly over the ham. Cover with foil and place inside the oven. Baste every half hour with the remaining sauce. Occasionally rock the ham to make sure it does not stick to the bottom of the pan with the caramelizing sugar and ginger. If necessary, drizzle the ham with stock from the stockpot to replenish some of the moisture lost during roasting.

5. Leave the foil cover off during the last half hour of cooking to enhance the color and glazed texture of the ham. The cooking time is approximately 5 hours, or until internal temperature reaches 185°. Once the roast is done, carefully remove from roasting pan and transfer to a serving tray for carving.

SERVING SUGGESTIONS: Serve with *Arroz con Gandules* (Rice with Pigeon Peas), Baked Yellow Plantains in Rum Sauce, and Avocado Salad.

Pork Chops Neo-Boricua

Chuletas Neo-Boricua

SERVES 4+

Pork chops, although not exclusive to Puerto Rico, are one of the many staples prepared and cooked with distinct Island and regional characteristics. The end cut pork chops are most commonly used in the Puerto Rican kitchen, followed by the *capa* variety, which is the loin cut with the skin attached. Center cuts are seldom used because they are lean and become very dry when seared.

Traditionally, all meats were either cooked on an open flame (*anafre*) or pan fried (*al sartén*). Whatever the method or cooking medium, the techniques employed have always aimed at taking advantage of the natural fibers and flavors of the meat, while at the same time protecting the integrity of the product. This is done by searing the meat to seal the juices, covering the pan or pot, and continuing the cooking process under moderate-to-low heat while basting occasionally.

Basic staples, such as rice or tubers, are often served alongside a main course like pork chops. They deserve a complementary side dish (a *mestura*) that is full of *salsa* (sauce) in order to provide more moisture to the meal and enhance the flavors being served. In the absence of a *salsa*, there are the natural juices and flavors of the meat which we call *salsita* or *mantequita* (fat drippings). Often these are drizzled over the rice or tubers. Therefore, great care should be taken in the preparation and cooking of the meat to ensure a respectable amount of intensely flavored drippings.

Since negative health consequences are associated with the consumption of extremely fatty foods, I suggest cutting off large portions of fat from the pork chops prior to cooking. Olive oil is called for instead of fat, for creating the sauce for the chops (the *sofrito*). I have named this dish *Chuletas Neo Boricua*. The name *Boricua* means an indigenous person of *Boriké*, the latter name being the original one given to The Island by the native Tainos.

In this dish I am trying to satisfy the best of both worlds.

> 8 pork chops (center cut)
>
> 8 garlic cloves, peeled
>
> 2 teaspoons whole peppercorns
>
> 2 teaspoons rock salt, pulverized

> ¹/₂ teaspoon ground cumin
> 1 tablespoon chopped fresh oregano (1 teaspoon dry)
> ¹/₃ cup olive oil
> 1 teaspoon wine vinegar
> 8 whole laurel leaves (soak in warm water until ready to use)
> ¹/₂ cup chopped onions
> ¹/₂ cup chopped green peppers
> ¹/₂ cup chopped celery
> ¹/₃ cup dry sherry
> 4 medium tomatoes, peeled and chopped
> 1 cup tomato puree
> ¹/₃ cup sliced black olives
> ¹/₃ cup chopped fresh cilantro

1. Wash pork chops and pat dry, then lay them flat on a cutting board and with the point of a sharp knife, trim off the fat, and superficially score the chops on both sides. Then place in a flat pan side by side.

2. In a mortar, combine garlic cloves, peppercorns, rock salt, cumin, and oregano and pound until a paste is achieved. Then carefully stir and blend in olive oil and vinegar. Spread mixture (you have just made an *adobo*) on both sides of the pork chops. Use the tips of your fingers to deeply penetrate the scored flesh of the chops. Use the entire amount of *adobo*. Blanket the chops with laurel leaves, then cover pan and refrigerate for at least 1 hour.

3. To cook pork chops: glaze the surface of a deep skillet with olive oil, then preheat the skillet over low-to-medium heat. Lay the pork chops side by side in the skillet, omitting the laurel leaves, and sear. Turn each chop over immediately after the natural juices appear on the top.

4. Once both sides have been browned, remove from skillet and quickly add to the skillet chopped onions, peppers, celery, and

sherry. Sauté for 1 minute, then stir in chopped tomatoes, tomato puree, and olives. Return the pork chops to the skillet, cover, and allow to simmer on low heat for approximately 25 minutes, occasionally rotating the position of the skillet and turning the chops to ensure that nothing sticks to the bottom of the skillet as the sauce cooks down.

5. Sprinkle chopped cilantro on top of the pork chops just before serving.

SERVING SUGGESTIONS: Serve along side White Rice or Yellow Rice, and with fried yellow plantains and Avocado Salad.

Taino Pot Roast

SERVES 6+

This pot roast is a succulent beef cut submerged in a classic red sauce made of blended fresh regional herbs and spices. The meat is cooked in the traditional slow method, on top of the stove, and dramatically served with a medley of ancient Taino staples, such as *yuca*, *batata*, and *apio* (cassava, sweet potato, and celery root). This wonderful dish is certainly one to be shared!

> 5 *pounds top round roast, excess fat trimmed off*
> 1/2 *cup Spanish olive oil*
> 8 *garlic cloves, minced*
> 1 *tablespoon minced fresh gingerroot*
> 4 *hot chili peppers, minced*
> 1/4 *teaspoon cracked black peppercorns*
> 1 *teaspoon crushed rock salt*
> 1/2 *teaspoon ground cumin*
> 1 *cup sweet sherry*
> 1 *medium yellow onion, diced*
> 1 *medium green bell pepper, cored, seeded and diced*
> 1 *heart of celery, chopped*

2 *tablespoons chopped fresh cilantro*

5 *medium tomatoes, cored and chopped*

2 *teaspoons chopped fresh oregano (1 teaspoon dry)*

2 *cups tomato puree*

6 *cups clear beef stock*

2 *pounds of celery root, peeled and cubed into 1-inch thick pieces*

2 *pounds of cassava root, peeled and cut into 1-inch pieces*

2 *pounds of sweet potatoes, peeled and cut into 1-inch thick pieces*

Garnish: *chopped mint*

1. Using a sharp knife, score the round roast approximately ¼-inch deep top and bottom, and set aside.

2. In a preheated kettle over medium heat, combine and blend the oil, garlic, ginger, chili peppers, black peppercorns, salt, cumin, and sweet sherry. Immediately place the round roast in the kettle, turning the roast on all sides until the meat is slightly brown.

3. Reset the heat to low and spread the chopped onion, green pepper, celery, and cilantro on the top and sides of the meat. Cover the kettle and allow to cook slowly until the onions caramelize.

4. Rotate the meat and add the chopped tomatoes, oregano, and tomato puree. Cover and cook down until a heavy sauce is formed. Then, begin thinning the sauce slowly with portions of the beef stock. Always rotate the meat for uniform cooking on all sides. Maintain the meat in liquid; do not allow the sauce to fall below three-quarters of the way below the top meat line. Keep extra beef stock on the side.

5. Kettle should be covered during cooking time, which is approximately 25 minutes per pound of meat. Once the roast is cooked (the internal temperature should be between 160–170°), remove from heat.

6. In a separate pot filled with boiling water, add the cassava, celery root, and sweet potatoes. Cook for 20 minutes or until tender. Drain the water and arrange the vegetables in a deep serving dish, alternating colors. Leave the center area open to arrange sliced roast pieces.

7. To serve: carefully transfer the meat to a cutting board and cut ¼-inch thick slices. Assemble the meat slices in the center of the deep serving dish containing the vegetable arrangement. Pour sauce from the roasting pan over the roast and vegetables. The sauce should be piping hot.

SERVING SUGGESTIONS: This is a full meal, which should be served with avocado slices on top of a bed of watercress, or Avocado Salad.

Goat Serenade
Cabrito Estofao
SERVES 6

Goat meat or *cabrito* (young goat) in Puerto Rico is considered by most to be a delicacy, something to be enjoyed on special festive occasions. It is often the main dish served during a christening of a young child, or at a wedding, a special birthday or at a family reunion.

Goats are inherently climbers and walkers and will eat and digest just about anything that is chewable. It is their climbing ability that makes the meat of an average goat somewhat tough, the result of hardened tissues and muscles; at times their meat tastes and smells very "gamy." But all that changes when the cooking is handled by someone who is well-versed on the subject of goat meat preparation.

In the past, the approach to preparing goat was always ritualistic in nature. The first part of the ritual consisted of selecting the best goat, a trek that often entailed an island-wide search for the farmer with the youngest kid goat. The best *cabrito* was usually under 1 year old, fed on coconut meat and sweet tubers. These candidates would invariably be found on or near the coastal towns, usually in areas called *parcelas* (land parcels) where the livestock were considered and treated as family members (pets) and the guarantee of a healthy animal was never an issue.

Preparing and cooking the goat meat ended up with a dish we call *cabrito estofao*, stewed goat meat. It is the slow cooking in a deep, covered kettle in a seasoned marinade that produces a meat that is tender and tasty. Enjoy the aroma, taste and tenderness of this young goat meat in one of our special Puerto Rican dishes.

FOR THE MARINADE:

- 2 tablespoons lime juice
- 2 tablespoons lemon juice
- 2 tablespoons white wine vinegar
- 2 teaspoons crushed rock salt
- 1 tablespoon whole black peppercorns
- 5 cracked garlic cloves, shell included
- 5 green onions, coarsely chopped
- 2 cups cold beer

FOR COOKING THE MEAT:

- 3 pounds goat meat, cubed into 2-inch pieces
- 1/3 cup olive oil
- 5 garlic cloves, minced
- 1 tablespoon chopped fresh gingerroot
- 1/2 cup chopped yellow onions
- 1/2 cup green peppers, chopped
- 4 tomatoes, cored and chopped
- 1/3 cup chopped fresh cilantro
- 1 teaspoon chopped fresh oregano leaves (1/2 teaspoon dry)
- 1 teaspoon chopped fresh sage (1/2 teaspoon dry)
- 1 teaspoon pulverized rock salt
- 1 teaspoon cracked black peppercorns
- 1/4 cup dark rum
- 2 cups concord grape juice
- 3 cups chicken stock
- 1/3 cup raisins
- 2 tablespoons capers
- 6 whole bay leaves
- 12 medium pitted olives
- 1/2 cup diced and broiled red bell pepper
- 1/3 cup chopped fresh parsley

1. To eliminate the gamy odor and taste of the goat meat, while at the same time tenderizing the meat, will require marinating the goat meat first, and then washing the meat prior to the final cooking. To make the marinade, combine and blend in a glass bowl the lemon juice, lime juice, white wine vinegar, salt, peppercorns, garlic, onions, and beer. Toss in the goat meat and make sure that all the pieces are uniformly coated. Cover and refrigerate overnight, or at least 10 hours. Prior to cooking, place the meat in a colander and wash under cold running water. Set aside.

2. In a preheated kettle over low-to-medium heat, combine the olive oil, minced garlic, ginger, chopped onions, green pepper, and goat meat. Brown the meat on all sides, then add the chopped tomatoes, cilantro, oregano, sage, salt, and peppercorns, and stir until tomatoes begin to break down.

3. Drizzle the meat with the rum and fold. Add one-half of the grape juice to deglaze the kettle, and then add half the chicken stock. Reserve the remaining half of both the grape juice and chicken stock. Add raisins, capers, and the bay leaves and stir. Cover and cook down slowly for $1/2$ hour.

4. Add the remainder of the grape juice and stock, and continue to cook slowly over low heat. Fold occasionally, until meat is soft, and trapped in a thick rich sauce. Gently fold in the olives and the diced and broiled red bell peppers. When meat is tender, remove from heat and serve on platter, garnished with sprinkles of chopped fresh parsley.

SERVING SUGGESTIONS: Traditionally, this exquisite goat meat dish is served with fluffy White Rice, boiled green bananas, a *Serenata* (see "Tubers & Vine-Grown Vegetables" chapter) and a green salad.

Puerto Rican Lasagna

Pastelón de Amarillo

SERVES 6

Over the centuries, outside cultures have influenced every aspect of Puerto Rican culture. The modern Italian influence on the island, and on those Puerto Ricans who migrated from The Island, is perhaps the least known and the most taken for granted. Even Columbus is not associated with Italy, the country of birth, but with Spain, since he traveled for the Spanish Crown.

In the middle of the nineteenth century, a Corsican named Juan Bertoli Calderoni was a municipal architect for the city of Ponce. He designed Hospital Tricoche (presently restored to its original state-of-the-art condition) and Teatro la Perla (considered an architectural gem, cut to perfection, and the place where all major theatrical productions have traditionally been held). He also built steel bridges still in use today, and designed private homes in the neo-classical style. Calle Bertoli (Bertoli Street) is in the center of Ponce, where most of these architectural treasures can be found and appreciated as superb nineteenth century classics. They are a reminder of the "golden years" of Ponce, a time of the Puerto Rican cultural renaissance.

For this recipe, I draw on my own personal experiences as a source of inspiration, blending the legacy of that which is culturally relevant and that which is universal in spirit. There is an Italian segment of my family—the Reginellos and the Arlottas. I'm sure they will appreciate this recipe for Puerto Rican Lasagna, as will you.

5   *yellow plantains, peeled and sliced vertically into 5 slices each*
1/2   *cup melted butter*
1   *pound lean ground beef*
1/3   *cup olive oil*
6   *garlic cloves, chopped*
1/3   *cup green onions, diced*
1/3   *cup chopped green bell peppers*
1/3   *cup chopped red bell peppers*

$1/3$	cup chopped tomatoes
$1/3$	cup tomato puree
1	tablespoon chopped cilantro
2	teaspoons chopped fresh oregano (or 1 teaspoon dry)
$1/4$	teaspoon cayenne pepper
1	teaspoon pulverized rock salt
$1/3$	cup red wine
12	ounces mozzarella cheese, grated
1	cup ricotta cheese
1	cup cottage cheese
	a dash of ground cloves
$1/3$	cup raisins
2	tablespoons fresh chopped parsley
$1/2$	cup sliced olives
$1/3$	cup capers
2	roasted red bell peppers, diced
6	whole eggs, well beaten
1	teaspoon paprika
$1/4$	teaspoon ground nutmeg
$1/4$	teaspoon ground cinnamon
$1/4$	teaspoon ground ginger
$1/4$	teaspoon orange zest

1. Preheat skillet over low-to-medium heat and coat with 1 tablespoon of butter. Place plantain slices in skillet and brown lightly on both sides. Carefully remove from skillet, blot with paper towel and set aside. Repeat until the entire batch is done.

2. To make meat filling, place ground beef in a saucepan over low-to-medium heat and brown. Add olive oil, garlic, chopped onions, chopped peppers, chopped tomatoes, tomato puree, cilantro, oregano, cayenne pepper, salt, and red wine, and stir. Cover and cook down slowly to a pasty consistency. Once done, remove from heat and allow to cool.

3. For the cheese mixture, combine the following in a cold glass bowl: mozzarella cheese, riccotta cheese, cottage cheese, a dash of ground cloves, raisins, and chopped parsley. Using a fork, press and fold the mixture until all ingredients are incorporated. Refrigerate until ready to use.

4. To assemble the *pastelón*, lightly coat the bottom of a deep baking pan (9 inches by 12 inches by 1 inch) with olive oil. Using the width of the pan, arrange first a layer of plantain slices (approximately 8 slices) and divide the meat filling into two parts. Using the first part, spread evenly, allowing for an inside margin of 1/4 inch. Sprinkle half of the sliced olives, capers, and red roasted peppers, then divide the cheese mixture into two parts.

5. Using a teaspoon, drop the cheese mixture in a pattern of one drop in the center and one drop each on the opposite end of each slice of amarillo, then drizzle layer with half of the beaten eggs. Arrange the second layer of plantain slices and carefully press down uniformly to pack and obtain a flat surface. Repeat the filling process, omitting the beaten eggs. Arrange the top layer of plantain slices, packed down carefully, then cover the entire surface evenly with the remaining beaten eggs.

6. In a salt shaker, combine and mix the paprika, salt, nutmeg, cinnamon, and ginger, and sprinkle on top layer, then sprinkle on the orange zest. Cover with aluminum foil and place inside the oven in another pan with about 1/2 inch of water. Bake for 1 hour at 350°. Remove foil during the last 15 minutes of cooking. Once done, remove from oven and allow to cool for a few minutes prior to serving.

7. To serve, cut a center line along the length of the pan, then portion out squares approximately 4 inches each. Portions can vary. Use the width of the plantain as a guide to control the size of the portion being served.

SERVING SUGGESTIONS: This dish is a complete meal served with salad on the side. It can also be served as *mestura* (side dish), with rice and beans. In smaller portions, the *pastelón* will make a superb appetizer.

Chicken

Pollo

May in Puerto Rico is the time when the *flamboyan* trees blossom, offering their bright reddish-orange flowers to The Island's grateful citizens. The last time we left Puerto Rico, it was the middle of May, and the glorious blooms were bursting, dotting city streets and highways with their colors. It was a beautiful memory that has remained with us all these years, while we have lived on the mainland.

If one drives the backroads from north to south on The Island in springtime—through Cayey, Caguas, and Coamo to Ponce—one will see the very best that the *flamboyan* trees have to offer.

Coamo is the largest poultry raising region on The Island. The majority of Puerto Rico's chickens come from here, whether they are of the *del pais* variety, or raised to meet the specifications of foreign customers. Passing through Coamo always makes me think of chicken, and most of the area's population make their living in this industry.

There was a time, however, when most homes in any town, or any *jíbaro* farm, would have a chicken coop under a shady corner of the patio, filled with chickens, hens, and two roosters. This provided the family with a trading commodity (eggs and meat), and an automatic alarm and security system by which to arise each morning or sleep safely each night. Roosters crowing at the break of dawn will get anyone up on time! And since the entire chicken coop would be stirred up by the sound of anyone—friend or foe—walking by, you didn't need a watchdog if you kept live chickens in your patio.

In traditional Puerto Rican culture, friends and family would drop by at all hours, without warning, and the custom was to offer food and drinks. While the family gathered in the living area, the men of the household would step out to the patio and pick out a nice healthy yardbird to prepare for dinner.

Although today's Puerto Rican city dwellers don't tend to have chicken coops, the fowl remains a standard in the Puerto Rican diet. The most common dish is *Arroz con Pollo*, but several traditional and new recipes are offered here for your experimentation and enjoyment.

Chicken in Orange–Rum Sauce

Pollo en Salsa de Naranja y Ron

SERVES 4

Chicken from the flatlands of Coamo, the chicken producing mecca of Puerto Rico, oranges from the south central mountain ranges of Tibes, ancient home of the Tainos, and rum from Juana Díaz, home to the oldest and finest rum distiller on The Island. This trilogy of ingredients seems like a perfectly logical composition to capture the culinary essence of Puerto Rico's historically rich southeastern and central regions. To prepare this dish outside of The Island, choose any good quality chicken breast and a juice orange with thin skin. Puerto Rican rum can be found in most spirits sections at well stocked markets.

> 4 chicken breasts, *approximately 8 ounces each, boned and skinned*
>
> 1/3 cup olive oil
>
> 1/2 teaspoon white wine vinegar
>
> 6 minced garlic cloves
>
> 1 tablespoon minced fresh gingerroot
>
> 1/4 teaspoon pulverized rock salt
>
> 1 teaspoon curry powder
>
> 1/4 teaspoon ground white pepper
>
> 2 teaspoons paprika
>
> 1/3 cup clear chicken stock
>
> 1 medium orange cut into 8 rings, peels intact
>
> 4 medium egg yolks

2 tablespoons light brown sugar

1½ cups freshly squeezed orange juice

3 ounces light Puerto Rican rum

Garnish: 8 fresh mint leaves, 8 slivers of red bell pepper

1. Rinse chicken breasts and pat dry, then arrange in a deep baking pan with at least ½ inch between each breast.

2. In a shaker, combine olive oil, garlic, ginger, salt, curry powder, white pepper, paprika, and chicken stock and shake vigorously. Pour mixture on the chicken breasts, cover with tin foil, and refrigerate for at least 1 hour.

3. To prepare the orange rum sauce, combine the egg yolks and brown sugar in a blender and cream at high speed. Reset the blender to low speed and, while blender is still running, break down the cream by adding, alternately, orange juice and rum.

4. Transfer liquid to a double boiler and cook over low-to-medium heat, stirring constantly with a wire whisk until a medium sauce consistency is achieved. Reset the heat to low and allow the sauce to sit until ready to serve. Keep an additional cup of orange juice and chicken stock mixture standing by to further break down the sauce in the event it becomes too thick as it cools down.

5. To cook the breasts, preheat oven to 375° for 5 minutes, then place the pan inside the oven. Bake for 25 minutes, uncover, and place 2 orange rings with a sliver of red pepper on top of each breast. Put back into the oven and finish cooking for approximately 10 more minutes.

6. To serve: transfer chicken breasts to a serving tray and ladle sauce on top of each portion. Garnish with 2 mint leaves.

SERVING SUGGESTIONS: Serve with Yellow Rice, Puerto Rican Style Black Beans, and Broiled Ripe Plantain slices.

Chicken Fricassee

Pollo en Fricasé

SERVES 4 TO 6

The *fricasé* (fricassee) method of cooking and serving a particular meat, like the *estofado* method, was intended to create an illusion of quantity, especially when there were more eaters than portions to go around, or when the economic situation was dismal. It was also used to take advantage of an old hen, rooster, or turkey.

The traditional prepping technique used was to cut the meat into the smallest workable sections while adding diced fat back, ham chunks, potatoes, and squash for greater volume to the dish, without suggesting that the household was too poor to feed the invited guest. And in many instances the guest would bring a second or third person. Bringing more people than planned for is a typical idiosyncrasy of Puerto Rican culture and condoned in most informal gatherings of families and friends. The saying, "from where one eats, all will eat" is taken seriously by my culture.

The fricassee (although the word may suggest French origin), is a perfect example of the the one stop batch cooking method employed on The Island. Unlike the French version, which simply means frying the meat and adding gravy, in the Puerto Rican version, everything goes into the pot and is cooked down to produce chunks and strands of meat hanging loosely from the bones, held together by a hearty sauce made flavorful with fresh herbs and spices. Once done, the dish is ladled out and served alongside rice and boiled tubers.

A roasting chicken or a fryer is adequate for this recipe. I recommend a 4-pound chicken, quartered. This can easily feed four people, but if the budget is tight, more can be fed by decreasing the sizes of the chicken parts. Each part can be divided in half, that is, by separating the drumsticks from the thighs, cutting the breast into quarters, and keeping wings and ribs together.

Great dishes are meant to feed and satisfy the craving for something wonderful without overindulgence. A little bit of fricassee sauce over rice is all you need.

> 1   *chicken, approximately 4 pounds, quartered and skinned*
>
> 1   *teaspoon pulverized rock salt*
>
> 1/4   *teaspoon cayenne pepper*

1   teaspoon paprika

2   tablespoons lime juice

1/3   cup olive oil

1   teaspoon vinegar

1/2   cup dry sherry

6   garlic cloves, peeled and chopped

1/2   cup chopped onions

1/2   cup chopped green peppers

2   cups chopped tomatoes

1   teaspoon chopped chili pepper

2   teaspoons chopped fresh oregano (1 teaspoon dry)

8   leaves of fresh sage, coarsely chopped

8   large pitted table olives

1   tablespoon capers

12   dry pitted prunes

12   medium closed cap mushrooms, stems trimmed

1   cup chicken stock

1   large roasted red bell pepper

2   tablespoons chopped fresh parsley

1. Rinse chicken parts and pat dry. Using the point of a sharp knife, make 2 superficial score marks diagonally, then sprinkle and rub the parts with salt, cayenne pepper, and paprika.

2. In a bowl or shaker, combine and blend the lime juice, olive oil, vinegar and dry sherry. Sprinkle the parts with half of the mixture and reserve the rest. Cover chicken parts and refrigerate for at least 1 hour.

3. To make the *fricasé*, preheat a deep skillet on low-to-medium heat. Place the chicken parts side by side and brown lightly on all sides. Then add chopped garlic, onions, and green peppers. Sauté until garlic and onions are caramelized. Add tomatoes, chili peppers, oregano, sage, olives, capers, pitted prunes, and mushrooms. Pour the remainder of the marinade and 1 cup of chicken stock into the skillet.

4. Cover and finish cooking on low-to-medium heat for approximately 1 hour, or until chicken is done. To ensure uniform cooking, and to prevent chicken from sticking to the bottom of the skillet, occasionally rotate the chicken parts.

5. Once chicken is done, arrange the parts in a deep serving tray, smother with sauce and garnish with red roasted peppers and chopped parsley.

SERVING SUGGESTIONS: Delicious with White Rice, Puerto Rican Style Red Beans, and avocado slices on a mat of crisp lettuce and watercress. Top with garlic sauce.

Lemon Lime Chicken
Pollo Limonado
SERVES 4

Lemons and limes are always ready to provide the eater with a reason to become excited, and to provide the cook with a reason to create new ways for using these citric wonders. Every day I walk into my backyard I stop to greet my lemon tree and carry on a one-way conversation, mostly about the potential kitchen use for its fruit, its fragrances, its oils, leaves and branches.

The following recipe offers a zesty lemon-lime sauce to wrap around crisp, oven-fried chicken parts. This recipe is inspired by a lemon-lime, garlic, and ginger-marinated chicken that my mother used to prepare and roast over a pit whenever we picnicked by the Maragüey river in Ponce.

> 1 *chicken, quartered (or 4 chicken parts 6 to 8 ounces each)*
> 6 *garlic cloves, minced*
> 1 *teaspoon minced fresh gingerroot*
> 1/2 *teaspoon cayenne pepper*
> 1/2 *teaspoon pulverized rock salt*
> 1/3 *cup dry sherry*
> 1/3 *cup fresh lime juice*
> 1/3 *cup fresh lemon juice*
> 1 *cup clear chicken stock*

1   cup flour

1   cup cracker meal

1   teaspoon ground oregano

$1/2$ teaspoon cumin

2   teaspoons paprika

4   tablespoons melted butter

4   lemon wheels (round slices)

4   lime wheels (round slices)

6   tablespoons dark brown sugar

2   tablespoons cornstarch

2   tablespoons water

1. Rinse chicken and pat dry, then place flat on a cutting board and using an ice pick or a sharp pointed instrument, perforate the chicken along the bone lines allowing approximately ¾ inch between each perforation.

2. In a bowl, combine and blend garlic, ginger, cayenne pepper, salt, sherry, lime juice, lemon juice, and chicken stock. Submerge the chicken parts, cover, and refrigerate for at least 1 hour.

3. Combine and mix dry ingredients in a deep pan: flour, cracker meal, oregano, cumin, and paprika; set aside.

4. Remove chicken from the refrigerator at least 10 minutes prior to executing the next steps. Shake off excess marinade and save, then dredge each chicken piece in the flour/cracker meal mixture and place on a roasting pan, allowing ½ inch space between pieces. Drizzle melted butter over the chicken and sprinkle 1 tablespoon of brown sugar over each piece. Place chicken in oven preheated to 375° for 40 minutes.

5. While chicken is baking, transfer marinade to a saucepan. Add 1 tablespoon of brown sugar and place over low-to-medium heat until simmering. Dissolve cornstarch in water and slowly add to simmering sauce, stirring constantly until sauce thickens.

6. Slide baking pan out of the oven and quickly place a lemon and lime wheel on top of each portion and ladle the lemon-lime sauce over each part. Put back into the oven and finish cooking for another 20 minutes.

SERVING SUGGESTIONS: Serve piping hot with Yellow Rice and broiled whole yellow plantains or *maduros*.

Pan Fried Chicken Legs

Muslo de Pollo Frito

SERVES 4

Fried chicken does not have to be messy to prepare and cook nor unhealthy to eat. Traditionally, fried chicken is breaded and deep fried in a tank of boiling cooking oil or shortening. This method, although popular in all cultures, has lately been considered unhealthy due to the saturated fats associated with deep frying. It is also difficult to control the temperature of the grease used to fry, and the breading used on the chicken becomes a sponge for the heavy fat deposits. There are other ways in which chicken can be fried. This recipe for pan fried chicken legs in the neo-Puerto Rican style is a healthy, delicious alternative.

The key factors in this method of prepping and cooking are using the *adobar* method to "marinate" the chicken, then trapping the moisture and flavors from within by searing the flesh and extending the cooking time in a covered pan or skillet at low-to-moderate heat. This allows the hot vapors to be trapped and recycled until most of the natural fat deposits have been eliminated through cooking and evaporation. The finished product has a crisp outer layer of flesh infused with herbs and spices, while the inside remains moist and bursting with the flavors and aromas of the typical Puerto Rican kitchen.

4   chicken legs (thighs and drumsticks)
8   garlic cloves, peeled
1   teaspoon black peppercorns
1   teaspoon crushed rock salt

1 *teaspoon paprika*

1 *teaspoon freshly chopped oregano (1/2 teaspoon dried)*

1 *teaspoon freshly chopped sage (1/2 teaspoon dried)*

1/2 *teaspoon white vinegar*

1/3 *cup olive oil*

1. Rinse the chicken legs and pat dry. With the point of a sharp knife, make 3 diagonal score marks on both sides of the legs.

2. Combine in the belly of a mortar the garlic, peppercorns, rock salt, paprika, oregano, and sage. Pound to a paste consistency. Break down with vinegar and oil. Using the tip of your fingers, rub each part of the chicken with the *adobo* you have just created, then cover and refrigerate for at least 1 hour.

3. Remove chicken from refrigerator and allow to sit at room temperature for approximately 15 minutes, then drain the marinade into a skillet or frying pan. Place skillet over low-to-medium heat until oil begins to sizzle, then arrange the chicken legs and sear one side. Turn chicken over, cover skillet, and continue to cook for approximately 12 minutes.

4. Uncover the skillet and using a spatula, turn chicken legs over and finish cooking. The chicken legs will be brown and crispy on the outside while the inside is moist and bursting with flavors. For an almost totally fat-free product, remove the skin before pan frying.

SERVING SUGGESTIONS: I enjoy this dish served with White Rice and Red Beans, *tostones,* and an Avocado Salad. This is a typically Puerto Rican way to eat Pan Fried Chicken. But black beans cooked in the New Puerto Rican style would be excellent with this dish, as would slices of avocado with a garlic sauce, or even my New Puerto Rican Fruit Salad.

Ponce Chicken

Pollo Ponceño

SERVES 4

The original dish from which my recipe is inspired was comprised of a large whole chicken stuffed with nuts and fruits, ground beef, and breadfruit chunks. It was roasted and served in a mildly spicy sauce. Because I don't recall ever having this unique dish outside my home town of Ponce, I have created my own version, which contains boneless and skinless chicken breasts seasoned with a marinade of dark rum mixed with herbs and spices, and stuffed with breadfruit, almonds, and raisins. The chicken is baked and laced with a spicy tamarind sauce.

In the absence of breadfruit, cooked *yuca* (cassava) would be the next preferable dressing substitute for this dish.

4 large chicken breast halves, skin removed

1/2 cup Spanish olive oil

3 garlic cloves, minced

3 ounces dark Puerto Rican rum

1 tablespoon fresh lime juice

1/2 teaspoon pulverized rock salt

1/2 teaspoon ground black pepper

1 medium breadfruit

1/3 cup sliced almonds

1/3 cup raisins

8 ripe pitted large Spanish olives, cut in quarters

1/3 cup Spanish capers

4 green onions, chopped

1/3 cup chopped red bell pepper

1/3 cup chopped green bell pepper

1/3 cup chopped celery heart

1 tablespoon chopped fresh cilantro

1/3 cup chicken stock

2   teaspoons paprika

2   cups of spicy Tamarind Sauce (see recipe in "Sauces" chapter)

1. Carefully butterfly the chicken breasts. This step can be executed by placing the breast on a flat surface or cutting board with the length running perpendicular to your body. Place the palm of one hand flatly over the chicken breast to hold it down in position and carefully, in one motion, run the blade of the knife halfway into the center of the breast. Start from the top of the breast and run knife to the bottom end. The breast is now split, with both flaps still attached. Repeat the process until the batch is completed. Spread the breasts flat on a deep pan and set aside.

2. To make a dark rum marinade, combine these ingredients in a shaker: olive oil, garlic, rum, lime juice, salt, black pepper, and oregano, and shake vigorously. Pour over the butterflied chicken breasts, then cover and refrigerate for at least 2 hours.

3. Peel, core and cut the breadfruit into 6 sections, then place in a stockpot, cover with water and bring to a quick boil. Lower heat, cover pot, and let simmer for 15 minutes. Remove from heat, drain, and allow to cool. Once the breadfruit is cool, and the excess moisture has been eliminated, transfer to a mixing bowl. Using a dough cutter or potato masher, coarsely mash the breadfruit sections. Then, using a wooden spoon or your hands, incorporate the almonds, raisins, olives, capers, onions, celery, red and green peppers, and cilantro.

4. To stuff the chicken breasts, remove each breast from the marinade. Divide the stuffing into equal parts and tightly pack each mound on the center of the chicken breast, close the flaps afterward, and fasten in place by inserting 1 or more toothpicks around the edges. Arrange the stuffed breasts on a baking pan side by side, allowing approximately 1/2 inch between each breast.

5. Incorporate 1/3 cup of chicken stock with the leftover marinade and pour it over the stuffed chicken breasts. Sprinkle paprika on top, cover pan with foil, place pan in oven preheated to 350° and bake for 20 minutes. Remove the foil and bake for an additional 20 minutes. Once done, assemble on dinner plate, topped lightly with spicy tamarind sauce.

SERVING SUGGESTIONS: Serve with White or Yellow Rice, and baked yellow plantains or sweet potatoes.

Spicy Taino Chicken

Taino Pollo Picante

• SERVES 4

The pre-Colombian Tainos had no significant form of domestic or wild livestock, other than some species of aquatic birds or parrots, to complement their diet of tubers and seafood. The arrival of Columbus, and later the Spanish colonists, changed life in Puerto Rico through the introduction of every imaginable European wild and domesticated fowl. Quails, pheasants, ducks, geese, turkeys, chickens, pigeons, guinea hens, soon became commonplace on The Island.

As happens in nature, adaptation to the environment dictates the ratio of survival for species. On The Island, none of the wildlife species survived, but the domestic variety adapted well, and some chickens and cocks eventually evolved into regional breeds identified as *del pais* ("from The Island"). These are still bred today in small numbers on farms and in backyards by sentimental individuals.

I call the following recipe *Taino Pollo Picante*, as a personal tribute to the Taino Indians, who were not able to overcome the hostilities of a newly-imposed environment, and who ultimately chose not to adapt.

1	4-pound chicken
8	garlic cloves, peeled
1	teaspoon rock salt
1	tablespoon chopped fresh oregano
1	teaspoon black peppercorns
4	small hot chili peppers
1	teaspoon minced fresh gingerroot
1/4	teaspoon saffron threads
1/2	teaspoon ground cumin seeds
1/2	cup olive oil
2	teaspoons paprika
1/3	cup Spanish brandy
3	chopped green onions
2	medium tomatoes, chopped

1/3 cup chicken stock

1/2 cup burgundy

1 tablespoon chopped fresh cilantro

Garnish: *lemon wedges*

1. Wash the chicken parts, pat dry and remove the skin. Place in a deep square pan and set aside. In the belly of a mortar, combine garlic, salt, oregano, and black peppercorns. Press down with the pestle until garlic is crushed and peppercorns are cracked, then add the chili peppers, minced ginger, and saffron threads. Slowly pound the mixture until achieving a paste and incorporate the oil slowly. At the same time, stir with a spoon to break down the paste.

2. Spread the mixture evenly over the chicken parts, lifting the chicken pieces to ensure distribution of the marinade to the bottom of the chicken parts. Sprinkle all parts with paprika. Cover and refrigerate overnight. If no mortar and pestle is available, execute the steps in a blender set on low speed until all the ingredients are coarsely chopped, then remove the canister, add the oil and shake or stir to break down the paste and blend the ingredients.

3. In a preheated deep skillet, over low-to-medium heat, arrange marinated chicken pieces side by side and brown the chicken on all sides. Spread the chopped onions, chopped tomatoes, and drizzle the burgundy over the chicken parts.

4. Cover and finish cooking on low heat for approximately 35 minutes. Remove from heat and sprinkle chopped cilantro on the chicken prior to serving. You may serve directly from the skillet.

SERVING SUGGESTIONS:
Serve with White Rice and
Black Beans, Puerto Rican style.
On the side, an Avocado Salad
would be great, as would any
tender root vegetable.

Tamarind Glazed Chicken

Pollo en Melao de Tamarindo

SERVES 4

The sweet and sour taste of the tamarind, interacting with a blend of garlic, peppercorns, red chili pepper, and curry powder, turns ordinary chicken into a mildly piquant and aromatic delight. Some consider tamarind to be an acquired taste, but this is a truly tropical dish, worth discovering.

1	chicken, cut in quarters and skinned
8	garlic cloves
2	teaspoons black peppercorns
1	teaspoon pulverized rock salt
2	dry red chili peppers
1	tablespoon curry powder
1/3	cup olive oil
1/3	cup chopped onions
1/3	cup chopped red bell peppers
1	cup seedless tamarind pulp
1/2	cup brown sugar
1/2	cup burgundy wine
1/2	cup chicken stock
1/2	cup tomato puree

Garnish: 1/3 cup freshly chopped mint

1. Rinse chicken pieces and pat dry. Using the point of a sharp knife, make 3 superficial diagonal score marks on the top of each portion, then place each piece on a baking sheet.

2. In the belly of a mortar, combine garlic cloves, peppercorns, salt, chili peppers, and curry powder. Pound together with the pestle to form a paste. Slowly, using a spoon, stir in the olive oil until all the ingredients are well blended. Use the tips

of your fingers to rub the mixture on the chicken parts. Spread the chopped onions and red peppers on top of the chicken parts. Cover and refrigerate for at least 1 hour.

3. In a blender, combine the tamarind pulp, brown sugar, and burgundy wine. Blend until the mixture becomes a paste, then break down slowly with chicken stock to create a smooth sauce. Transfer sauce to a sauce pan, stir in the tomato puree and cook down slowly until reaching a boiling point. Remove from heat and set aside.

4. To cook the chicken pieces, place the sheet pan with chicken under the broiler for 5 minutes; turn chicken pieces over so that each side becomes broiled. Remove the chicken pieces and transfer to a deep baking pan, with the scored sides up. Blanket the chicken pieces with sauce, cover with tin foil, reset oven to 375° and place chicken in the oven for approximately 1 hour.

5. To serve, transfer the chicken to a serving tray, ladle with any remaining sauce, and sprinkle chopped mint to garnish.

SERVING SUGGESTIONS: Serve with *Arroz con Gandules*, baked *batata* slices and an avocado salad.

Seafood

Mariscos

My family and I lived very close to the seashore so we had access to the once abundant supply of Puerto Rican marine life: fish, conch, octopus, oysters, clams, squids, shrimps, sea turtles, and the gray land crabs. This bounty was available to everyone willing to get up at 4:00 A.M. on any given morning during the height of the season.

I made many trips to the *playa* with my father. For a 5¢ fare, we would be packed, standing room only, inside a cattle transport truck and driven 15 miles on unpaved slippery roads and through thick marshlands to a fisherman's paradise.

The entire stretch of virgin beach was filled with people as far as the eye could see, some manually working their nets filled with the catch of the day. Whole families huddled together, cleaning, counting, and classifying the fish by size, species, and potential market value. Other groups would form to trade with one another and exchange the commodities they had just caught.

Eating freshly fried fish with *tostones* was the height of adventure whenever I made this trip to the *playa*. It was in this environment, and among the people who handled seafood, that many ideas and techniques for seafood preparation were exchanged. Just about everyone had a personal recipe for a particular item to be prepared and cooked for a special occasion.

I tend to believe that working with seafood is more of a process than a recipe, but in the following dishes, I introduce some of my favorite seafood. My family and I have enjoyed these dishes most of our lives both in Puerto Rico and here in the United States.

Unless you live in a coastal area where there is always an abundance of seasonal catch, the best place to buy fish is at a fresh fish market or a specialty store. To choose a fresh whole fish that is not swimming about in the tank, but laid out motionless on the display counter, there are a couple of things to remember. First, poke the fish gently; the flesh should be firm, the tail resilient rather than stiff. The eyes should be clear and transparent, the inside of the gills intensely pink to bright red in color. Ask for permission to pick the fish up, then hold it up to your nose and smell it—the smell should be like clean ocean water and not like ammonia.

The other factor to consider is the amount of bones in the fish's skeletal structure. Unless you are an islander or come from a fish-eating culture, I would recommend a fish with little or no bones, cut into fillets 6 to 8 ounces each, or steaks cut about 1-inch in thickness. We islanders seem to be taught from an early age to devour fish the same way we eat sunflower seeds, cherries and watermelons, that is, by chewing the meat of the fruit or seed and spitting out the pits. If you want to be adventurous, buy the whole fish, complete with the head on. For me, this is the only way to go.

Stewed Codfish
Bacalao Guisado
SERVES 4+

A *mestura* is a side dish served alongside the typical one-plate dinner served in the Puerto Rican home. The meal is usually planned around a carbohydrate such as rice or tubers, and in some cases, pasta. The *mestura* that will give the basic dish balance and dignity can either be beans, meat, poultry, fish, salad or vegetables.

The dish known as *Bacalao Guisado* (salted codfish seasoned with fresh herbs and spices, and held together by a light fresh tomato sauce) is a perfect example of Puerto Rican country-cooking ingenuity, addressing the issue of a *mestura para viandas* (side dish for vegetables or tubers). The delightful quality of the tuber medley, *serenata* (vegetable serenade) or other country favorites such as *guanimes* (corn pies) and the *Funche de Maiz* (a close approximation to polenta) would perhaps be less exciting if not for the superb embellishment of this complex flavored codfish dish.

1 *pound salted codfish*
2 *quarts warm water*
1 *lemon, cut in half*

1   *lime, cut in half*

¹/₂   *cup olive oil*

5   *garlic cloves, minced*

1   *teaspoon minced fresh gingerroot*

¹/₃   *cup chopped green onion*

¹/₄   *teaspoon ground cumin*

¹/₄   *teaspoon saffron threads*

2   *teaspoons paprika*

¹/₄   *teaspoon cayenne pepper*

¹/₃   *cup dry sherry*

²/₃   *cup tomato puree*

2   *teaspoons chopped fresh oregano*

¹/₂   *cup chopped tomatoes*

¹/₃   *cup diced green bell pepper*

¹/₃   *cup diced red bell pepper*

¹/₃   *cup Spanish olives*

1   *tablespoon Spanish capers*

1   *tablespoon chopped cilantro*

1. In a stockpot, combine warm water, codfish, lemon, and lime, and allow the codfish to soak for at least 20 minutes. Discard the water, lemon and lime shells, and rinse codfish under running cold tap water for 2 to 3 minutes. Blot the codfish with a kitchen towel and place it on a cutting board. Cut the codfish into 8 sections, then cut the 8 section into thirds, making 24 squares. Place all the pieces into a colander or a sieve, and rinse again under running water and set aside.

2. In a deep skillet over low-to-medium heat, combine olive oil, garlic, green onions and sauté lightly. Stir in codfish, cumin, saffron threads, paprika, and cayenne pepper until all of the codfish is coated with the yellow tint. Add sherry, tomato puree, and oregano, and rock the skillet back and forth for uniform distribution of the liquid.

3. Reset heat to low and continue cooking until the liquid starts to bubble, then fold in the chopped tomatoes, green and red bell peppers, olives, capers, and sprinkle with cilantro. Cover skillet and continue to cook for an additional 5 minutes.

4. To serve: arrange the tubers on the center of the plate and smother with a generous portion of the stewed codfish.

SERVING SUGGESTIONS: Serve with sliced avocados or watercress salad to complete the balance of the plate. Serve corn *guanimes* or *funche* in the same manner. Cold beer is imperative!

Crab
Jueyes
SERVES 4

When I was growing up, the Puerto Rican land crab population was so enormous that they used to walk themselves into waiting pots filled with cooking water. The land crab, a most cherished source of food and used in exquisite local dishes, has all but disappeared. Their demise was due partly to contamination and pollution of their natural habitats and breeding grounds, and partly to the elimination of mangroves, wetlands, beach fronts, and sugar cane fields to make way for housing developments, and the new pharmaceutical and chemical industries. Individual efforts to save this precious crustacean from total extinction came too late.

Today, genuine local land crabs (*del pais*) are somewhat of a luxury item and very expensive. Over the years, attempts to crossbreed local crabs with those of neighboring islands, have been unsuccessful. The off-island crabs do not adjust, therefore, they do not live long enough to reproduce in a controlled environment.

Since Puerto Rican land crabs are a thing of the past, the crabmeat that is available on The Island comes from neighboring islands, precooked and frozen. In the absence of genuine Puerto Rican land crabs, I use the fresh live Dungeness crab which I discovered on the San Francisco wharf, and have come to appreciate and have adapted to all of my favorite crabmeat dishes.

4 Dungeness crabs, approximately 10 to 12 ounces each

6 quarts of boiling water

1 tablespoon coarsely ground rock salt

2   *teaspoons cracked black peppercorns*
1   *lemon, cut in half*
1   *lime, cut in half*
1   *tablespoon white vinegar*
4   *laurel leaves*
1   *tablespoon olive oil*
6   *garlic cloves, minced*
1/2 *cup chopped onions*
1/3 *cup dry sherry*

1. Using a set of tongs, place the crabs, one at a time, into the stockpot of boiling water for approximately 5 minutes, or until the crabs turn over on their side. Remove the crabs and pour out the water.

2. Using a vegetable brush, scrub the crabs and rinse under running tap water. Remove and discard the apron and gills, and inspect to make certain that all foreign matter, seaweed, rubber bands, sand, etc., have been eliminated.

3. Once the crabs have been scrubbed clean, arrange each one in the stockpot. Add fresh water to approximately 1/2 inch from the top of the crabs, then add salt and black peppercorns. Squeeze some juice out of the lemon and lime pieces and throw them (include the shells) into the pot. Add the vinegar and laurel leaves and place over high heat. Bring to a quick boil, then lower heat.

4. While the crabs are simmering, in a preheated skillet, combine the olive oil, garlic and chopped onions, and sauté lightly. Deglaze skillet with dry sherry and pour into the stockpot. Allow the crabs to continue simmering for 12 to 15 minutes. Remove crabs to a cold glass tray and allow to cool. Use a fine mesh sieve to strain the stock into a bowl and set aside.

5. To separate the meat from the shell, first remove the wide back shell. You can execute this movement by holding the base of the crab with one hand, inserting the thumb of the other hand at mid-point and lifting the back off as though opening a book. Use a spoon to scrape off all the creamy mass attached to the cavity of the body and place into the bowl. You may use a brush dipped in the stock to wash the body clean. Remove the claws and legs, and set aside. Carefully remove the stomach sac inside the back shell and discard. Scrape off the remainder into the

bowl and fold to incorporate the mixture, and to obtain a balanced blend of liquids and solids. You now have a base stock for an intensely flavored, natural crab sauce which can be used in most of the crab dish recipes. If the stock is not intended for immediate use, cover and freeze for future use.

6. The empty shells can be used as natural boats for serving cold crabmeat salad. To preserve the shells, wash them thoroughly. Prepare a lemon, salt, and vinegar solution consisting of the juice of 1 lemon, 1 teaspoon salt, and 1 tablespoon vinegar combined with 1 quart of ice water. Place the empty crab shells into the solution and refrigerate until ready to use. Make sure to blot dry prior to using. Do not use this process for shells intended to be used in a hot crab meat dish such as stuffed crabs, but rather keep the shells as is and refrigerate until ready to stuff.

7. To separate the meat from the body, legs and claws, take body first. Using a sharp knife, cut the body lengthwise in half. Then using either the needle point of a crab leg or a seafood fork, carefully (to minimize the shell flecks) pluck the flesh that is imbedded in the cavity of the body and place in glass bowl. Toss out empty shells.

8. For the claws, first position the claws with the seams up on top of a cutting board. Hold one down with the tip of your fingers while tapping with a kitchen mallet or a pestle, uniformly up and down the seam until it cracks. (Do not bang or smash, or the meat will become contaminated with shell fragments, creating an unpleasant chewing and ingesting experience.) Once cracked, use the tip of your fingers to pry open the claw and pluck out the meat.

9. For the legs, there may be pieces of meat attached to the bases. Remove that first; it is the only easily obtainable meat. Use a sharp knife to cut the stubs off the legs at the joint that was attached to the base of the body. Then eliminate the nails on the other end by snapping back in the opposite direction. Place the leg perpendicular to your body on top of a cutting board, take a rolling pin, press down firmly and with one forward stroke squeeze the meat out. Followed by one backward stroke. Discard the shells and save the meat. One 12-ounce crab will yield approximately 1 cup of crabmeat.

Neo-Hot Crab Salad

Neo-Salmorejo de Jueyes

SERVES 4

1	pound cooked crabmeat
1	lemon
1	lime
1	teaspoon pulverized rock salt
1/4	teaspoon white pepper
1/3	cup olive oil
6	garlic cloves, minced
1/3	cup sliced shallots
1	tablespoon chopped scallions
2	tablespoons white wine vinegar
1/3	cup cooked garbanzo beans
1/3	cup thinly sliced celery heart
1	teaspoon chopped fresh sage
1	teaspoon chopped fresh oregano
1/3	cup dry sherry
1	cup cored, seeded, diced tomatoes
1	tablespoon chopped fresh cilantro
1	chopped fresh mint sprig
1	bunch of watercress, washed and blotted dry
16	fresh spinach leaves, washed, blotted dry, stems cropped
2	medium red bell peppers, broiled and sliced
2	medium green bell peppers, broiled and sliced

1. Place cooked crabmeat in a bowl. Cut the lemon and lime into halves, remove pits, and drizzle the crabmeat with the juice. Sprinkle the salt and white pepper. Use the tips of your fingers to toss the meat. Cover and set aside.

2. Preheat skillet over low-to-medium heat. Add olive oil, stir in garlic, shallots, scallions, and vinegar, and sauté lightly. Spread the crabmeat into the skillet, sauté for 1 minute, then use a spatula to flip the crabmeat. Spread the garbanzos and the celery heart, sprinkle the sage and oregano, then incorporate the mixture by folding. Drizzle the sherry over the mixture, cover skillet, lower the heat, and continue to cook for approximately 5 minutes. Remove from heat and fold in tomatoes, then sprinkle cilantro and cover.

3. To assemble salad on individual dinner plates, first core the peppers and eliminate the seeds. Hold them carefully, so as not to tear the sensitive shell. Slice the peppers into quarters the long way and set aside.

4. Arrange 4 spinach leaves on the center of a plate to form a doily. Divide the watercress into 4 mounds and arrange 1 mound on the center of the spinach leaves. In a circle around the watercress, arrange the red pepper and green bell pepper slices, alternating the colors. Then divide the crab mixture into 4 groups. Place 1 portion on each plate, on top of the vegetables, and then top with a sprinkle of chopped mint.

SERVING SUGGESTIONS: Serve with Yellow Rice, New Puerto Rican Style Red Beans and *tostones* topped with garlic sauce.

Stuffed Baked Crabs
Jueyes Rellenos
SERVES 4

    4 *processed crabs, both meat and shells*
  1/3 *cup olive oil*
    6 *garlic cloves, minced*
    1 *teaspoon minced fresh gingerroot*
  1/3 *cup sliced unblanched almonds*
  1/3 *cup diced yellow onions*

^{1}/$_3$ cup diced green bell peppers

^{1}/$_3$ cup diced red bell peppers

1 teaspoon fresh oregano (^{1}/$_2$ teaspoon dried)

1 tablespoon chopped fresh cilantro

^{1}/$_2$ teaspoon pulverized rock salt

^{1}/$_3$ cup raisins

^{1}/$_3$ cup sliced pitted black olives

1 tablespoon capers

^{1}/$_3$ cup dry sherry

2 cups coarsely ground cornbread crumbs

^{1}/$_4$ teaspoon ground cumin

^{1}/$_4$ teaspoon cayenne pepper

1 teaspoon chopped fresh sage (^{1}/$_2$ teaspoon dried)

2 teaspoons Spanish paprika

2 cups crab stock base

1. Arrange the empty crab shells, cavity side up, in a deep baking pan and set aside.

2. In a preheated skillet over low-to-medium heat, combine oil, garlic, ginger, onions, almonds, green and red bell peppers, and sauté lightly. Add oregano, cilantro, salt, raisins, olives, and capers. Incorporate the crabmeat and continue to sauté for 1 to 2 minutes before removing from heat.

3. Using a slotted spoon, and allowing for some of the liquid to strain back into the skillet, start to fill each crab shell with crabmeat mixture. Press down gently to pack well. Once the shells have been filled with the crabmeat, place the skillet over low heat, add the sherry to deglaze the skillet, then quickly add the cornbread crumbs, cumin, cayenne pepper, and sage. Stir for 2 minutes.

4. Remove skillet from heat. Pack the stuffing on top of each crab and sprinkle with paprika. Pour the crab stock base into the baking pan, then place the baking pan with the crabs in oven preheated to 375° for approximately 15 minutes. Spoon baste the crabs 5 minutes prior to removing from oven.

SERVING SUGGESTIONS: Serve hot with *amarillos* (yellow plantain slices) on the side.

Island Crab Stew

Jueyes Guisado

SERVES 4

4 *fresh processed crabs with stock base*
1/3 *cup olive oil*
6 *garlic cloves, minced*
1 *teaspoon pulverized rock salt*
2 *chili peppers, seeded and chopped*
1 *teaspoon oregano*
1 *tablespoon chopped fresh cilantro*
1/3 *cup diced green bell pepper*
1/3 *cup diced red bell pepper*
1/3 *cup diced yellow onion*
1/3 *cup chopped celery hearts*
1 1/2 *cups chopped tomatoes*
2 *teaspoons lime juice*
1/3 *cup dry sherry*
3 *quarts fish head stock (see recipe in "Soups, Stocks, and Brothy Rice" chapter)*
3 *medium white potatoes, peeled and cut into 4 wedges*
4 *baby carrots*
2 *ears of white or yellow corn, divided into 4 sections each*
3/4 *pound butternut squash, diced into 1-inch pieces*
2 *green bananas, peeled and sliced into 1/2-inch medallions*
1 *yellow plantain, peeled and sliced into 1-inch medallions*
1/2 *pound celery root, peeled and diced into 1/2-inch pieces*
2 *medium chayote pears, peeled, cored and cut into 1-inch cubes*

1. In a preheated skillet on low-to-medium heat, combine olive oil, garlic, salt, chili pepper, oregano, cilantro, bell peppers, onion, and celery. Sauté until onions are translucent. Then stir in tomatoes, sherry, and lime juice. Fold in the crabmeat and set mixture aside until ready to use.

2. In a stockpot or soup kettle, incorporate the crab stock base with the fish head stock. Add the potatoes, carrots, corn, squash, green banana, yellow plantain, celery root, and chayote pears. Cover and simmer over medium heat until the bananas are tender and the liquid is reduced by 50 percent. Fold in the crabmeat mixture, cover, and continue to cook on low heat for 10 minutes more, or until a thick, heavy sauce is achieved.

SERVING SUGGESTIONS: Serve piping hot alongside White or Yellow Rice, and Avocado Salad, avocado slices, or New Puerto Rican Fruit Salad.

Creole Salmon
Salmon Criollo
SERVES 4

Salmon is a northern climate fish, so the only way we could eat it in Puerto Rico was to purchase the canned variety, carried by most of the dry goods stores as an imported item. However, with the introduction of new technologies to The Island, and the presence of giant food retailers, imported fresh produce became a reality, and access to many new food items became more widespread.

Canned salmon had to be treated and processed differently than fresh fish in the kitchen in order to obtain a decent palatable dish. From removing the can's contents to selecting the appropriate herbs and spices that would neutralize the after-canning taste of the item, there was always something to be considered when using a canned fish. Most of the canned goods came already cooked, or packed in salt water and other preservatives. There was the problem of contamination every time a can was opened. Most people would automatically know how to look for contamination. Over time, the canned and processed foods have become more reliable, while in many cases, today's fresh foods have to be as carefully scrutinized as the commercially processed foods of earlier years.

In this recipe, I will use the same method of prepping and cooking fresh salmon as we did with the canned variety, in order to introduce to a new generation of cooks, an old delectable dish that time has forgotten.

> 4 *salmon steaks, each divided into 4 sections*
> 1/2 *cup cold beer*

juice of 2 fresh limes

8   *garlic cloves, peeled*

1/2   *teaspoon black peppercorns*

2   *hot chili peppers*

1   *teaspoon rock salt, pulverized*

1   *teaspoon vinegar*

1/3   *cup olive oil*

1/2   *cup sweet Spanish sherry*

5   *green onions, chopped*

1/3   *cup clear fish head stock or boullion*

6   *sweet cherry peppers (3 red and 3 green), seeded and sliced*

6   *large pimiento-stuffed table olives, cut in halves*

4   *medium tomatoes, diced and broiled*

4   *fresh mint leaves, chopped*

1. Arrange salmon chunks in a glass bowl and drizzle with cold beer. Toss lightly, then add the lime juice and toss again. Cover and refrigerate for 1 hour.

2. In the belly of a mortar, combine garlic, black peppercorns, hot chili peppers, and rock salt. Use the pestle to pound the ingredients into a paste, then break the paste down with vinegar, incorporate olive oil and set aside until ready to use.

3. To cook the salmon, drain the excess liquid and add the condiments contained in the mortar. Toss well. Preheat a deep skillet over low-to-medium heat and glaze the bottom of the skillet with 1 tablespoon of olive oil. Immediately pour the salmon chunks into the skillet and rock the skillet back and forth to prevent the salmon from sticking to the bottom. Use a spatula to flip the salmon chunks and drizzle the sherry over them. Blanket the salmon with a mat of green onions, drizzle the fish stock and allow the liquid to be reduced by half. Carefully flip the salmon chunks and cover with a blanket of sweet cherry peppers, olives, diced tomatoes, and chopped fresh mint. Cover and finish cooking for approximately 6 to 8 minutes, rocking the skillet back and forth a few times to mix all the ingredients.

SERVING SUGGESTIONS: Serve alongside a mound of White Rice, Avocado Salad, and Rum Glazed *Maduros.*

Oven Fried Fish

Pescado Frito

SERVES 4

Pescado frito is Spanish for fried fish, usually a whole fish that has been dusted with spices, dredged in flour, and fried in hot grease. It is usually eaten with *tostones* (plantain chips) and washed down with a cup of freshly made fish head *caldo* (broth).

Sundays were the days that my family—and many families—went on a picnic at the beach. Imagine sitting under the shade of a coconut palm, gazing at the gentle rolling waves, listening to the ocean's soothing sounds, and feeling the warm trade winds blowing against your face. Luxurious cloud formations on the horizon, and the fragrances of spices and fish frying in the background, provided the finishing touches to a perfect setting, devoid of the stresses of daily life.

If you don't live along the beach, create your own ambiance with a selection of tropical music and let your imagination take over while you prepare this recipe. Although I use whole perch, the following process can be applied to any whole fish up to 2 pounds in weight. In this recipe I eliminate the hassle of frying fish, while at the same time creating a luscious and comparable finished product.

4   *whole perch, approximately 1 to 2 pounds, cleaned, head left on*

12   *garlic cloves, peeled*

2   *teaspoons black peppercorns*

3   *teaspoons rock salt*

1   *teaspoon dry oregano*

1/2   *teaspoon ground cumin*

1/2   *teaspoon ground coriander*

1   *tablespoon fresh lime juice*

1/2   *cup olive oil*

Garnish: *lemon and lime wedges*

1. Rinse fish and pat dry, then place on a flat surface or cutting board. Using the point of a sharp knife, make 3 uniform diagonal cuts on both sides of the fish;

arrange fish on a flat sheet pan or non-stick cookie sheet, allowing approximately ½ inch between each fish.

2. In the belly of a mortar, combine the garlic cloves, black peppercorns, and rock salt, and pound with the pestle. Incorporate the oregano, cumin, coriander, and lemon juice. Use a spoon to blend and break down the paste with olive oil.

3. Use a basting brush to apply the *adobo* that you have just made inside the cavity of the fish, and on the outside, making sure that the *adobo* gets trapped inside the diagonal cuts. Do not allow the *adobo* to separate; stir periodically with a spoon or brush to maintain the integrity of the herbs and spices. Cover and refrigerate the fish for approximately 1 hour.

4. To cook, preheat the oven to 375°. First allow fish to rest at room temperature for 10 to 15 minutes, uncover it and place inside the oven for 15 to 20 minutes. When done, the fish should be crisp on the outside and flaky on the inside. Test with a fork.

5. Transfer to a serving plate and garnish.

SERVING SUGGESTIONS: This fish is great with a *Mojo Isleño* (Island Sauce). Serve also with *tostones* or garlic bread, fish head broth, and salad. This dish is also good with Black Rice and New Puerto Rican Style Red Beans.

Swordfish Boricua

SERVES 4

The Igneris and the Tainos, whose name for Puerto Rico was *Boriké*, depended on the sea for much of their subsistence. Today, many older generation Puerto Ricans still refer to themselves as *Boricuas*, as a statement of ethnic consciousness and cultural pride. I named this recipe in tribute to the great fishermen of that earlier time.

The swordfish is abundant in the Caribbean and has been considered a game fish by sportsmen, sometimes reaching a weight of 600 pounds. Although it has always been a superb food source, it wasn't until more recently that it soared to great popularity and was sought after as a commercially feasible food item, which could be sold for $10 to $12 a pound. Swordfish steaks are now commonplace at fresh fish markets and supermarkets.

These swordfish steaks are marinated in a combination of white wine, lemon and lime juices, herbs and spices. Then they are broiled, basted with the marinade, and served on banana leaves.

4 *swordfish steaks, 6 to 8 ounces each*
6 *garlic cloves, minced*
1 *teaspoon pulverized rock salt*
1/2 *teaspoon cracked black peppercorns*
2 *teaspoons chopped fresh oregano*
1 *teaspoon minced fresh gingerroot*
1/4 *teaspoon cayenne pepper*
1 *teaspoon paprika*
1/3 *cup olive oil*
2 *teaspoons lemon juice*
2 *teaspoons lime juice*
1/2 *cup dry sherry*
1 *cup clear fish head stock (see "Soups, Stocks, and Brothy Rice" chapter)*
4 *sheets of banana leaves*
4 *green bell pepper rings*
4 *red bell pepper rings*
4 *thick slices of tomatoes*
4 *teaspoons chopped black olives*
2 *teaspoons capers*
2 *teaspoons chopped cilantro*

1. In a glass bowl combine and blend the following: garlic, salt, peppercorns, oregano, ginger, cayenne pepper, paprika, olive oil, lemon juice, lime juice, dry sherry, and fish stock. Submerge fish steaks in the marinade, cover and refrigerate for 4 hours.

2. With a set of kitchen scissors, carefully trim the banana leaves to a size 1 inch smaller than the dinner plate to be used for serving the fish. Spread the leaves on a flat

surface, then use a cloth dampened with hot water to wipe the leaves very carefully. Do not tear the fibers. Arrange the leaves on a sheet pan until ready to use.

3. To cook, preheat the broiler and remove the fish from the refrigerator. Shake the steaks lightly over a bowl to loosen and reserve any excess marinade. Place steaks side by side on a sheet pan with at least ½ inch between each steak. Place under the broiler 4 minutes for each side of the steaks.

4. Carefully, with a spatula, transfer each steak and arrange on top of banana leaves, then assemble on the center of each steak a crown of green bell pepper, tomato slice, and red bell pepper. Drizzle with the reserved marinade and place back into the broiler. Continue to baste and finish cooking for approximately 5 to 6 minutes more.

5. Transfer the swordfish steaks to the banana leaves, each steak atop a banana leaf placed on a serving plate. Garnish with sprinkles of chopped olives, capers, and cilantro.

SERVING SUGGESTIONS: Serve with *tostones* (green plantain or breadfruit) and Avocado Salad. For a heartier meal, serve Yellow Rice alongside the swordfish.

Marinated Kingfish
Sierra en Escabeche

SERVES 4

Escabeche de pescado is fish that has been fried and subjected to a pickling or curing process. This dish is not to be mistaken with the Mexican *ceviche*, which consists of raw fish submerged in citrus juices, then mixed in hot salsa. The *sierra* (kingfish) has been traditionally used for this dish in Puerto Rico, because of its abundance during Lent.

The natural characteristics of this fish are a solid flesh, held together by a large center bone structure. This allows the fish to be submerged in a marinade (cured) for a long period of time without falling apart. When the fish is served, the bones are very visible, thus eliminating the risk and fear of choking, so commonly associated with eating fish.

In addition, the *sierra* is able to perfectly assimilate and absorb the blends of herbs, spices and pickling juices without falling apart, while at the same time lessening the intensity of the pickling elements of vinegar and citrus juices. During the curing process, the flavor of the fish becomes intense, bursting with the aromas and fragrances of Island condiments.

Once made, the *escabeche* would be placed in a glass jar with a tight lid and kept in a cool place or refrigerated for at least 5 days. On Good Friday, the marinated fish would be transferred to a deep glass serving tray and used as the centerpiece. Other items like green bananas in *escabeche* would follow, or gazpacho, and garlic bread, and a pitcher of orange-lime water made sweet with brown sugar crystals. Fresh fruit was often served for dessert.

Escabeche de Pescado is not a dish limited to Lent. It can be prepared and served all year round as a main course. It is handy to have for quick meals or snacks, and can be served as an appetizer, a salad and as an addition to a salad.

   8   *kingfish steaks, each 1 to 1¹/2-inch thick*

  10   *garlic cloves, minced*

   1   *teaspoon freshly chopped gingerroot*

   2   *teaspoons coarsely ground rock salt*

   2   *teaspoons fresh chopped oregano (1 teaspoon dry)*

 ¹/2   *teaspoon cayenne pepper*

 ¹/4   *teaspoon ground cumin*

   2   *tablespoons lemon juice*

   2   *tablespoons lime juice*

 ³/4   *cup white wine vinegar*

   2   *teaspoons dark brown sugar*

   2   *cups olive oil*

   1   *large white or yellow onion, sliced into ¹/4-inch rings*

   1   *large green pepper, roasted and diced*

   1   *large red pepper, roasted and diced*

   1   *large Anaheim pepper (long green chili pepper) roasted and diced*

16　large pitted Spanish table olives

1/3　cup capers

1　teaspoon cracked peppercorns

6　laurel leaves

1. Rinse fish steaks and pat dry. Arrange on a non-stick sheet pan or cookie sheet. In a mixing bowl, combine garlic, gingerroot, salt, oregano, cayenne pepper, cumin, lemon juice, lime juice, 2 tablespoons white vinegar (reserve the rest), brown sugar, and 1/3 cup olive oil (reserve the rest). Blend with a wire whisk. Using a basting brush, apply a light coat of the mixture on all sides of the fish steaks. Save remaining mixture.

2. Place the fish in oven preheated to 375° for 20 minutes. Bake 10 minutes on each side.

3. While the fish is baking, add the remaining vinegar and oil to the bowl containing the mixture of herbs and spices. Fold in the onion slices, diced green and red roasted bell peppers, diced Anaheim roasted pepper, olives, capers, and laurel leaves. Cover and set aside.

4. Once the fish steaks are done baking, remove from the oven and arrange them in a deep glass serving tray. Immediately blanket the steaks with the marinade. Rock the tray back and forth to make sure there is plenty of juice on the bottom and that each steak is saturated with the mixture. Cover and refrigerate.

5. The kingfish will be ready to eat in 24 hours. Allow to sit at room temperature for at least 15 minutes before serving.

SERVING SUGGESTIONS: Serve with Boiled Green Bananas, New Puerto Rican Style Black or Red Beans, White Rice or Yellow Rice, and perhaps a dish of *Serenata.*

Sauces

Salsa

As in Puerto Rican music, *salsa* is the spice, sauce, flavor and mood of the country and the cuisine. The *coquí*, chirping in the shrubbery and moist gardens as soon as dusk sets in, is completing the rhythm and the magic of Puerto Rico. His evening song is ever present, whether one is on a country road or a city street. He hides by day, beginning his song only when life on The Island quiets down, and we can clearly hear him: *ko-kee, ko-kee!*

The Island's dances and its music-making are the human echoes of the natural rhythms of Puerto Rico. The adaptation of popular songs to the *salsa* or *merengue* beat is heard everywhere—as difficult to miss as the *coquí's* song.

The rhythm and splash of flavors in Puerto Rican sauces, the *salsas* of the cuisine, reflect the harmonious mix of sweet and tender flavors—the fast beat of the drum, the dance rhythm of the *mambo*. These sauces wind up the palate for intense or spicy flavors. And they soothe with a fruity covering for a warm dessert. The *adobos* and *sofritos* make Puerto Rican cuisine what it is. The unique combination of ingredients provide rich flavor to a cut of meat or poultry that might otherwise have been rather dry and dull. They enhance a piece of fish or perhaps a tuber with an intense garlic taste, often mixed with fresh oregano or cilantro.

This is the best in country eating—the freshest tastes combined with the lively rhythms and flavors of Puerto Rico. Eat and enjoy these sauces and you will come to know more about the soul of the cuisine and The Island itself.

SOFRITO

The soul of Puerto Rican food lies in the composition of the following basic ingredients: garlic, salt, oregano, black peppercorns, cilantro, *culantro* (wide leaf coriander), parsley, sweet cherry peppers, onions, green peppers, tomatoes, olive oil and annatto (*achiote*). Once combined and sautéed with diced smoked ham, Spanish sausage or cured bacon, this sauce will produce an excellent flavoring that we call *sofrito*.

Traditionally *sofrito* (the word means to cook slowly) has always been red in color or intensely orange, depending on whether tomato sauce or *achiote* (annatto seed) emulsion predominates in the mixture. Since I want to present traditional dishes in a contemporary light, I have created a diversity of color schemes, and have introduced a varied combination of the herbs and spices for the purpose of enhancing the look and texture of the dish to be prepared, without sacrificing the distinct flavors of the food or the essence of the *sofrito*.

Although the *sofrito* can be made ahead of time, packed in a glass jar and stored in the refrigerator for several days, the propensity for a high acidity level is present. Therefore, I recommend using freshly made *sofrito* or a batch that is not more than one day old. The recipes below will acquaint you with three different versions of Puerto Rican *sofrito*.

New Wave Red Sofrito

MAKES APPROXIMATELY 1 CUP

1/3 cup olive oil

1/3 cup diced smoke-cured ham, diced into 1/4-inch pieces

8 minced garlic cloves

1/3 cup chopped red bell pepper

1/3 cup chopped red onions

2 medium tomatoes, peeled, cored and chopped

2 teaspoons chopped fresh oregano (1 teaspoon dry)

1 tablespoon chopped fresh cilantro

1 tablespoon chopped fresh parsley

1/4 cup burgundy wine

1 cup tomato puree

1/2 teaspoon pulverized rock salt

1 teaspoon freshly milled black peppercorns

1. In a preheated deep skillet over medium heat, combine olive oil, ham, garlic, red peppers, red onions. Sauté until ham turns slightly dark. Then stir in chopped tomatoes, oregano, cilantro, parsley, and cook down until tomatoes begin to bubble. Add wine and stir to deglaze skillet. Stir in the pureed tomato, salt and black pepper.

2. Reset heat to low, cover and continue to cook slowly for approximately 1/2 hour. Uncover, stir, and set aside until ready to use.

Yellow Sofrito

Sofrito Amarillo

The Yellow Sofrito is intended to highlight the texture and intrinsic flavors of a particular dish, especially mixed rice dishes with seafood and poultry. Because I want chicken to taste like chicken, and I want the rice to be fluffy and bursting with the chicken flavors, I have revisited the classic *sofrito* and extracted from it this lighter yellow version. It will definitely provide the palate with an excellent balance of tastes and textures.

In this recipe, the essence of the Caribbean and the Mediterranean is captured in the combination of ginger, cumin, saffron, cayenne pepper, paprika, and sage. When combined with the basic or standard ingredients of *sofrito*, these will add a resonance and will offer a new alternative to the classic *sofrito*. Use this *sofrito* as a color and flavor base for all mixed dishes.

1/3 cup olive oil

2 Spanish sausages, cut into 1/4-inch slices

5 garlic cloves, minced

1 teaspoon minced fresh gingerroot

1/3 cup finely chopped yellow onion

1/3 cup finely chopped yellow pepper

4 medium tomatoes, peeled and chopped

1/2 teaspoon ground cumin

1/3 cup dry sherry

2 teaspoons chopped fresh sage (1 teaspoon dry)

1/4 teaspoon saffron threads

2 teaspoons Spanish paprika

1/2 teaspoon pulverized rock salt

1/4 teaspoon cayenne pepper

1. In a preheated skillet on low-to-medium heat, combine olive oil and sliced sausages. Sauté sausages until they begin to sizzle, then stir in garlic, ginger,

onions, peppers, tomatoes and cumin. Set heat to low and cook slowly until tomatoes break down. Then stir in the dry sherry, sage, saffron threads, paprika, salt, and cayenne pepper.

2. Continue to cook down until achieving an intense yellow color and heavy sauce consistency. Then remove from heat and place in a glass container.

VARIATIONS: The recipe is intended to be a base or a point of reference and can be built upon to satisfy the mood of the cook. To achieve greater color, aroma, and flavor intensity, simply increase the proportional amounts of combined ingredients. Color intensity: increase the amounts of the following ingredients by one-half: 1/2 teaspoon paprika, 1/4 teaspoon saffron, 1 tablespoon olive oil, etc.

For greater aroma and flavor, increase the amounts of garlic, onion, cumin, salt, sage, and/or dry sherry.

For greater pungency and spiciness, increase the hot sausage, garlic, ginger, onion, cayenne pepper.

For greater moisture, increase yellow peppers, tomatoes, and dry sherry.

Green Sofrito
Sofrito Verde

The *recao* is a blend of all the green herbs. Use as the main components of the classic *sofrito*. The fresh *recao* leaves, wide leaf coriander and the sweet cherry peppers which we call *aji dulce* are two of the essential ingredients that contribute to the distinct *criollo* flavor. Unfortunately, these are not readily available in the United States.

Processed *recao*, however, can be purchased frozen at most Latino produce stores within Puerto Rican communities in the States. I have made use of fresh ingredients that are universally available and recognizable to create this Green *Sofrito*. This new element presents an alternative and adds to the dynamics of instant green garden freshness in my cooked dishes, and is one of my favorite uses for neutralizing the sometimes heavy taste of charred meats and vegetables cooked over an open flame. The color is green and the result is freshness with a *criollo* twist.

1/3 cup olive oil

5 garlic cloves, minced

4 medium green tomatoes, chopped

1 teaspoon white wine vinegar

1/2 teaspoon pulverized rock salt

2 teaspoons chopped fresh oregano (1 teaspoon dry)

1 teaspoon seeded and chopped green chile pepper

1/4 cup dry sherry

1/3 cup chopped green onions

1/3 cup finely chopped green peppers

2 tablespoons chopped fresh parsley

2 tablespoons chopped fresh cilantro

2 tablespoons chopped fresh mint

1. In a preheated skillet on low-to-medium heat, combine olive oil, garlic, tomatoes, salt, vinegar, oregano, and chili pepper. Sauté until tomatoes break down. Then stir in dry sherry, onions, green peppers, parsley, cilantro, and mint. Sauté for 1 additional minute and remove from heat. Transfer to a glass container, cover and save until needed. Be sure to shake or stir to reincorporate the blend prior to using.

SUGGESTED USES: Use at the last minute at room temperature as a topping or marinade for cooked meats and vegetables. Use to lace and baste roasting meats, as a natural green food coloring, for added texture in pastas and rice, or even on scrambled eggs or omelets.

Island Adobo

Adobo Isleño

MAKES APPROXIMATELY ¹/₄ CUP

This condiment is a blend of dry spices used for rubbing and sprinkling on meat, poultry, and seafood. Most of the spices come in seed form and can be purchased in bulk at tea and spice shops or in small packaged amounts in supermarkets. The amounts suggested are a starting point and can be increased, decreased, combined or omitted, to modify flavors and aromas depending on the mood of the cook and the dish to be prepared.

In addition to marinating meat, seafood and poultry, *adobo* also works well as an accent and a base seasoning for vegetables, rice, salads, soups, dips, pastas, butters, and oils.

The benefits derived from preparing the *adobo* at home, as opposed to purchasing a commercially packaged mixture, is that the cook is able to control the amount of any one of the ingredients, and highlight those flavors and aromas that will best accent the dish and create the desired overtones. Another benefit is that the strength of the spices is best preserved when the spices are kept whole and processed immediately prior to using.

Textures are as important to me as flavors. In fact, a texture can dramatically alter the flavor of a particular dish. For example, black pepper, when ground, cracked or coarsely milled, will provide a very different experience each time. The texture of any spice in the *adobo* can be determined by the cook to achieve the desired seasoning results and quality of the dish. Differing textures also affect the visual outcome of the dish, and by giving yourself greater control over the texture, flavor, and visual appeal of the dish, you will create greater opportunities for a successful dish or meal.

> 2 teaspoons pulverized rock salt
>
> 1 tablespoon coarsely ground oregano leaves
>
> ¹/₂ teaspoon ground cumin
>
> ¹/₂ teaspoon ground coriander
>
> ¹/₄ teaspoon ground ginger
>
> ¹/₄ teaspoon cayenne pepper
>
> 2 teaspoons paprika
>
> 3 cloves fresh garlic, minced

1. Mix all the ingredients well and save in a lid-covered glass jar. Store in a cool, dry place until ready to use. When I make the *adobo*, I generally use the mortar and pestle to pound and crack the spices to the texture I want.

2. Once the dry ingredients are pounded and mixed together, add fresh minced garlic. I usually do this just prior to marinating the food item.

VARIATION: For *Adobo Isleño* made with fresh herbs, combine in the belly of a mortar the following ingredients and pound to a paste: 6 garlic cloves, 1 teaspoon coarse rock salt, 1 teaspoon black peppercorns, 1 teaspoon minced fresh ginger-root, 2 teaspoons chopped fresh oregano, and 2 teaspoons fresh cilantro. Stir in ½ cup olive oil.

If coloring (for bronzing) is needed, stir in 2 teaspoons paprika with the olive oil. Use the fresh *adobo* straight from the *pilón* (mortar) or transfer it to a glass bowl.

Garlic Sauce
Salsa de Ajo
MAKES 2+ CUPS

Garlic sauce is always popular, as a natural topping or as a wraparound, creating enhanced flavor in most hot or cold, bland dishes. It is also used as a base for other sauces and marinades. Whenever the need arises for perking up a salad dressing, lacing pasta, tubers, or bread with zest and pungency, garlic sauce is the agent to fall back on. It can be made ahead of time and refrigerated for a long time. Since the oils can become dormant while in the cold, it is advisable to allow the sauce to sit at room temperature prior to using. Shake to invigorate the blend of herbs and spices, and then coat the food using a pastry brush, or drizzle when applying it to soft or delicate food items.

1 large garlic bulb, peeled
1 teaspoon rock salt, pulverized
1 teaspoon fresh oregano, crushed
1 teaspoon chopped mint

1 teaspoon *white peppercorns*
2 cup *Spanish olive oil*
1 teaspoon *lime juice*

1. If you own a mortar and pestle (*pilón y maceta*) combine the garlic, peppercorns, salt, oregano and mint. Pound with the pestle until forming a coarse paste. Add the lime juice, mix with a spoon, then transfer garlic paste to a glass container with a lid. Add the olive oil to the paste, cover the container tightly and shake vigorously to blend. Always shake prior to using.

2. If you don't own a *pilón*, use a blender. Combine the garlic, cracked peppercorns, salt, and mint, and chop. Reset the blender on low speed and incorporate the olive oil and lime juice. Reset to high speed for a quick blend, then transfer sauce to a glass bowl or jar. Garlic sauce should be coarse (with fibers or strands) and not smooth. Do not overblend.

Island Sauce

Mojo Isleño

MAKES 2 CUPS

Mojo Isleño is the Puerto Rican island sauce most favored as a topping for seafood. It is especially good on a crispy, fried catch of the day. What makes this sauce so wonderful is the burst of intense flavors and aromas of fresh local herbs and spices blending with those of the sea. The delicate sweet cherry peppers used and the *culantro* leaf (wide coriander leaf) are among the leading components of this Island regional specialty. These herbs are not widely available in the United States, and most likely limited to the east coast. The *habanero* peppers are a close approximation to the *aji dulce* of Puerto Rico, and are carried by many supermarkets. These peppers, and cilantro in place of *culantro*, will do the job nicely.

2/3 cup *Spanish olive oil*
8 *garlic cloves, minced*
1/2 cup *diced yellow onions*

$1/3$ cup habanero peppers, seeded and diced

$1/3$ cup dry sherry

1 cup tomato puree

2 teaspoons chopped fresh oregano

$1/2$ teaspoon pulverized rock salt

$1/4$ teaspoon cayenne pepper

$1/2$ cup diced red bell pepper

$1/2$ cup diced green bell pepper

2 cups diced fresh tomatoes

1 teaspoon fresh lime juice

$1/3$ cup fresh cilantro, chopped

Garnish: lemon and lime wedges

1. In a preheated skillet, combine olive oil, garlic, onions, *habanero* peppers, and sauté lightly until onions become translucent. Deglaze the pan with sherry. Stir in tomato puree, oregano, salt, cayenne pepper, and bring to a simmer. Fold in diced tomatoes, red and green bell peppers, drizzle the lime juice, and sprinkle with chopped cilantro. Serve over your favorite seafood or meat dish.

VARIATIONS: For a spicier sauce, add the following after the tomatoes: 3 minced hot chili peppers, 1 teaspoon chopped fresh gingerroot, and 2 teaspoons chopped fresh mint. Garnish with lemon and lime wedges.

Island Hot Cocktail Sauce
Salsa Isleña Picante
MAKES APPROXIMATELY 1+ CUPS

Most of the traditional Puerto Rican sauces are a composition of nicely blended fresh ingredients balanced for flavor and aroma. Most fresh seafood dishes will invariably be marinated, thus flavors are sealed in prior to cooking, making a "cocktail sauce" rather unnecessary. This sauce is suggested to provide moisture and complexity to the accompanying side dish traditionally served, usually tubers or rice, dishes that are inherently *seco* (dry).

Many wonderful sauces can be ruined when an individual eater looking for a hot bite of food reaches over to the condiment tray for a bottle of hot sauce, and mercilessly splashes the stuff all over the plate. After witnessing this barbaric behavior once too often, I decided that I would offer a delightful sauce along the lines of the *Mojo Isleño* with a "hot bite" to appease the jaded palates.

1/3   *cup Spanish olive oil*

8   *minced garlic cloves*

4   *finely chopped green onions*

1   *teaspoon chopped fresh oregano*

2   *teaspoons minced fresh gingerroot*

4   *red chili peppers, seeded and minced*

1   *cup tomato puree*

1/2   *teaspoon pulverized rock salt*

1/4   *tablespoon cayenne pepper*

1   *teaspoon dark brown sugar*

1   *tablespoon dark Puerto Rican rum*

1   *tablespoon lime juice*

1   *cup chopped fresh tomatoes*

2   *tablespoons fresh chopped cilantro*

Garnish: *lemon and lime wedges*

1. In a saucepan over medium heat, combine oil, garlic, chopped onions, oregano, ginger, chili peppers, and sauté lightly. Stir in the tomato puree, salt, cayenne pepper, sugar, rum and lime juice. Cook down slowly for 5 minutes, then stir in fresh tomatoes.

2. Remove from heat and transfer to a glass bowl. Fold in chopped cilantro. Allow to cool at room temperature, then cover and refrigerate. Serve hot or chilled.

Puerto Rican Seafood Marinade

Marinada para Marisco

MAKES 2 CUPS

This basic marinade for seasoning fresh seafood will guarantee an exquisite finished product bursting with the distinct flavors and aromas of traditionally prepared Island *mariscos* (seafood dishes). The sauce makes an eye-appealing and mouth-watering experience for visitors to Puerto Rico's seafood restaurants.

    1   cup olive oil
    2   tablespoons wine vinegar
    1   teaspoon lemon juice
    1   teaspoon lime juice
    8   garlic cloves, crushed
    1   teaspoon minced fresh oregano
    1   teaspoon ground black pepper
    6   bay leaves, crushed
    1   tablespoon chopped cilantro
    1   teaspoon fresh chopped gingerroot
  1/2   cup chopped onions (yellow, red or green)
    1   teaspoon rock salt, pulverized

1. Place all the ingredients in a glass jar. Cover with a lid and shake vigorously, then pour over the seafood to be marinated. Refrigerate until ready to use.

Rum Sauce

Salsa de Ron

MAKES APPROXIMATELY 1 CUP

An excellent quality rum, like that produced in Puerto Rico, is difficult to pass over for its potential use in the kitchen. The essence of the smooth, velvety taste and aroma of this spirit mixes with the natural spices of cinnamon, star anise, cloves, fresh gingerroot, and nutmeg to render a delightful base from which to create an excellent sauce for cooked dishes and desserts.

> 3   cups water
>
> 2   cinnamon sticks
>
> 4   stars of anise
>
> 5   cloves
>
> 1   ounce fresh gingerroot
>
> 1/8 teaspoon ground nutmeg
>
> 1/3 cup raisins
>
> 1/2 cup dark brown sugar
>
> 1/3 cup dark Puerto Rican rum
>
> 2   tablespoons cornstarch

1. Combine in saucepan 2½ cups of water; reserve ½ cup. Add cinnamon, anise, cloves, ginger, raisins, and sugar. Bring to a quick boil, lower heat, then cover and simmer for 15 minutes.

2. Stir the rum into the spice stock, then dissolve the cornstarch in ½ cup of water. Make sure there are no lumps. Stir in the cornstarch-water mixture until the stock thickens.

3. Bring to a quick boil, then remove from heat, strain the sauce into a glass container and keep at room temperature for immediate use. Or cover and refrigerate for future use.

4. For extra stock, add 1 cup of water to the already strained spices. Add 1 tablespoon of rum and simmer. Strain into a glass container and save. The extra stock should be used to thin down the sauce if it becomes too stiff while stored in the refrigerator.

Tamarind Sauce
Salsa de Tamarindo

MAKES APPROXIMATELY 2 CUPS

Commercially packaged tamarind pulp, with or without seeds, can be found in most Latino, Asian, and East Indian produce markets. When shopping for this ingredient, keep in mind that the tamarind pulp has many uses and can be taken advantage of to make such items as glazes for meat and poultry, desserts, and beverages.

The sweet and sour quality of the tamarind makes it an ideal element for adding zest to salads or white meat, especially pork and chicken, and of course, in sweet or spicy sauces. It also makes a superb base for a barbeque sauce.

   1   cup seeded tamarind pulp
   3   cups water
   2/3 cup dark brown sugar
   1   Island Bouquet Garní (see recipe, this chapter)
   2   teaspoons cornstarch

1. To separate the seeds from the pulp, combine the pulp with the water and, using a fork, stir and flake the pulp until the seeds separate. Pick the seeds out with a spoon.

2. Combine tamarind pulp, 2½ cups water, and Island Bouquet Garní in a saucepan. Bring to a quick boil. Lower heat and allow to simmer for 15 minutes.

3. Remove Bouquet Garní and stir in brown sugar. Dissolve cornstarch in ½ cup water and slowly stir it into the simmering tamarind mixture, until it thickens.

4. Remove from heat and allow to cool to the touch. Transfer sauce to a blender set at low speed and blend for approximately 10 seconds. Transfer sauce to a glass container, cover and refrigerate until needed.

VARIATION: To make a hot and spicy tamarind sauce place the following in a preheated skillet and sauté lightly for approximately 2 minutes: 1 tablespoon olive oil, 3 minced hot chili peppers, 4 garlic cloves, 1 teaspoon minced fresh ginger. Incorporate these ingredients after adding the sugar in the original recipe.

Island Bouquet Garní

The Island Bouquet Garní is a medley of powerful aromatics and inherently pungent spices, sensitive to heat and moisture. When exposed to hot liquids, it will instantly release the exotic perfume that is so strongly associated with the Caribbean and other regions of the tropics.

When lightly used in stocks and sauces, the Bouquet Garní will add a hint of Caribbean accent to the cooked dish. However, care must be taken not to exceed the suggested time for submergence and removal of the garní from the hot liquid, as any overextended time will cause the spices to release a larger dose of oils and intensify the taste and aromas.

2   *cinnamon sticks, divided into 4 pieces*
1   *inch-cube of fresh gingerroot*
4   *cloves*
2   *anise stars*
1   *nutmeg*
4   *inch-square piece of cheesecloth*

1. Turn the cheesecloth to a diagonal position. Break the cinnamon sticks into halves. Group all the pieces together in the center of the cloth, then pull the corners together and twist, forming a ball. Tie with a piece of string. Use for aromatic accent in your soups, sauces, and beverages. Remove from the pot when you can smell the perfume rising up during the cooking process. To add pungency or zest to the taste of the cooked dish, allow the bouquet to remain in the pot for the entire cooking time of the dish, then remove.

Brandy Sauce

The use of brandy and other spirits has been limited in many typical food dishes of The Island's kitchens. According to my mother, Puerto Rican women were not only discouraged from but, in most cases, prohibited from consuming beverages with high alcohol content. It was the cultural belief at that time that this type of indulgence was exclusively for men and *mujeres callejeras* (street ladies of the night), therefore, morally and socially unacceptable for the *señoras de la casa* (decent home-bound women).

This belief prevented women—in the vast majority of cases the predominant cook in the house—from working freely and openly with strong spirits in the kitchen, because most of the preparation required constant tasting and sampling by the cook. My mother speculates that the use of sweet wines, grape juice, and sweet spices were used to substitute, and often to camouflage the traces of a strong spirit snuck into the dish by bolder cooks.

> 1 cup water
> 1 Island Bouquet Garní (see recipe, this chapter)
> 1/2 cup freshly squeezed orange juice, strained
> 3 egg yolks
> 3/4 cup brown sugar
> 1/2 cup Spanish brandy

1. Add water to a saucepan and place pan over high heat. Bring water to a roaring boil, add Island Bouquet Garní to water, lower heat, cover and simmer for approximately 3 minutes. Incorporate orange juice, cover and continue to simmer for 3 minutes more.

2. While orange juice stock is simmering, set a blender at medium speed and combine egg yolks and brown sugar. Cream the ingredients, then reset the blender to low speed and, while the blender is still running, slowly incorporate the brandy. Quickly remove the garní from the saucepan and slowly incorporate the hot orange juice stock to the brandy until a smooth blend is achieved. Transfer the sauce to a glass bowl and refrigerate. Use in recipes calling for hot or chilled brandy sauce.

3. To reheat the sauce, use a double boiler and whip with a wire whisk to reincorporate the ingredients. In the case where a chilled sauce is called for, set the bowl in an ice cold bath and whip to a smooth consistency.

Tropical Dressing

This dressing is a delightful flavoring for many salads such as the Mango Chicken Salad (see recipe in "Salads" chapter).

2 large egg yolks
2 garlic cloves
1 teaspoon dijon mustard
2 tablespoons olive oil
1 tablespoon vinegar
2 tablespoons honey
4 ounces plain yogurt
2 tablespoons finely chopped pineapple, strained

1. Combine egg yolks and garlic in a blender, and set at medium speed. While blender is still running, add mustard, olive oil, vinegar, and honey. Blend until achieving a creamy consistency.

2. Transfer cream to a cold bowl, then incorporate the plain yogurt, and fold in a chopped pineapple.

3. Refrigerate until ready to use.

Desserts

Postres

> *My mother opened her eyes wide*
> *at the edge of the field*
> *ready for cutting.*
> *'Take a deep breath,' she whispered,*
> *'There is nothing as sweet:*
> *Nada mas dulce.'*
>
> JUDITH ORTIZ COFER

The sweet tooth of Puerto Rican islanders was influenced not only by the Spanish, but the Danish, French, and British also had a tremendous impact on our dessert enjoyment. European concepts of preparing fruits and cheese-based desserts, compotes, custards, puddings, and pastries made with regional ingredients and preparation methods, provided the laboratory for *panaderos* (bread bakers) and *reposteros* (pastry confectioners) to recreate desserts with distinct Island flair and characteristics. Most homemade desserts had been traditionally rich and sweet, and before the electric oven, most desserts were made on top of the stove using the dutch oven method or a double boiler.

Sugar and spices were always in abundance, and there was always fruit around for the picking. The hens would frequently lay an extra egg or two, and the neighbors had odds and ends to mix in the pot, in exchange for a share in the end results. My mother was great at assembling these ingredients to produce batch-cooked desserts, like puddings and fruit compotes.

In this chapter, I introduce some of my favorite homemade and typical desserts from the Puerto Rican kitchen. The custards and puddings are usually served with caramelized sugar, or topped with sauces or combined with a complement of fruit compote. This is not a rule, but an option for enhancing the complexity of the dessert and aesthetically balancing the dish, thus making the presentation much more appealing and enjoyable. It will also allow for minimizing the size of the portions to be served, thereby making it possible for the dessert to be enjoyed by a greater number of guests, or more frequently by family members. In our house, a pan of *Arroz con Dulce*, for example, will last the four of us for several days of repeated enjoyment.

I hope you enjoy the Puerto Rican *postres* enough to make them repeatedly yourself!

Basic Bread Pudding

Budín de Pan Basico

MAKES 12+ SERVINGS

One of my favorites is a very typical and "down home" dish, the bread pudding or *budin de pan*. Although very basic in its components, it can provide the cook with a base for a more complex and elaborate dessert dish. As a perfect example of the potential of a simple dish, I follow up with a delightfully delicate custard bread pudding draped with rum or brandy sauce.

The perfect way to use leftover bread is to make bread pudding. In addition to being a satisfying dessert, the bread pudding can be served as a warm or cold breakfast dish and, of course, as a snack. The most effective way to save bread for an indefinite amount of time is to keep a plastic bag in the freezer and whenever there is a piece of leftover bread, put it in the plastic bag and freeze immediately before the bread turns stale. Once enough pieces have been accumulated, you can turn it into a delicious dessert.

4	*cups chopped leftover bread*
3/4	*cup hot water*
1/3	*cup melted butter*
1	*cup dark brown sugar*
1	*tablespoon cinnamon*
1	*teaspoon vanilla*
2	*teaspoons almond extract*
2	*teaspoons coarsely chopped lemon rind*
1/2	*cup raisins*
1	*cup hot milk*

1. Place bread in a mixing bowl and add hot water. Press down with a masher or a dough cutter until the chopped bread is incorporated to form a paste. Then stir in, one at a time, the butter, sugar, cinnamon, vanilla, almond extract, lemon rind, raisins and milk.

2. Pour the batter into a lightly buttered 9 inch by 11 inch cake pan and place in the oven. Bake at 350° for 1 hour.

3. Remove bread pudding from the oven and allow to cool at room temperature, then run the point of a knife along the inside edges of the pan to facilitate the cutting of the pudding. Cut into squares. The bread pudding can be served at room temperature or cold. It can be served plain or dressed up with a sauce or a fruit compote.

VARIATIONS: In addition to raisins in the batter, add any other dried fruit or combination of dried fruit. Try soaking the dried fruit in a ½ cup of brandy prior to adding to the batter.

Custard Bread Pudding
Flan Budín
MAKES 12+ SERVINGS

4	cups coarsely chopped leftover white bread (Italian, French, etc.)
2	teaspoons ground cinnamon
1/4	teaspoon ground nutmeg
1/4	teaspoon ground ginger
1	teaspoon grated lemon zest
1/2	cup raisins
9	medium egg yolks
1/2	cup white sugar
1/2	cup condensed milk
2	cups evaporated milk
2	teaspoons vanilla
1	teaspoon almond extract
1/3	cup caramelized sugar

1. Preheat oven to 350°. Set a large pan in the oven, fill 1 inch high with water.

2. In a mixing bowl, combine and mix chopped bread, cinnamon, nutmeg, ginger, lemon zest and raisins. Set aside.

3. Place egg yolks into a blender. Add sugar and cream at medium speed until smooth. Then, while blender is still running, add the condensed milk, vanilla and almond extracts. Slowly add the evaporated milk and blend for 7 seconds.

4. Slowly stir the cream into the chopped bread mixture and whisk to a thick batter consistency. Carefully (wear kitchen gloves) spread the inside bottom and sides of a 9 inch by 11 inch cake pan with caramelized sugar. Allow to cool and form a crystallized base. Pour the batter into the cake pan, leaving approximately ¼ inch of space from the top of the rim. Place the cake pan into the pan of water inside the oven and bake for 1 hour.

5. Once done, remove from pan of water and allow to cool. Cover with plastic or aluminum wrap and refrigerate. Place pan in hot water (180°) for approximately 2 minutes, remove the pan from the hot bath, then run a knife along the sides to dislodge the pudding from the pan. Place a serving dish or platter on top of the pan. Then, while holding down the platter firmly against the rim of the pan, and with the other hand supporting the pan from the bottom, in one movement quickly turn upside down and set on top of the table. Tap on the cake pan until the pudding has been released.

6. To serve, cut into squares, rectangles or diamond shapes and serve plain or with fruit slices or ice cream on the side.

Cheese Flan with Green Papaya Compote

Flan de Queso con Dulce de Lechosa

SERVES 8

The flan is perhaps the number one dessert on The Island. There is always room for a new type of flan, and pastry chefs look for the opportunities to explore and experiment with different variations of flan. All that is needed is a basic custard blend of eggs, sugar, and milk, and some unrestricted imagination. The results can be surprisingly delightful.

8	*large egg yolks*
1/2	*cup sugar*
1/2	*cup condensed milk*
8	*ounces cream cheese*
1	*teaspoon almond extract*
1/2	*teaspoon vanilla*
2	*cups warm evaporated milk (110°)*
	Papaya compote (see recipe, this chapter)
	Garnish: *fresh mint leaves*

1. Preheat oven to 350°, and set up a pan with about 1½ inches of water.

2. Combine egg yolks and sugar in blender, set at medium speed, and cream until smooth. While the blender is still running, add the condensed milk, cream cheese, almond, and vanilla extract, and slowly incorporate the evaporated milk. Continue to blend until foam appears. Pour equal amounts of the mixture into 8 individual custard cups (or 3-ounce soufflé dishes) and place in pan of water.

3. Bake for 45 to 60 minutes or until the center is firm. Carefully remove the pan from the oven, transfer the cups to a cold tray and allow to cool. Cover with a wrap and refrigerate overnight.

4. To serve: place the flan cups in a hot bath for about 25 seconds. Remove the cups and wipe dry, then run the tip of a knife around the inside edge to dislodge the

flan. Position the dessert dish on top of the flan cup and turn upside down; the flan will slide into position. Arrange 3 slivers of papaya compote on the side. Allow for a couple of cloves to conspicuously fall on top of the papaya slivers for accent. Delicately spoon papaya sauce on top of the flan and garnish.

VARIATION: Any fruit compote or sauce will work well.

Coconut Flan with Squash

Flan de Calabaza con Coco

SERVES 8

A squash flan for dessert is another great way to take advantage of the many wonderful varieties of squash during the fall and winter months. Traditionally, fresh coconut is used in the preparation of all cooked dishes as base agent or for accents. This requires processing the coconut (see "Tools, Techniques, & Ingredients" chapter), therefore, for the sake of convenience I suggest using commercially processed and packaged coconut, either the canned cream variety or the grated or shredded frozen type. They can be found in the frozen food section of most Latino and Asian markets.

> $1^{1}/_{2}$ *pounds butternut squash*
>
> 9 *large egg yolks*
>
> $^{1}/_{2}$ *cup white sugar*
>
> $^{1}/_{4}$ *cup condensed milk*
>
> $^{3}/_{4}$ *cup coconut cream*

1 cup *evaporated milk*

1 teaspoon *vanilla*

1/4 teaspoon *ground nutmeg*

1/2 teaspoon *ground cinnamon*

1/4 teaspoon *ground ginger*

1/8 teaspoon *ground cloves*

1. Peel the squash, dice into 1-inch cubes and place in a stockpot. Add enough water to reach a level of 1 inch over the top of the squash, then cover and simmer until the squash is cooked (approximately 7 minutes).

2. Remove from heat, strain, and transfer to a cold mixing bowl. Add nutmeg, cinnamon, ginger, and cloves. Then, using a beater or a wire whisk, whip to a puree consistency. Set aside and allow to cool.

3. Combine eggs and sugar in a blender set at medium speed and cream. While the blender is still running slowly, add the condensed milk, coconut cream, and evaporated milk. Then, slowly incorporate all the liquid into the squash.

4. Pour into a glass baking mold, or individual custard cups glazed with caramelized sugar (optional). Place in a larger pan filled with an inch of water and bake in a preheated oven for 45 minutes at 350°.

5. Make sure the center is firm before taking the flan out of the oven. Allow to cool at room temperature, then refrigerate. Prior to serving, run a knife all around the inside edges of the pan or cups. Place the pan or cups in a hot bath for about 2 minutes then invert onto a serving platter if using the large mold, or onto dessert plates if using the cups.

6. To serve: top with Rum Sauce and garnish with sprinkles of toasted coconut or toasted almond slivers.

VARIATION: For a superb variation, substitute squash with an equal amount of uncooked breadfruit. To use the breadfruit, it must be allowed to ripen to the point where the breadfruit is spongy and soft to the touch. Peel, core, dice, and blend as per recipe instructions.

Green Papaya Compote

Dulce de Lechosa

SERVES 6 TO 8

The *lechosa*, which is the green and unripened papaya, actually translates to mean "full of milk," and describes the natural characteristic of the fruit during the green stage, when the papaya contains a very high level of pure white, sticky, and highly staining sap. The *lechosa* is much like a watermelon rind, but once cooked, it transforms into a very silky and delicate texture which we enjoy in a *dulce* (compote) by itself or in a classic combination with homemade cheese.

One of the natural methods that has been replaced by the use of baking soda, was the employment of wood coal ashes to clean, prepare, and condition the papaya for the transformation from a seemingly inedible mass to a superb and enticing dessert. Selecting and preparing papayas is still somewhat of a mystery for a large number of mainstream Americans, who are sometimes not sure of what to purchase or what to do with the fruit. The amazing thing is that even with the overwhelming popularity and demand for the fruit, the papayas have not lost their exotic qualities.

One of the methods used in the Caribbean to accelerate the ripening process is to run the points of a fork uniformly down the entire length and on all sides of the unripened fruit in order to scratch the surface and set it out on a basket where there is sunlight or natural light and a warm room temperature. The papaya sugar level is at its highest when the outer skin thins down and exhibits patches of tarnished areas. This is the perfect time to prepare the fruit. Peel the skin, cut open the papaya, and spoon out the seeds in the center. Now the papaya is ready to be used in ripe papaya dishes.

However, the following recipe uses green papaya; the greener the papaya the greater the success in turning out a wonderful dessert. The small Hawaiian papaya seems to be the most common in the States. However, there are wonderful species from Central America and Mexico that are much larger, and with textural qualities that can withstand exposure to intense heat and remain intact during the cooking process.

    1 green papaya (1 to 1 1/2 pounds)
    2 tablespoons baking soda (or 1/2 cup of wood coal ashes)
  2 1/2 cups raw sugar

$^1/_3$ *cup fresh lime juice*

4   *cups water*

8   *spice cloves*

2   *sticks of cinnamon*

Garnish: *toasted coconut or almond slivers*

1. Cut the papaya in half the long way and spoon out the seeds. Turn the papaya pieces flat side down and peel with a knife. Then cut the papaya into 2-inch slices.

2. Place the papaya slices in a pot and add enough water to rise approximately 2 inches over the slices. Add the baking soda, immerse your hand in the pot, and swirl the slices a couple of time to activate the solution. Allow the slices to soak for at least 15 minutes. The solution will neutralize the papaya milk, the same way the lye contained in the ashes would behave.

3. Wash the papaya slices under running water, then transfer to a kettle and add the sugar, lime juice, water, cloves, and cinnamon sticks. Place over low heat, cover and simmer for approximately 45 minutes. Uncover and carefully flip the slices to rotate position. Continue to cook for approximately 30 minutes or, if using a candy thermometer, when the temperature reaches between 220–230°. The sauce should exhibit a heavy consistency. The slices will appear glazed and almost translucent with a silky texture. The bite is crunchy on the outside, and velvety on the inside. Once done, remove and transfer to a cold container and allow to cool, then refrigerate. To serve: the compote can be served alone or with cheese, or in combination with pudding or custards.

Mango Compote

Dulce de Mango

SERVES 4

Ripe mango is a wonderful natural dessert all by itself. But the volatile attributes of the fruit are unlimited when used as a base ingredient in hot or cold prepared dishes, or in beverages and pastries. Ripe mangoes are wonderful too, but the green unripened mango is used to create *Dulce de Mango*. I'm sure you will enjoy it!

4   *medium unripened mangoes*

3   *cups water*

1   *Island Bouquet Garní*

2   *cups sugar*

1   *tablespoon fresh lime juice*

1. Wash the mangoes thoroughly. Dry and peel, saving the peel, and dice the mangoes into 1 to 1½-inch cubes. Set aside. Save the large pits. In a saucepan, combine 3 cups water, mango peels, pits, and 1 Island Bouquet Garní. Bring to a quick boil, then reduce heat and allow to simmer until water level is reduced by one-third.

2. Strain, using a fine sieve, catching the stock in another saucepan. Add the mango to the stock and incorporate the sugar and lime juice. Place over low heat and simmer for approximately 10 minutes.

3. Fold gently to incorporate moisture and solid fruit and continue to cook for an additional 8 minutes (or when a candy thermometer reaches 225°).

4. Transfer to a cold dish, allow to cool, cover, and refrigerate. Makes an excellent partner for cheese, ice cream or puddings, and a superb breakfast alternative to jams or jellies.

Coconut Earthquake
Tembleque de Coco

SERVES 4 TO 6

Following the dessert repertoire of the typical Puerto Rican kitchen, the next is the most coveted dessert, enjoyed by children, and one that I like to refer to as a true Puerto Rican heirloom. No matter what pieces of culinary culture may have been assimilated into oblivion, the *Tembleque* continues to be a household favorite with Puerto Ricans. *Tembleque* (the name means "shaky") derives from the gelatin-like quality of the body and texture of this fun dish and from the word *temblor* (to shake, as in earthquake) which is how the dessert behaves on a dish. It rocks back and forth, much to the delight of both children and adults. Eating was always fun and having a fun dessert always made it that much better at the dinner table.

> 4 *large egg yolks*
> 1/2 *cup sugar*
> 2 *cups coconut milk*
> 1 *teaspoon almond extract*
> 1 *cup evaporated milk*
> 1/3 *cup cornstarch*
> 1 *tablespoon soft salted butter*

1. Prepare a double boiler on top of the range. Dissolve cornstarch in evaporated milk and set aside. Combine egg yolks and sugar in a blender at medium speed and cream. While the blender is still running, gradually pour in coconut milk and almond extract, and blend until foam appears.

2. Transfer mixture to saucepan in double boiler and bring to a simmer, then stir in the soft butter. Make certain that the cornstarch is thoroughly dissolved in the evaporated milk, then gradually stir it into the simmering coconut egg cream. Continue stirring until you have a smooth thick batter.

3. Remove from heat source when the batter begins to bubble. Transfer to a square glass mold and sprinkle with ground cinnamon. Cover and refrigerate overnight. To serve, cut into 3-inch squares.

VARIATION: The last breakfast that my mother served us on the day we departed The Island for the mainland was this corn version of the *Tembleque.*

- ¹/₂ cup shredded coconut
- 2 cups water
- 3 cinnamon sticks
- 1 tablespoon soft salted butter
- ¹/₂ cup sugar
- 1 cup yellow cornmeal
- 2 cups coconut milk

1. In a kettle, combine shredded coconut and water and bring to a quick boil, then reset the heat to low. Break the cinnamon sticks into halves and add to the simmering coconut. Stir in butter and sugar and continue to simmer for 10 minutes.

2. In a separate bowl, mix cornmeal with coconut milk to make a batter, then stir the batter gradually into the simmering stock. Continue to cook and stir until the batter stiffens and separates from the sides of the pot. Remove from heat and transfer to a cold serving platter or glass mold and allow to cool.

3. To serve: cut into wedges or squares. The cinnamon sticks should be spread strategically when pouring the *Tembleque* onto the platter. This will ensure uniform cutting of the *Tembleque,* and will provide at least one piece of cinnamon (for accent) to each portion of *Tembleque.*

Rice Pudding with Gingerroot and Anise

Arroz con Dulce

SERVES 12+

My mother has been making this exquisite dessert for over 50 years. Her mother and grandmother made it too. I happily continue the Puerto Rican tradition of preparing and sharing *Arroz con Dulce* during the Christmas holidays with family and friends.

This dessert is made from rice, with sugar and sweet spices. However, the preparation and traditional cooking method is labor intensive, and will require a few hours of work with a wooden spoon by someone standing over the pot, continually stirring to break down the raw rice. I have modified the original method (from using raw rice straight from the bag, to presoaking the rice overnight) to conform to a more acceptable time frame, without sacrificing the integrity of the finished product. My mother agrees that a quicker cooking process is required by modern life!

At home, getting ready for the holidays was, and still remains, an exciting and special time, partly because every member of the family gets to participate in the preparation of holiday dishes—main courses, desserts, and beverages. The kitchen comes alive with aromas and flavors. I can still hear the improvised rhythm of the utensils in my brother Mike's hands, keeping time with the *salsa* beat playing in the background, and see my sisters' choreographed waists swaying in sassy unison in the kitchen. These impromptu gatherings always established the mood for holiday merrymaking and provided a focal point for reaffirmation of family love and unity.

Making and eating *Arroz con Dulce* at Christmastime always brings back memories of my childhood. When I enjoy it with my wife and young son, Adam, it is heartwarming to see them appreciate this dish, and to know we are creating new memories of our own.

 4 *cups medium or short grain rice*

 4 *ounces fresh gingerroot*

 8 *cinnamon sticks, cut in half*

10 *stars of anise*

10 *spice cloves*

1   teaspoon ground nutmeg
3   quarts water
1/4   pound soft butter
4   cups sugar
1   cup raisins
2   cups coconut milk
1/2   cup anisette
1/2   cup cracker meal

1. The night or day before cooking the dessert, put rice in a large (6 to 8 quart) kettle and fill with water. Allow the rice to soak overnight at room temperature in order to soften the grain.

2. Wash the gingerroot to clean away any impurities. Pat dry and use a kitchen mallet or a pestle to tap on both sides and crack open the gingerroot. Do not mash the gingerroot. Place it in a stockpot, add cinnamon sticks, anise stars, cloves, nutmeg, and water. Bring to a quick boil, lower heat, cover, and simmer for 1 hour. Remove from heat, allow to cool, and refrigerate overnight.

3. To cook the dessert, use a fine sieve to drain all the water, then rinse the rice under running water. This rinse will eliminate most of the starch residue that accumulates and floats to the top during the soaking phase. Transfer to a kettle. Using a wooden kitchen spoon or a paddle, stir the spice stock to reincorporate the mixture, then hold a sieve over the rice and strain all the spice stock into the rice kettle. Reserve the spices. Stir and place on top of the burner, bring to a quick boil, and add soft butter. Lower heat, cover, and simmer for 10 minutes.

4. Uncover the kettle and stir in the sugar, raisins, coconut milk, and anisette. Most of the moisture will be quickly absorbed by the rice and will also be lost in evaporation.

5. The sugar will crystallize and cause the rice to stick to the bottom. It is therefore imperative to maintain a balance of moisture and solids. Place the reserved spices in a stockpot and add 1 quart of water. Bring to a quick boil, reduce heat and allow to simmer. Keep the stock near the rice pot and add 1 to 2 ladles of stock as needed. As the rice thickens, continue to stir. Do not allow rice to settle at the bottom of the pot. This will prevent the rice from sticking and burning. The rhythm is

to stir in the stock, scrape and fold the mixture. Continue the rhythm until the rice grains turn puffy and tender. If available, insert a candy thermometer until it reads between 225–230°. Remove from heat and pour the rice dessert immediately into a 2-inch deep glass mold. Using a flat spatula, apply a light coat of butter and shake the entire surface to make it tight and smooth.

6. Carefully place the cracker meal in a sifter, hold the sifter approximately 6 inches over the rice pudding, and shake back and forth to blanket the entire surface of the dessert. Allow to cool. Cover with a food wrap and refrigerate overnight. To serve: cut into squares and assemble on individual dessert plates.

VARIATIONS: For a special treat, combine with papaya compote and accompany with a glass of Puerto Rican Eggnog (*Coquito*) (see recipe in the "Island Beverages" chapter).

Island Beverages

Refrescos del Pais

> *Soul pushing out of tamarind husk*
> *Coffee in coconut shell, it's all lost . . .*
>
> VICTOR HERNÁNDEZ CRUZ

When Columbus discovered the tiny island of Puerto Rico on his second voyage to the New World, he found the island's inhabitants very hospitable. This tradition of hospitality continues to this day, coined in the national phrases, *mi casa es su casa* (my house is your house) and *a donde come uno, comen todos* (where one eats, all eat). The offering of food and drink is the most sincere gesture to make anyone feel welcome and at home. The beverages that follow are the friendliest and most authentic The Island has to offer. They can be enjoyed at various times of the day.

Natural fruit drinks are refreshing because they are light and are not overbearing in their sweetness. While the ingredients may be easier to find in Puerto Rico, a determined search, made in person or through the mail, should enable you to turn up some of these fruits or barks.

Coffee enjoyed the Puerto Rican way is a strong drink, closer to cappuccino or cafe latté than to the American house coffee. If you cannot find Puerto Rican coffee beans, you may want to try a strong blend of your choice, finely ground.

Years ago, coffee was a more important crop on The Island. Puerto Rican coffee has been exported since the 17th century, although it occupies a less significant share of the world coffee market today. You may find the *Bustelo* or *Café Rico* brands in Latino stores or many supermarkets throughout the country.

Rum production has fared somewhat better than coffee growing in Puerto Rico, and it is still widely enjoyed throughout the world. Visitors to The Island tour rum distilleries and see the sugar and molasses industry that are linked to rum production.

The drinks included here are the most typical beverages made with rum spirits or wine. We purposely do not include many of the tropical drinks one may have seen in a bartender's guide; such drinks are made mainly for the tourist trade. But for the occasional rum-based drinks, those included here are the most typical.

Whether you first choose a natural fruit drink, or a cup of *Café Puertorriqueño*, or a beverage with spirits, we're sure you will enjoy your experience with Puerto Rican beverages.

NATURAL TROPICAL DRINKS
Bebidas Naturales

Because of Puerto Rico's warm tropical climate, it is customary to keep cold drinks in the refrigerator or fresh fruit on hand in baskets, from which to make thirst-quenching beverages. The most common drinks are *limonada*, *maví*, *jágua*, and *güarapo de caña*—all are said to be our national fruit drinks. There is also *parcha* (passion fruit), which is frequently made into a fruit drink.

Limonada is lemon juice or lemonade, made from the small cherry-sized lemons that abound on The Island. They are smaller than lemons found in American supermarkets, and more closely approximate the size of a lime.

Maví is a drink made from the fermentation of the bark of the *maví* tree. Not only does it quench the thirst, but it is also said to have medicinal properties, such as being good for the kidneys. *Maví* will invariably be seen fermenting in glass jars on the tops of counters facing the sun in stores and homes.

Jágua is a wrinkled pulp fruit the size of an orange that, when open, resembles the inside of a ripe cantaloupe. The *jágua* is also cut up into quarters and placed inside a glass jar and fermented, always facing the sun. The condensed fruit and juice are strained, and the liquid is then mixed with cold water and sweetened with sugar or molasses. Or it can be drunk unsweetened. The *jágua* is also thought to have medicinal properties, like many of The Island's fruits and roots.

Güarapo de Caña is a drink made from sugar cane—the thin bark variety. It is peeled and the juice squeezed out by a hand-cranked cylinder. Or you can buy cane spears, strain the extract, and then add water and ice. Or you can simply purchase the extract, add cold water and ice, and you have an instant drink. Add a wedge of lemon or lime. It's refreshingly wonderful!

Parcha, or passion fruit, is high in vitamin C. It grows on a vine, round and green, and when ripe it turns yellow. Bitter like a lemon, it is a perfect sphere, naturally glossy, and pretty to look at. It goes through a metamorphosis and transforms its flavor from a bitter vine-like taste to one that is tangy and sweet. *Parchas* can be purchased at most major supermarkets in the

United States. To process the fruit, simply cut one open in half and spoon out the seedy pulp. Place the pulp in a blender, add 1 cup of water and make a puree. Then strain the puree through a fine sieve, catching the extract in a container. To make the drink, dilute the extract with 1 cup of water per fruit used in making the extract. Add sugar to sweeten to your taste. Serve over ice. Also a great mixer with your favorite spirit.

In the States, these fruits can be purchased at some of the fresh produce stores in Latino neighborhoods. You will find it worth your while to make a fresh batch of any one of these natural tropical drinks.

Lemonade

Limonada

MAKES 2 QUARTS

In this version, fruits widely available in the United States are used.

> 2 *quarts water*
> 6 *lemons, cut in halves*
> 6 *limes, cut in halves*
> 1 *cup sugar*
>
> **Garnish:** *mint leaves*

1. Place stockpot of water over high heat and bring to a quick boil. Remove from heat, then squeeze out most of the lemon and lime juice from the fruits and mix into the boiling water. Include the shells of the fruit. Stir, cover, and allow to cool.

2. Once cool, strain the juice through a fine sieve, and use a spoon to press out the juice from the shells. Stir in the sugar or serve over ice and sweeten with your preferred sweetener.

Maví

FOR THE STARTER:

- 1/2 cup *maví bark*
- 2 *quarts water*
- 3 *sticks of cinnamon*
- 4 *cloves*
- 1 *tablespoon gingerroot, minced*

1. Combine all the ingredients in a 6-quart stockpot. Bring to a roaring boil, lower heat, and simmer for 10 minutes. Remove from heat and allow to cool.

2. Once cool, strain through a linen strainer or colander draped with a tight mesh cloth. Reserve the *maví* bark and spices. Liquid should be dark brown. Pour into a glass container and refrigerate until ready to use.

FOR THE MAVÍ DRINK:

- 2 *quarts water*
- 5 *cups brown sugar*
- 2 *cups maví starter*

1. Combine in a stockpot 2 quarts of water with 5 cups of brown sugar and stir. Add the 2 quarts of *maví* starter and continue to stir until creating a layer of foam.

2. Pour foamy liquid into a glass 1-gallon bottle. Cover the mouth of the bottle by tying a piece of cheesecloth around the open top or place a paper cup to cover the open top. This will protect the drink from becoming contaminated with external impurities.

3. Place the bottle in a clean area near a window where it can be exposed to sunlight, and allow to ferment undisturbed for 3 days. After the third day, refrigerate. To serve, prepare a tall glass with ice cubes and fill.

VARIATIONS: To make a zestier drink, add 1 part ginger ale to 1 part *maví*. For an adult cocktail drink, add 1 part beer to 1 part *maví*. The leftover cooked bark and spices can be placed in plastic wrap and stored in the freezer for an indefinite time to be used for making one more batch.

Tamarind Drink
Refresco de Tamarindo

Among the other Island drinks, the *tamarindo* (tamarind) is an old favorite, easy to make, and very refreshing. The pods or pulp can be purchased in bulk at most Latino fresh produce markets and East Indian produce stores in the United States.

> *4 cups of tamarind pulp*
> *4 cups of water*
> *1 cup of cold water*
> *2 cups sugar*
>
> ***Garnish:*** *mint leaves*

1. To make the tamarind extract, combine tamarind pulp and 4 cups of water in a 6-quart saucepan; bring to a quick boil. Lower heat and simmer for approximately 10 minutes, stirring occasionally until the seeds separate from the pulp.

2. Pass the liquid through a fine strainer or a sieve, and press in a circular motion using a spoon or a wire whisk. Empty the sieve or strainer into another pan and stir in 1 cup of cold water. Eliminate the seeds and incorporate the pulp and the liquid into the first batch of extracted juice.

3. Stir in sugar and transfer extract to a blender. Set the blender at high speed and liquefy the pulpy extract. Transfer the concentrated juice to a glass container and refrigerate. Use it as a base for thirst-quenching drinks.

VARIATIONS: For individual servings, mix in a tall glass with ice, equal parts concentrate to equal parts water, sweeten to taste, and garnish. For daiquiris, slushes, and ices, mix 2 parts concentrate to 1 part water. Blend well and fill ice cube trays. Sweeten to taste.

Oatmeal Drink

Refresco de Avena

Another excellent summer drink that my mother kept in her repertoire of home remedies is the oatmeal drink. This drink is believed to help stabilize and control the itching caused by body rashes associated with the summer season, such as prickly heat, and mild cases of exposure to poisonous plants.

Whenever we had a rash, my mother would apply calamine lotion on the outside and give us oatmeal juice to drink.

> 1   cup toasted oats
> 4   cups lukewarm water
> 1/2 tablespoon vanilla extract
> 1   cup whole milk

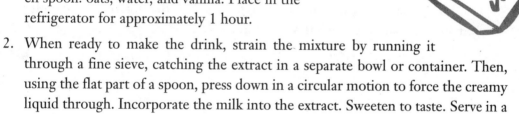

1. In a mixing bowl, combine and stir with a wooden spoon: oats, water, and vanilla. Place in the refrigerator for approximately 1 hour.

2. When ready to make the drink, strain the mixture by running it through a fine sieve, catching the extract in a separate bowl or container. Then, using the flat part of a spoon, press down in a circular motion to force the creamy liquid through. Incorporate the milk into the extract. Sweeten to taste. Serve in a tall glass over ice.

PUERTO RICAN COFFEE
Cafe Puertorriqueño

> The coffee trees of my time
> bloomed with flowers of hope.
>
> Juan Avilés

Excellent coffee is still being planted and harvested in Puerto Rico for commercial purposes, mostly destined for the shelves of Puerto Rican *bodegas* (grocery stores). But The Island's coffee can also be found in the ethnic food sections at some American supermarkets, waiting to be discovered by curious and interested coffee lovers.

This wonderful eye opener is guaranteed to get you going in the morning! To make it, you will need a *colador* (a cloth strainer with a metal handle), which can be purchased at any Latino market. It is the boiling of the coffee in the water that produces the strong brew.

Coffee with Steamed Milk

Café con Leche

MAKES 4+ CUPS

To keep the coffee and milk hot prior to serving, set the pots in a double boiler on top of the stove. However, as a rule, coffee is always served freshly made, therefore only the amount to be served and consumed on the spot is prepared. To serve reheated coffee, or coffee that has been sitting too long, was considered offensive. The older members of the family, who felt that having excellent coffee was a protected and undisputed part of life, were very *exigentes* (demanding), to the absurd extent that some would refuse the coffee unless it was strained directly into the cup.

> *4 tablespoons ground Puerto Rican coffee*
> *4 cups water*

1. Add water to a 2-quart saucepan, place over medium heat, and allow water to reach a simmering point. Set up the *colador* (cloth strainer) in a tall coffeepot and have it standing by.

2. Add the coffee grounds to the simmering water and continue to simmer until coffee begins to foam and rise up. Quickly remove the saucepan from the burner before coffee bubbles over the sides.

3. Pour into cloth strainer, allowing the coffee to filter through. For a stronger brew, run the coffee through the strainer a second time.

4. Bring milk to a simmer. Then add milk to each cup as you serve the coffee.

VARIATIONS: If you prefer *tinta* (full strength, black coffee), run the coffee through the strainer 3 times and serve it in a *posillo* (demitasse). For *prieto* (regular cup), run one time through the strainer. For *café ralo* (thin) dilute it with a little hot water.

Spanish After–Dinner Coffee

1   *teaspoon raw sugar*
1   *tablespoon rum, cognac, or brandy*
    cafe tinta (strong-brewed coffee, see recipe above)
    fresh whipped cream
    ground ginger
    nutmeg
    cinnamon

1. To each serving cup, add raw sugar and stir in rum, cognac, or brandy.

2. Add the hot coffee, leaving room to top it with fresh whipped cream. Sprinkle with a dash of mixed (equal parts) ground ginger, nutmeg, and cinnamon.

Piña Colada

Piña Colada is a unique blend of pineapple juice and coconut milk, with rum added, and served cold. Omit the rum and serve the children a virgin *Piña Colada*.

   Piña Colada translates to strained pineapple. This popular drink originated in the Old San Juan area in the middle of the twentieth century on *Calle Fortaleza*. There is actually a metal plaque on the side of the existing building commemorating the event. A "good *Piña Colada*," as is beauty, is "in the eyes of the beholder." It is also relative to the experience of the bartender who makes it. My interpretation of the *Piña Colada* consists of 1 part coconut cream, 2 parts rum, 3 parts pineapple juice.

> 1   *cup coconut cream*
> 1/2   *cup evaporated milk*
> 1/4   *tablespoon almond extract*
> 1/3   *cup powdered sugar*
> 3   *cups pure pineapple juice*
>   *white Puerto Rican rum*
>
> **Garnish:** *one of each per serving—fresh pineapple spears,*
> *orange slices, cherries, fresh mint leaves*

1. In a blender, put the coconut cream, evaporated milk, almond extract, and powdered sugar; mix for 30 seconds at low speed. Then, while the blender is still running, incorporate all of the pineapple juice and blend for 30 more seconds.

2. Fill ice trays with the *Piña Colada* mix and freeze.

3. To serve *Piña Colada*: place the ice cube mixture into the blender (8 cubes per serving), add 1 to 2 jiggers of white Puerto Rican rum and frappé. Pour into a tall glass. Garnish with fresh pineapple spear, orange ring, mint leaf and maraschino cherry, or preferably a real bing cherry.

Puerto Rican Eggnog
Coquito

The word *coquito* translates to "small coconut," the base ingredient of this drink. Once made, it was served in cups fashioned from coconut shells. Traditionally, this drink has always been prepared and served during the Christmas and New Years celebrations, with or without alcohol.

Noche Buena (Christmas Eve) and *Año Nuevo* (New Year's Eve and New Year's Day) are not complete without the *coquito*. It is usually made in large batches, preserved in bottles, and stored in the refrigerator a few days ahead of time. The *coquito* is made into a heavy consistency, to be sipped slowly and enjoyed in small quantities. This deliciously rich creamy drink is so enticing that it is difficult not to be tempted to have "one more." Beware of its alcohol subtleties. One can go from inhibition to euphoria to a drunken stupor, depending on the amount of spirit in the coquito!

The eggnog will keep for an indefinite time in the refrigerator. The longer it is allowed to sit,the thicker the consistency will become. Shake well before serving. You can thin it down with any of the milk used in the recipe (1 part milk to 3 parts *coquito*) for an after-dinner dessert. Serve with any of the traditional puddings or with *Arroz con Dulce*.

2   *cups whole milk*

2   *cups evaporated milk*

2   *cups coconut milk or cream*

5   *whole cinnamon sticks*

5   *spice cloves*

1/4 *teaspoon ground nutmeg*

1   *ounce cracked fresh ginger*

6   *large egg yolks*

1   *cup white sugar*

1   *pint light Puerto Rican rum*

Garnish: *fresh coconut slivers, ground cinnamon, and nutmeg*

1. Set up a double boiler on top of the stove over medium heat in a 6-quart saucepan. Incorporate whole milk, evaporated milk, coconut milk, cinnamon, nutmeg, and ginger. Bring to a simmer (when a bubbly ring begins to appear on the inside of the pan). While the milk and spices are simmering, combine egg yolks and sugar in a blender and cream well (sugar must be totally dissolved).

2. Strain the simmering milk to eliminate the spices. Reset the blender to low speed, and while the blender is still running, slowly incorporate the milk and rum into the creamed egg yolks. Once all the milk and rum has been poured in, cover the blender and reset it to high speed until achieving a high foam.

VARIATIONS: The rum can be omitted from the batch and mixed into individual servings. Transfer the *coquito* into a glass decanter and refrigerate. Shake well before serving. Serve in a wine glass garnished with a cinnamon stick. *Coquito* can also be set out in a chilled punch bowl (place on top of ice mat). Garnish with slivers or flakes of fresh coconut, and sprinkle with ground cinnamon and nutmeg.

Sangría

Sangría is a delightful and refreshing drink that can be enjoyed with almost any meal under any circumstances, especially when the guests are many and the budget is limited. It is also a way to salvage wine that is of less than "perfect quality" whether it is red, white, or bubbly. *Sangría* basically is a wine and fruit punch that is enhanced by the personality of the individual who puts it together.

My interpretation of the *sangría* is the following:

> 1 *liter of burgundy*
> 2 *cups light Puerto Rican rum*
> 1 *cup lime juice, freshly squeezed*
> 1 *cup sugar*
> 30 *ice cubes*
> 6 *spice cloves*

2 liters of ginger ale
2 oranges, cut in halves and crosscut sliced

1. In a punch bowl, combine the burgundy, rum, lime juice, and sugar, and stir. Add ice cubes and spice cloves, and carefully stir in the ginger ale. Add the orange slices and serve in a tall glass.

For Further Reading

Historically, literature about Puerto Rico has not been very abundant. We were encouraged to see more books on the shelves of libraries and bookstores that we visited during the last year or two. We hope this trend continues. Here are some books from a variety of categories that will enhance the knowledge of you or any member of your family about the island of Puerto Rico and its people.

TRAVEL AND PHOTOGRAPHY

Ames, Tad and Caldwell, Chris. *Insight Guides: Puerto Rico.* Hong Kong: Apa Productions, Ltd., 1987.

LaBrucherie, Roger A. *Images of Puerto Rico.* El Centro, Calif.: Imágenes Press, 1984.

Phelps de Córdova, Loretta. *Ponce: Rebirth of a Valuable Heritage.* San Juan, P.R.: Publishing Resources, Inc., 1991.

FOODS OF THE REGION

Grigson, Jane. *Exotic Fruits and Vegetables.* New York: Henry Holt and Company, Inc., 1987.

Margolis, Carolyn and Viola, Herman J., ed. *Seeds of Change: Five Hundred Years Since Columbus.* Washington, D.C.: Smithsonian Institution Press, 1991.

Schneider, Elizabeth. *Uncommon Fruits and Vegetables: A Commonsense Guide.* New York: Harper and Row Publishers, Inc., 1986.

Sokolov, Raymond. *Why We Eat What We Eat: How the Encounter Between the New World and the Old Changed the Way Everyone on the Planet Eats.* New York: Summit Books, 1991.

CULTURE

Babín, María Teresa. *The Puerto Ricans' Spirit: Their History, Life, and Culture*. New York: The Macmillan Company, 1971.

Glasser, Ruth. *My Music is My Flag: Puerto Rican Musicians and Their New York Communities, 1917–1940*. Berkeley, Calif.: University of California Press, 1995.

Maldonado-Denis, Manuel. *Puerto Rico: A Socio-Historic Interpretation*. New York: Vintage Books, 1972.

Mintz, Sidney W. *Worker in the Cane: A Puerto Rican Life History*. New York: W. W. Norton and Co., Inc., 1974.

Wagenheim, Kal. *Puerto Rico: A Profile*. New York: Praeger Publishers, Inc., 1970.

Wagenheim, Kal and Jiménez de Wagenheim, Olga. *The Puerto Ricans—A Documentary History*. Princeton, N.J.: Markus Wiener Publishers, 1994.

HISTORY AND POLITICS

Beckles, Dr. Hilary and Shepherd, Verene, ed. *Caribbean Slave Society and Economy*. New York: The New Press, 1991.

Carr, Raymond. *Puerto Rico: A Colonial Experiment*. New York: Vintage Books, 1984.

Columbus, Christopher. *The Log of Christopher Columbus*. Translated by Robert Henderson Fuson, and based on the abstract of the Log and *Historia* by Bartolomé de las Casas and Fernando Columbus's *Historie* [of the Columbus family]. Camden, Maine: International Marine Publishing, 1987.

de las Casas, Bartolomé. *The Devastation of the Indies: A Brief Account*. Baltimore, Md.: The John Hopkins University Press. English translation by Herma Briffault, The Crossroad Publishing Co., 1974. Introduction c. 1992, The Johns Hopkins University Press.

Fernandez, Ronald. *Prisoners of Colonialism: The Struggle for Justice in Puerto Rico*. Monroe, Maine: Common Courage Press, 1994.

Gudmundson, Lowell; Kutschbach, Mario Samper; and Roseberry, William, ed. *Coffee, Society and Power in Latin America.* Baltimore, Md.: The Johns Hopkins University Press, 1995.

Jiménez de Wagenheim, Olga. *Puerto Rico's Revolt for Independence: El Grito de Lares.* Princeton, N.J.: Markus Wiener Publishing, 1993.

Rogozinski, Jan. *A Brief History of the Caribbean From the Arawak and the Carib to the Present.* New York: Facts on File, Inc., 1992.

Rouse, Irving. *The Tainos: Rise and Decline of the People Who Greeted Columbus.* New Haven, Conn.: Yale University Press, 1992.

Williams, Eric. *From Columbus to Castro: The History of the Caribbean, 1492–1969.* New York: Harper and Row, 1970.

LITERATURE

Babín, María Teresa and Steiner, Stan, ed. *Borinquen, An Anthology of Puerto Rican Literature.* New York: Alfred A. Knopf, 1974.

Ballester, Manuel Mendez. *Isla Cerrera: Novela Basada en la Conquista de Puerto Rico.* Mexico: Editorial Diana, S.A.; 1949.

Cofer, Judith Ortiz. *The Latin Deli: Telling the Lives of Barrio Women.* Athens, Ga.: University of Georgia Press, 1993.

Curl, John. *Columbus in the Bay of Pigs.* Berkeley, Calif.: Homeward Press, 1988.

Hernández-Cruz, Victor. *By Lingual Wholes.* San Francisco: Momo's Press, 1982.

Hernández-Cruz, Victor. *Red Beans.* Minneapolis, Minn.: Coffee House Press, 1991.

Santiago, Esmeralda. *When I Was Puerto Rican.* New York: Addison Wesley, 1993.

Thomas, Piri. *Down These Mean Streets.* New York: Vintage Books, 1974.

CHILDREN'S AND YOUNG PEOPLE'S LITERATURE

Adoff, Arnold. *Flamboyan*. Orlando, Fla.: Harcourt Brace Jovanovich, 1988.

Crespo, George. *How the Sea Began: A Taino Myth Retold and Illustrated*. New York: Clarion Books, 1993.

Delacre, Lulu. *Vejigante (Masquerader)*. New York: Scholastic, Inc., 1993.

Jacobs, Francine. *The Tainos: The People Who Welcomed Columbus*. New York: G.P. Putnam's Sons, 1992.

Kent, Deborah. *America the Beautiful: Puerto Rico*. Chicago: Children's Press, 1992.

Index